SUBLIME WORLDS
EARLY MODERN FRENCH LITERATURE

LEGENDA

LEGENDA, founded in 1995 by the European Humanities Research Centre of the University of Oxford, is now a joint imprint of the Modern Humanities Research Association and Maney Publishing. Titles range from medieval texts to contemporary cinema and form a widely comparative view of the modern humanities, including works on Arabic, Catalan, English, French, German, Greek, Italian, Portuguese, Russian, Spanish, and Yiddish literature. An Editorial Board of distinguished academic specialists works in collaboration with leading scholarly bodies such as the Society for French Studies and the British Comparative Literature Association.

MHRA

The Modern Humanities Research Association (MHRA) encourages and promotes advanced study and research in the field of the modern humanities, especially modern European languages and literature, including English, and also cinema. It also aims to break down the barriers between scholars working in different disciplines and to maintain the unity of humanistic scholarship in the face of increasing specialization. The Association fulfils this purpose primarily through the publication of journals, bibliographies, monographs and other aids to research.

MANEY
publishing

Maney Publishing is one of the few remaining independent British academic publishers. Founded in 1900 the company has offices both in the UK, in Leeds and London, and in North America, in Boston. Since 1945 Maney Publishing has worked closely with learned societies, their editors, authors, and members, in publishing academic books and journals to the highest traditional standards of materials and production.

Sublime Worlds

Early Modern French Literature

❖

Emma Gilby

l

LEGENDA

Modern Humanities Research Association and Maney Publishing
2006

Published by the
Modern Humanities Research Association and Maney Publishing
1 Carlton House Terrace
London SW1Y 5DB
United Kingdom

LEGENDA is an imprint of the
Modern Humanities Research Association and Maney Publishing

Maney Publishing is the trading name of W. S. Maney & Son Ltd,
whose registered office is at Suite 1C, Joseph's Well, Hanover Walk, Leeds LS3 1AB

ISBN 1 904350 65 8 / 978-1-904350-65-1

First published 2006

Printed in Great Britain

Cover: 875 Design

Copy-Editor: Polly Fallows

CONTENTS

❖

ACKNOWLEDGEMENTS

❖

During the writing of this book, and the thesis on which it is based, I was fortunate to receive financial assistance from the Arts and Humanities Research Council and the Newton Trust, Cambridge. Among the friends and colleagues (many of them happily both) who have encouraged and inspired me, I should like to mention in particular Anne Chassagnol, Tim Chesters, Hannah Dawson, Katja Haustein, Nick Hammond, Christophe Hirat, Katherine Ibbett, John Leigh, Tim Lewens, Helen Macdonald, Christina McLeish, Nicole Moreham, Richard Scholar, and Nick White. I am indebted to my Ph.D. examiners, Peter Bayley and Richard Parish, as well as to Terence Cave, John D. Lyons, and Michael Moriarty, for their readings and their support. Emmanuel College granted me a research position as the thesis was drawing to a close, and Sidney Sussex College has subsequently admitted me into its Fellowship; it is a great pleasure to thank the people who make up these institutions. Similarly, I should like to offer my thanks to the Department of French at the University of Cambridge, headed by Emma Wilson, for providing such a lovely atmosphere in which to work. Some of these chapters touch upon work I have published elsewhere and list in my bibliography: I'd like to thank in this regard the editors of *Seventeenth-Century French Studies* and *Papers on French Seventeenth-Century Literature*, as well as Frédéric Gabriel at Éditions Comp'Act. The people with whom I have been in contact at Legenda, and especially my editor, Graham Nelson, and my copy-editor, Polly Fallows, have been models of friendly efficiency. Thanks, finally, to my parents, who have given me so many wonderful books. Thanks to Nick Hammond, who has taught me since my first year as an undergraduate, who continues to do so, and who has been so generous throughout. And thanks to Tim, to whom I dedicate all that follows.

Emma Gilby
Cambridge, July 2006

What is a quote? A quote (cognate with *quota*) is a cut, a section, a slice of someone else's orange. You suck the slice, toss the rind, skate away. Part of what you enjoy in a documentary technique is the sense of banditry. To loot someone else's life or sentences and make off with a point of view, which is called 'objective' because you can make anything into an object by treating it in this way, is exciting and dangerous. Let us see who controls the danger.

ANNE CARSON, '(Essay with Rhapsody): On the Sublime in Longinus and Antonioni', in *Decreation: Poetry, Essays, Opera* (New York: Knopf, 2005), pp. 43–51 (p. 45)

INTRODUCTION

❖

At the point of putting pen to paper, the 'déjà-dit' can be a dead weight. But then some of the language we come across moves us. Words spoken or on the page mediate forceful understanding or insight. They can seem to anticipate an intimacy with us or to require a response from us; they occupy us and involve us. Writers are fascinated and inspired by this phenomenon. This truth, trivial as it is, became the subject of the classical treatise *On the Sublime*, traditionally attributed to Longinus.[1]

Longinus's overwhelming preoccupation, described well by Boileau in one of his reflections on the sublime, is with 'la petitesse energique des paroles'.[2] Energy always carries a sense of transference: it turns to entropy unless it is reassigned as work done to or upon another. Longinian sublimity carries this sense of transference too. The 'sublime' of the treatise's title is always an encounter. Language is sublime when it gives us, as readers or listeners, such a deep understanding of what its author communicates that the words seem somehow to have come from within ourselves. Longinus raises the absorbing matter of self-absorption: how we can be met in a moment of communication, how this leaves us to view ourselves and the world around us in a new light.

Longinus's paraphrases of sublime experience, as my introductory comments already suggest, show that moment to be bewilderingly bound to the intellectual structures of its participants — authors, readers, speakers, listeners — as well as to the language they use. Longinus looks to give many examples of texts that have affected him powerfully, in the interests of analysing what makes them work on him thus. One of his most famous examples is the *Fiat lux*: that 'let there be light' which, says Longinus, gives the reader an immediate understanding of the power of the divine being who is conceived and portrayed there. Longinus's examples deal with human worlds too: Sappho's telling of her glimpse of a woman; Homer's recounting of lives threatened in battle or at sea. Longinus often dramatizes encounters between human beings, takes discourse to be inseparable from the moments it depicts as well as from the reactions and re-enactments it encourages in its readers: he deals in, as he puts it, 'images drawn from real life'.[3] Sublime moments are also human. The ineffable can be thought through in terms of human interaction. And if his authors are, he says, great, Longinus discusses them because he wants to be useful to all those who, interested in reading and writing, can learn something from illustrations, examples, experimentation.

In no sense is the Longinian sublime to be confused with a discussion of the 'sublime style' in the tradition of a rhetoric of stylistic gradation: a style characterized by complex figurative language. Indeed, sublime experience can be — although is by no means always — triggered by the simplest discourse, as with the *Fiat lux*. Simple, everyday language can produce the revelatory, transformative experiences with which Longinus is concerned. And Longinus knows and insists that his questioning of these experiences, and their strange relationship to language, gives him a due entitlement to his readers' attention.

The work of three major early modern French authors — Pierre Corneille, Blaise Pascal, and Nicolas Boileau — can be usefully situated in relation to this Longinian way of thinking. This introduction will explain how I go about my juxtapositions and why I think they are worthwhile.

Before Boileau's Translation

Marc Fumaroli notes that 'comme il nous manque une étude sur la fortune d'Aristote aux XVIᵉ et XVIIᵉ siècles, il nous manque tout aussi cruellement une histoire du *Traité du sublime* du Pseudo-Longin avant Boileau'.[4] Faced with Nicolas Boileau-Despréaux's renowned translation of Longinus in 1674, critics still think occasionally that 'in rescuing Longinus from almost complete oblivion, Boileau put an end to a long story of neglect'; that 'le sublime était apparu à la fin du XVIIᵉ siècle comme un cheval de Troie introduit dans la forteresse classique'.[5] Indeed, not just the reception but everything about the age, authorship, and history of the treatise *Peri hypsous* is controversial. Thus it has proved seductive for generations of readers who engage in literary detective work, who dissect in order to date, name, enumerate.

This much is clear: the words that remain of *Peri hypsous* are sourced from a lacunary tenth-century manuscript, Parisinus 2036, which also contains sections of Aristotle's *Problemata*. Parisinus 2036 presents the author of *Peri hypsous* as 'Dionysius Longinus' on its title page but as 'Dionysius or Longinus' on its contents page. The ambiguous 'or' means that, historically, two men have been identified as the author in question: the Augustan Dionysius of Halicarnassus and the third-century Cassius Longinus. Both these options, however, had been rejected by the time of the early nineteenth century; and current scholarship, supposing that an unknown first-century 'Dionysius Longinus' must be responsible for the treatise, uses the appellation 'Longinus' for the sake of convenience.[6] Muret translated Longinus, but his text has been lost.[7] Robortello's Greek text and Latin notes were published in 1554, six years after his important commentary on Aristotle's *Poetics*.[8] Domenico Pizzimenti's Latin version is the earliest printed translation, published in 1566. Giovanni di Niccolò da Falgano's Italian manuscript version is the earliest extant vernacular translation, dating from 1575. Longinus circulated in various Greek and Latin editions in the early decades of the seventeenth century, the most substantial of these being Petra's 1612 Greek text with Latin translation and notes. John Hall of Oxford brought out an English translation in 1652. In 1663 the Greek text came out for the first time in France in an edition by Tanneguy Le Fèvre. We know that an anonymous translation was undertaken in the middle decades of the seventeenth century, and we know that several copies of Longinus were at this point available in the personal collection of the Dupuy brothers, as well as in that of the Du Thou library.[9]

Longinus is profoundly important to, and widely conveyed by, Jesuit rhetoricians. Francesco Benci, who had been taught by Muret for seven years and remained a friend for over thirty, mentions Longinus and indeed translates some of his treatise in his *Orationes*.[10] Caussin (*Eloquentiae sacrae et humanae parallela*, 1619, and *Reginae palatium eloquentiae*, 1641) and Louis de Cressolles (*Vacationes autumnales*, 1620) make significant use of Longinus.[11] *Peri hypsous* corresponds well to a broad Jesuit interest in a rhetoric of vividness: the communicative potential of the arts, their ability to have an effect on audiences, moving and involving them. Moreover, as the post-Tridentine church made a move to occupy the whole of social and political space, to regenerate spirituality in all sections of the community,[12] the fact that a pagan Greek writer had cited the 'let there be light' of Genesis as an example of supremely powerful discourse could be very useful. It could justify Caussin, for example, in an ambition which had 'quelque chose de pantagruélique: en un seul programme organique, il embrasse l'éloquence "héroïque", celle de l'Eglise, et l'éloquence humaine, celle de la société civile'.[13] The glory of God could be seen in all aspects of human life. As Fumaroli continues, this was 'une façon délibérée [...] de faire percevoir d'un seul regard tous les étages du *Logos*, tous ses compartiments, en même temps que son unité profonde' (p. 286).[14]

So Longinus was, from 1554–55, published, paraphrased, and commented upon in the 'savant' domain of the *Respublica litteraria*, to which 'les écrivains en langue française, médiateurs entre deux degrés de culture, avaient naturellement accès'.[15] Particularly influential in this mediation was Leone Allacci, who published in Rome in 1634 an essay entitled *Des fautes des grands hommes dans le discours*, in which Longinus 'sert à la fois de point de départ et d'autorité dans l'argumentation'.[16] Allacci was 'bien connu à Paris, non seulement dans le cénacle des frères Dupuy, en relations constantes avec les milieux doctes de Rome, mais d'un "médiateur" aussi averti que Chapelain'.[17] Jules Brody notes references to Longinus in Giulio Mazarini's *Pratica breve del predicare* (1615), translated by Jean Baudoin in 1618; in Charles de Saint-Paul (*Tableau de l'éloquence française*, 1632); in La Mothe Le Vayer (*Considérations sur l'éloquence*, 1638); in Dumas (*Triomphe de l'académie chrétienne*, 1641); and in Le Grand (*Discours sur la rhétorique française*, 1658).[18]

Guez de Balzac is also, as Sophie Hache in particular has shown, associated with Longinus in the various quarrels that mark his career.[19] One defence of Balzac's work, published in the name of François Ogier although (according to Tallemant des Réaux) written in collaboration with Balzac himself, makes direct reference to 'le Sophiste Longin', while Balzac's later *Socrate chrestien* points to 'la Critique payenne' which finds 'son Genre sublime, dans le style de Moïse'.[20] A subtle use of Longinus emerges in the virulent polemic of 1653 around the publication by Costar of his *Defense des ouvrages de Monsieur de Voiture, à Monsieur de Balzac*, and, two years later, his *Suite de la Defense des oeuvres de Mr. de Voiture, à M. Ménage*. The following citation refers to the Longinian move away from the 'sublime style' in the tradition of a rhetoric of stylistic gradation:

> Un Poëte de la Cour d'Auguste, parle d'une médiocrité toute d'or, qui a le prix & l'éclat de ce beau metal, & c'est indubitablement celle-là, ou les Philosophes ont establi le thrône de la Vertu. Si les oeuvres sérieuses de Monsieur de Voiture sont mediocres, j'ose dire que c'est de cette loüable mediocrité.[21]

Costar berates Monsieur de Girac, who does not appreciate the discourse 'sans contrainte, sans affectation et sans vice' of his contemporaries, even if 'veritablement il sauroit tout cela par cœur si c'estoit un passage de Demetrius Phalereus, ou de Longin, ou d'Hermogene'.[22] He also paraphrases Longinus when he writes that '*mesme les ouvrages naturels perdent une partie de leur force & de leur bonté par la subtilité des preceptes de l'Escole qui rendent le discours plus sec & plus décharné, & qui au lieu de former un beau corps ne font qu'un squelette*'.[23] The sublime is aligned with the rejection of a servile adherence to the 'precceptes de l'Escole'. Well before Boileau's translation, then, the themes and motifs of Longinus's treatise were available to writers in the vernacular.

Corneille, Pascal, Boileau

Taking Pascal as his subject, Fumaroli writes that 'les *Pensées* demeurent le *Traité du sublime* de la prose française classique', not least 'par leur dédain pour la "rhétorique" scolaire ou pédante'.[24] Fumaroli notes, in a comment which he would presumably extend to other seventeenth-century authors, that 'il importe peu que Pascal ait lu ou non le traité *Du Sublime*: ici, et dans les *Pensées*, il ne cesse de répondre à la question que pose le traité, et qui était ouverte obstinément depuis le XVIe siècle: qu'est-ce que la grandeur?'.[25]

Fumaroli picks up on a particular concept: grandeur. We shall see that sublimity and grandeur are often taken as easily coterminous in Corneille studies, too. 'Le mot sublime,' writes Georges Forestier, 'renvoie à une esthétique et une éthique de la *grandeur*'.[26] Let us engage, though, with another question, while maintaining an interest in Pascal and Corneille. How does language move? Before getting to the matter of grandeur (whatever it is), Longinus deals with human beings affected by the words they encounter. This is his basic premise, and the basic premise of all readings of his work. Giving his examples, Longinus engages with variegated texts, his responses to these, and the matter of how their own responses may inflect the way his readers live and interact. Worlds clash in the sublime; and as our world merges with and is changed by the worlds portrayed by others, so distinctions between ordinary and extraordinary (great), or between intimate and forceful (grand), bear less weight. Thinking about this indistinction is one of the goals of this book.

I argue that work by Corneille, Pascal, and Boileau can be analysed in terms of the relationships set up between the different strands of Longinus's *On the Sublime*: its argumentational juxtapositions and intratextual resonances. I start from the basis that the quirky ways in which these three seventeenth-century writers use the term 'sublime' can — not because it stands for, sums up, or is believed to point to a particular concept, but because it happens to be used in Longinian constellations of motifs — provide an anchor for our reading of their arguments.

It is possible to look at the term 'sublime', I argue, as it crops up within a cluster of concerns which are those of the treatise on the sublime. This cluster makes ineffably affective responses clash with the discursive provocation of those. It comprises communication, encounter, and the kinds of knowledge open to human beings. These broad themes will be identified through such terms as 'connaissance', 'expérience', and 'rapport', all of which will, as they deflect off the term 'sublime' and off each other, be vitally important at various points in what follows. So first I observe that Corneille and Pascal, as well as Boileau, use the term 'sublime' at critical — crucial and interrogatory — moments: moments that look at different levels of 'connaissance', for instance, or 'rapport'. Then I use my close readings of the passages in question to catalyse wider analyses of these motifs. My preference for connections made glancingly, it is tempting to emphasize, serves a purpose: the way connections glance off each other in Longinus is the energy of his text, and also finds instructive echoes in the authors I consider here. In my study, then, Longinus's questions about the literary and the lived are not mapped through the term 'sublime' alone. Nor is the sublime taken as a definable concept ('grandeur', for example). I am dealing here with argumentational connections, constellations.

I hold then, with Fumaroli, that the place of the treatise before Boileau has been underestimated. I also hold that, even if Longinus's treatise had not been available in multiple copies in important seventeenth-century libraries, discussed, referred to, and indeed, in at least one case, translated by an anonymous seventeenth-century writer, the existence of sixteenth-century translations by figures of the highest importance in the early modern republic of letters would be enough to justify an interest in idiosyncratic uses of the term 'sublime' and in Longinus's many-layered argumentation. And I hold, more generally, that an interesting way of proceeding with literary criticism is, as Terence Cave suggests, 'de créer un champ virtuel pour lequel l'avenir que nous connaissons n'a pas (encore) eu lieu'.[27] Here the 'avenir que nous connaissons' is the modern mass of writing on the sublime and its catalysis by Boileau. Cave is interested, not in 'la transmission ou l'évolution d'un ensemble conceptuel', an ensemble with which it is in any case impossible for us to come to accurate terms, but in 'des symptômes de trouble ou d'inquiétude dans le champ de réception de cet ensemble' (p. 178).

For the sake of clarity, then, one has to accept in reading what follows that it is not impossible for writers in the seventeenth century to have had access, either directly or indirectly, to Longinian theories of the sublime before Boileau's translation, which explains the background discussion above. But one does not have to accept that Corneille and Pascal had been influenced in any specific or demonstrable sense by Longinus. The fact that Corneille and Pascal do use the term 'sublime' at a few points certainly does not prove the latter. It seems a matter of common sense that cast-iron influence is a limited and limiting criterion for the discussion of what can be seen, I think, as 'symptômes de trouble ou d'inquiétude'. It is, moreover, possible entirely to occlude intentionality and influence while still talking about one writer's text having recourse to or picking up on another's terms. The extent to which these authors are explicitly directing our attention towards Longinus is undecidable, as is the place that Longinus holds within their work (I shall not be offering tidy or strict delineations of references which Corneille, Pascal, and Boileau have tried to make tidy or strict: they have not). But when intertextuality is seen as a dynamic process, which does not necessarily have to be footnoted through specific reference, then the juxtapositions I propose can have fruitful lessons to teach — both in giving us new readings of these authors and in enabling us to rethink questions about sublimity in relation to the seventeenth century.

It is perhaps worth looking briefly at that kind of philology which does insist on clearly delineated 'influence' as the only possible tool for the establishment of working relationships with ideas and motifs, and the field of Latin allusive studies is useful here. As Stephen Hinds notes, 'At a time when semiological approaches in the academy at large have increasingly emphasized the implicatedness of *all* literary language in intertextual negotiations [...] the mainstream of Latin allusive studies has moved in the opposite direction, by circumscribing more narrowly the kinds of intertextual event which merit study.'[28] The traditional philological delimitation of conscious imitation runs as follows, and aims to differentiate this phenomenon from mere 'similarities of word or thought or phrase':

> Similarities of word or thought or phrase can occur because writers are indebted to a common source, or because they are describing similar or conventional situations, or because their works belong to the same generic type of poem. Only patient scholarship and a thorough familiarity with the relevant material can reveal whether the similarities cannot be explained by any of these three reasons. In such cases we may be fairly certain that direct imitation of one author by another is taking place.[29]

The dangers of intertextuality are averted here by 'patient scholarship'. Hinds is excellent in taking to pieces the assumption that the background noise of shared language use gets in the way of the rigorous study of 'direct imitation'. He extends the kind of closeness of attention promoted by the philologists he cites into less tidy areas, and offers 'a more exact account of allusive inexactitude' (p. 25). (In the course of this account, he is equally damning about that kind of writing on intertextuality which is so excitable that it is possible to wonder what a particular author brought to his or her enterprise at all.) The work I propose here moves in the area of this allusive inexactitude, this play on similarity and difference, which I put in the service of an account of Corneille, Pascal, and Boileau. It rejoins that kind of 'dépistage de trouble' which 'permet de localiser une région problématique de la perception, de retrouver une sorte de fêlure dont l'auteur et ses contemporains ne sont peut-être pas pleinement conscients, mais qu'ils ressentent comme un malaise, une tache floue à l'horizon de la pensée'.[30]

Other Approaches to the 'Sublime'

Examples of studies which pursue non-period-specific conceptual histories of the sublime abound. Countless critics have taken it upon themselves to assimilate *Peri hypsous* into the broadest conceptual schemas of literary criticism.[31] They step from Longinus to Burke, who did much for the seductiveness of the sublime when he wrote his *Philosophical Enquiry*, making the term 'sublime' refer to the intermingling of terror and pleasure inspired by the ruins and the Alpine passes which were to provide some of the standard imagery of the Gothic.[32] They take Longinus and Burke to Kant, who looks at the aesthetic consequences of the interplay between our sensory reception of formless, oceanic or tempestuous phenomena in the natural world and our rational comprehension of these.[33] They cite any and all of the above in looking at Lyotard, who, in his writing on the avant-garde, makes the sublime a 'sentiment', a sensation of shock upon being confronted with an art object that neither corresponds to existing models nor testifies to reality. Lyotard's gloss on the problems facing the critic who seeks to analyse the work of Barnet Newman lends itself particularly easily to citation:

> Que dire, qui ne soit donné? La description est aisée, mais plate comme une paraphrase. La meilleure glose consiste dans l'interrogation: que dire?, dans l'exclamation: ah!, dans la surprise: ça alors!. Autant d'expressions d'un sentiment qui porte un nom dans la tradition esthétique moderne (et dans l'œuvre de Newman): le sublime. C'est le sentiment que: voilà.[34]

Longinus can be taken to any of these end points, and many more.[35] One critic of the Romantic sublime notes that 'we can begin with the hypothesis that the encounter with literary greatness — the so-called rhetorical sublime — is structurally cognate with the transcendence, gentle or terrible, excited in the encounter with landscape, the "natural" sublime'.[36] The sublime transcends its local manifestations. Theories of the sublime are, here, 'structurally cognate' because their structure is clearly defined by the critic in question as 'transcendence, whether gentle or terrible'.

Because it is difficult to separate the 'sentiment que: voilà' posited in these transhistorical theories of the sublime from the problem of the adequacy of discourse to that sentiment, it has been important to many critics to make sure that they deflate, demask, and demystify all notions of sublime exaltation. Uses of the term 'sublime' are primarily, from this point of view, a citation of impossibility, reminding us of the shortfalls and rootless repetitions of a language which aims to evaluate or symbolize:

> The Longinian sublime is [...] an event, a force of enunciation as coming to act, which, as such, can never be represented, was never present, because of the blinding force of its effect, which acts as a dissimulation or a withdrawal. It can only be reproduced, reenacted, through the nonmimetic repetition of citation as repetition of the act of enunciation.[37]

Paul de Man, writing on Kant, succinctly has the sublime 'determined by linguistic structures which are not within the author's control'.[38] Sublimity as a movement beyond oneself is a 'moribund aesthetic':

> In contemporary criticism and the general development of structuralist thinking we are instructed how little, really, of our creations belong to individual vision and choice. It is against this sense of an increasingly constricted and structured world that the ideology of the sublime looms up retrospectively as a moribund aesthetic.[39]

All texts on sublimity can — and, for some, should — be retrospectively read as proving that experience or encounter can never supersede linguistic alienation. Sublimity can never transcend, but only repeat and sustain, scepticism.[40]

Thus, for Louis Marin, what is of interest in Boileau's reference to a 'je ne scay quoy qu'on peut beaucoup mieux sentir que dire' is precisely the writer's inability to describe sublimity in terms other than the irretrievably periphrastic.[41] The 'je ne sais quoi', emblematic of sublime experience, can therefore be read only in its literal sense: that which cannot be known or guaranteed:

> Le sublime est un 'je ne sais quoi' dans la mesure même où il apparaît difficile voire impossible de produire, de construire le 'concept' du sublime, dans la mesure même où la définition du sublime fait question, une question qui est partie intégrante de la notion même du sublime. (p. 186)

Sublimity stands in Marin for the impossibility of aesthetics:

> Le sublime nommerait [...] avec le 'je ne sais quoi' un écart de la théorie avec elle-même, interne à la théorie même, avec le 'je ne sais quoi', une fin de l'art même qui en désignerait à la fois la destination et la cessation. (p. 189)

Marin's terms are precisely those of Jean-Luc Nancy, aiming to show that sublimity is not reducible, or even relatable, to dialectical theories of art:

> Pour la pensée dialectique, le contour d'un dessein, le cadre d'un tableau, la trace d'une écriture renvoient hors d'eux-mêmes à l'absolu d'une présentation totale. [...] Pour la pensée sublime, le contour, le cadre et la trace ne renvoient à rien qu'eux-mêmes.[42]

In discovering in Longinus and Boileau that which he seeks, Marin's end point is the original premise of deconstructive theory. Interpretations such as this, coruscatingly expressed as they are, see nothing but transhistorical flotillas of floating signifiers.

Often, then, in writing about the sublime, we find seepages from one set of material to another. Whether in deconstructive or in more traditionally historical mode, these seepages bring with them dramatic risks of imprecision: risks pertaining to the construction of 'mythologies', to borrow Quentin Skinner's term.[43] Skinner writes of the contamination of historical study 'by the unconscious application of paradigms whose familiarity to the historian disguises an essential inapplicability to the past' (p. 7). The danger here, as he puts it, is that 'the doctrine to be investigated so readily becomes hypostatized into an entity' (p. 10). Samuel Monk provides *dix-septiémistes* with a cast-iron example of Skinner's 'mythology of doctrines' ('a form of non-history which is entirely given over to pointing out earlier "anticipations" of later doctrines, and to crediting each writer in terms of their clairvoyance', p. 11): it is 'the new, the eighteenth-century, sublime for which Boileau is responsible'; and 'just as eighteenth-century literature has as its unconscious goal, in the fulness of time, the literature of the early nineteenth century, so it may be said that eighteenth-century aesthetics has as its unconscious goal the *Critique of Judgment*, the book in which it was to be refined and re-interpreted'.[44] In a similar vein, Louis Marin takes care to make Pascal anticipate Kant on the basis of a common concern with 'the infinite': 'More than a century before Immanuel Kant's *Critique of Judgment* (1796), Pascal describes the mind's encounter with the infinite in terms that announce the sublime.'[45]

The Sublime and 'Classicism'

As my preceding comments on the work of Marc Fumaroli have already suggested, some critics have refurnished theories of the sublime in their seventeenth-century context by focusing on an aesthetic of ineffable greatness or grandeur — 'l'esthétique de la grandeur merveilleuse', says Georges Forestier[46] — which may redefine 'classicism'. 'Classicism' has generally been understood, since Bray's *La Formation de la doctrine classique*, as being profoundly Aristotelian in character, with Aristotelianism in turn being viewed as a belief in the perfectibility of method.[47] Individual facts, according to this understanding of Aristotelianism, are supplanted by the workings of a rationale which connects them; this rationale is known as 'technē', defined in the *Nicomachean Ethics* as a capacity to make, or productive state, involving a true course of reasoning.[48] 'No art [technē]', states Aristotle in his *Rhetoric*, 'has the particular in view'; and this preoccupation with paradigms of axiomatic thinking is seen by Bray and those who follow him to define overwhelmingly both Aristotle's thinking and classical French theory.[49] Some critics have tended to see Boileau's reflections on the sublime as fundamentally incompatible with the espousal of classical doctrine he is supposed to evince in his *Art poétique*. The latter text is viewed as nothing other than an attempt to reduce literature to rational rules and concepts: 'Boileau's *L'Art poétique* is a complete expression of the neo-classic code.'[50] Following Monk, Théodore Litman states that 'un grand nombre d'éléments de la conception du sublime ne s'accordent nullement avec les principes généreux que Boileau lui-même avait exposés dans ses *Satires*, ses *Epîtres* et son *Art poétique*'.[51] Clearly, if 'classicism' is seen as nothing other than a harmoniously rule-bound body of material, then the *Traité du sublime*, with its emphasis on the experiential, does not 'fit'.

Jules Brody's significant 1958 study *Boileau and Longinus* does not see the classical and the sublime as mutually exclusive. Brody engages in a minutely detailed study of Boileau's translation and how its emphases and cadences differ from the original Greek and from the available Latin translations. Hostile to that view according to which Boileau's 'standard of excellence is not the ability to move and astound but to write according to the rules', Brody suggests that 'when the nature and limits of his respect for the rules are properly established it will be apparent that for Boileau their role was to heighten and sustain emotive effort and not to negate them' (p. 100).

Brody's critique influentially integrates 'emotive effort' and the entire related semantic field of the inexpressible, the ineffable, the intuitive, the affective, and so on into critical accounts of classical literature. In other words, classicism is seen as no less 'definable' because it happens to encompass that which cannot be defined. Typical is Boudhors's comment:

> L'ennemi né des fausses noblesses et des fades emphases [Boileau] s'est pris de sympathie pour une œuvre qui discernait le vrai et le faux sublime, et fondait l'union intime de la grandeur et de la simplicité [...] Le Sublime est devenu pour lui l'auxiliaire et le garant de l'Art Poétique.[52]

Gilles Declercq also makes a telling move in this regard when he entitles an article 'Topique de l'ineffable dans l'esthétique classique: rhétorique et sublime'.[53] Declercq examines texts 'dont la cohérence permet à nos yeux de parler d'une topique de l'ineffable' (p. 203). His assertion is that Boileau's *Œuvres diverses* de 1674 formulent un équilibre spécifique au "classicisme français"', a concept 'dont on sait aujourd'hui qu'il ne saurait se réduire à la notion de clarté'.[54]

Working from a similar standpoint, Fumaroli cites in a comparison of Retz and Longinus the Cardinal's statement that 'j'observai aussi en cette rencontre qu'il y a des points inexplicables dans les affaires, et inexplicables même dans leurs instants'; this statement is proof of a 'perception de l'"inexplicable", ce contact direct avec ce qui dépasse l'humaine raison'.[55] For Fumaroli, 'l'art du récit dans les *Mémoires* semble obéir avec une intelligence consommée aux préceptes énoncés par le Ps. Longin', helping Retz to present himself 'dans une lumière de grandeur classique' (p. 47). Declercq claims exactly the same about Racine's work, citing 'la conjonction de simplicité dramaturgique et d'acmé pathétique dont se prévaut la préface de *Bérénice*' (p. 214). In the most recent monograph on the sublime to emerge from French criticism, Sophie Hache echoes the assertion that sublimity introduces into seventeenth-century French literature an element of inexplicable affect which can itself be seen as defining classicism: 'Les termes du débat engagé sur la question du sublime sont riches de paradoxes pour Boileau et ses contemporains, fructueux en questionnements qui contribuent à l'édification d'une esthétique classique française.'[56]

Both Hache and the author of another recently published monograph on the sublime, Nicholas Cronk, seek to illustrate in extremely detailed terms the embeddedness of theories of affect in seventeenth-century thought.[57] Hache homes in on the reception of Longinus via seventeenth-century texts which ally simple language with a power to move. Her expressed hope is to be able to investigate this critical coupling by means of a corpus which consists of 'traités d'éloquence', with a further section devoted to rhetorical commentaries.

Cronk takes his own preoccupation with the simple yet powerfully moving discourse theorized by Longinus into related domains, considering not just the appearance of Longinian themes in seventeenth-century literature but the threatening questions and debates to which this appearance was a response. He is interested, namely, in seventeenth-century undercurrents of Platonism and poetic enthusiasm. He relates Boileau's *Traité du sublime* to broader neo-Platonist ideas of poetic fury and divine inspiration, to hermetic discourse, and to minor genres such as the 'devise', arguing that certain classical theorists, using the emblem as a metaphor for poetic discourse more generally, are able to discuss Plato's ideas without appearing to affront a rational Aristotelianism which Cronk takes to be the dominant mode of discourse. Correspondingly,

> Boileau's distinctive achievement is to have discovered a strategy for discussing platonism which allows him to challenge the prevailing tenets of classical poetic theory, while apparently remaining (just) within them. Adopting the borrowed authority of a seemingly innocuous classical author, he publishes a treatise on poetic theory with strongly platonist undercurrents, and he invents a term, *le sublime*, which permits him to discuss openly the notion of poetic fury — and posing all the while as the humble translator. (pp. 109–10)

So Boileau's translation of Longinus (with indeed the very decision to translate Longinus) constitutes a participation in a taboo aesthetic, a reaction against an officially sanctioned obsession with clear and distinct ideas.

Cronk goes into much detail about the contrast between the ineffable power granted to discourse in the *Traité du sublime* and the 'nomenclaturism' of contemporary linguistic debate:

> If words are nothing more than the tokens of preconceived ideas, then poetic
> language can be nothing more than the arrangement of poetic ideas. The logic
> of nomenclaturism is to reduce poetic discourse to invisibility, and ultimately
> to deny poetry altogether. (p. 174)

There is no logical space, in the notion that words are mere tokens depicting ideas
of an external reality, for transport, rapture. But there are grey areas in seventeenth-
century nomenclaturism, arguably embodied even in Arnauld and Nicole's
renowned statement that 'il est nécessaire dans *La Logique* de considérer les idées
jointes aux mots et les mots joints aux idées'.[58] The 'il est nécessaire dans', here, is
an internal check and control which, showing itself for what it is, points to domains
other than *La Logique* in which its limitations might not apply. Thomas M. Carr,
moreover, notes of Arnauld and Nicole's theory that 'whether it is a question of the
subject matter itself, the speaker's relation to the subject, or the relation between
speaker and audience, a legitimate space for eloquence alongside logic appears'.[59]
Looking at Arnauld and Nicole's theory of accessory ideas, Carr concludes
that 'they account for the communication of passion, as well as ideas, through
language' (p. 87).

   We can trouble the idea that the dynamic set up by the reception of the treatise in
question is to be summed up as sublime exaltation versus explanation, transcendence
versus rationalism, poetic fury versus a categorical 'classicism'. Longinus's own aim
to write a useful, pragmatic treatise is of itself relevant here. But both Hache and
Cronk do illustrate that, as far as rhetorical theory is concerned, and notably by
combining simplicity and stunning rhetorical force, 'la question du sublime apparaît
comme l'occasion d'un profond renouvellement des termes du débat'.[60]

   Although the debates about defining sublime style are not those with which I
am primarily concerned, it is perhaps worth nodding to Racine's mention, in his
preface to *Esther*, of 'les grandes vérités de l'Ecriture, et la manière sublime dont
elles y sont énoncées' (these, 'pour peu qu'on les présente, même imparfaitement,
aux yeux des hommes, sont si propres à les frapper'), which clearly brings us into
this area.[61] The same is true of his reference in the *Abrégé de l'histoire de Port-Royal*
to Montdidier's 'sublime oraison'.[62] I shall moreover be neglecting here the case of
Guez de Balzac, whose references to Longinus I have mentioned already. Hache
sums up well the rhetorical toings and froings about his work:

> C'est sans doute la reconnaissance par un certain nombre d'auteurs de la
> distinction entre style longinien et style sublime — ce que défendait pourtant
> le *Socrate chrestien* lorsqu'il établissait que la grandeur de l'éloquence peut naître
> de sa modestie — qui aboutit à une dégradation de la réputation de l'épistolier
> dans la seconde moitié du siècle.[63]

   I shall not be considering the texts of Bossuet, Fénelon, or Le Maistre de Sacy,
although these too use the term 'sublime' in Longinian ways. One might cite
Fénelon's appreciation of Saint Paul: 'Tout le monde ne peut pas atteindre à cette
sublime simplicité'; Sacy's chapter of his translation of Genesis entitled 'Simplicité
sublime de l'écriture'; or Bossuet's statement about Psalm 148, '*Ipse dixit, et facta sunt:
ipse mandavit, et creata sunt*; prorsus ex dignitate atque ex sublimitate Mosis'.[64] These
writers use the term 'sublime' to reject the notion that rhetorical force is achieved

only by fancy figurative means.[65] An alternative preference for a lively use of figures is demonstrated by Arnauld d'Andilly in his quarrel with Goibaud du Bois: 'Rien n'est plus grand, plus sublime, plus animé, & rien ne présente à l'esprit des images plus vivantes que les Cantiques & les Pseaumes de l'ancien Testament.'[66] But once again, I pass largely over — pointing the reader to the other recent critical work on the topic I have mentioned — these seventeenth-century debates about what a sublime style might be (straightforwardness versus 'discours pompeux').

Overview

The first chapter will offer a more detailed analysis of Longinus's *On the Sublime*, in the interests of backing up my introductory claims that certain concatenations of ideas are important in Longinus's text. These concatenations of ideas will, in the subsequent sections on Corneille, Pascal, and the wider work of Boileau, manifest themselves as themes and motifs and argumentational possibilities. It is vital to the seventeenth-century texts I consider that they, like *On the Sublime*, consider the ineffability of some kinds of experience alongside everyday human communication and encounters. Corneille does so, we shall see in the remainder of this study, when rethinking dramatic theory in the 1650s; Pascal does so when rethinking apology; Boileau does so when formulating moral negotiations in the debates known as the *Querelle des Anciens et des Modernes*.

Pierre Corneille returns repeatedly to the possibilities presented by Longinus, staking out some of his own most important and controversial theories via the term 'sublime'; and I look in this context at his theoretical discourses about the identification of the observer with the character on stage (when the term 'identification' is used in what follows, it will be in this general sense).[67] Here, liaisons and proximities inject unpredictability into proceedings in ways that bear upon 'connaissance' and upon sublimity in tragedy. We can read Corneille's theoretical emphases and re-emphases through his treatment of the canonical figure of Oedipus (*Œdipe* being contemporaneous with the *Discours* and granted a particularly useful exemplary status within them). Some of the most striking contemporary criticisms of Corneille are rolled up in the concept of 'vraisemblance', and Corneille's concept of 'vraisemblance' can also be seen to collaborate fully in the original critical discourse facilitated by his appropriation of the term 'sublime'. Finally, the diffuse seventeenth-century insistence upon the association of sublimity with Corneille is often connected to a specifically Longinian understanding of the term 'sublime'.

Pascal acknowledges the power of spirituality and the possibility of spiritual conversion. He cannot supply his readers with this kind of reorientation or the ensuing experience of God's grace. His text can only ever hope to leave his readers in such a state that grace might potentially be open to them. I suggest that Pascal inserts into his writing a pragmatically Longinian examination of knowledge as, and knowledge through, interaction; and that overlapping terms such as 'sublime', 'connaissance', 'expérience', and 'rapport' are useful to us here. Taking us via Pascal's engagements with Descartes, Montaigne, and the Augustine of the *Confessions*, I shall look at how Pascal is an intimate explorer of human encounters.

Turning to Boileau's 1674 translation of *Peri hypsous*, and a hitherto unknown, unidentified translation written at some unspecified point in the mid-seventeenth century, I shall consider particularly striking passages of emphasis or alteration within these texts. I shall not go about a systematic comparison of these texts bearing, for example, on accuracy of translation (indeed, the text of *Peri hypsous* itself is, throughout this book, given in English rather than Greek). But I shall look at the filaments of Longinian argumentation which are picked up on and worked with interestingly. Looking at this argumentation in Boileau's critical writings then opens up a new way of understanding the sublime in relation to the *Querelle des Anciens et des Modernes*. In his *Réflexions critiques*, Boileau has to respond to the Moderns' criticism that he, in looking to classical writers, is interested in the irrational and unreasonable elements of ancient culture. He uses Longinus to heap complex moral negotiations about knowledge, encounter and 'rapport' upon his adversaries.

In all the authors with whom I am concerned, the ineffable is indissociable from and theorized through an interrogation of the encounters lived out, and written about, in the course of a life. These texts conduct separate, but interrelated, literary and moral experiments, looking, sometimes painfully, at the incursion of alterity and the external world into existence. They admit of 'liaisons d'amour ou d'amitié', of 'la vie ordinaire des hommes', of 'l'emploi et le maniement des affaires du monde'.[68] The ethical dilemmas they present in so doing are acute, as the 'querelles' they precipitate show.

Early Modern Experience

The indecisiveness of Longinus's treatise is that he writes about words, the mind, and the world as these hold some dim relationship with one another. The question of the accessibility or inaccessibility of experience in text subtends this study, as it does other recent work.

Neil Kenny, for instance, offers a word history of the term 'curiosity', and its cognates, in the overarching interest of entering into 'an arena in which some of the period's basic anxieties and aspirations about knowledge and behaviour were thrashed out', in which people attempted, as he says, 'to get things done'.[69] His approach, he says, is 'openly anachronistic': his word history presupposes that 'language is constitutive of meaning and that meaning arises from the relations between signifiers rather than from any dualistic harnessing of signifiers to referents'.[70] But this also means that he follows the contours of the period's ordinary language, rather than reorganizing those contours himself, sorting them out, or tidying them into those of a concept; and the result of his work is a powerful recognition of idiosyncrasy, the day–to–dayness of use. Richard Scholar, unlike Kenny, styles himself as a 'modern mentalist', assuming a distinction between the word, or lexeme, with which he is concerned (the *je-ne-sais-quoi*) and its meaning, or seme.[71] Preoccupied with those 'encounters with a certain something' in which 'certain' can, it seems, only ever mean its opposite, he sketches his own provisional definition of the *je-ne-sais-quoi*, and assesses whether particular lexical instances of the *je-ne-sais-quoi* fit this core meaning, observing the 'interactions and rifts' between them (p. 58). Examining preceding disparate and mobile traces that appear to participate in the subsequent interest in the *je-ne-sais-quoi*, he also suggests that these traces 'offer a more faithful image of the *je-ne-sais-quoi* than its subsequent historical development' (p. 6). He thereby 'moves the *je-ne-sais-quoi* outside its history in order to remain faithful to the thing itself' (p. 7): to forceful first-person experiences that are difficult to account for.

As I have already indicated in my introductory comments on Corneille, Pascal, and Boileau, I do not here seek to give an account of what 'the sublime' as a concept is, does, or allows authors to do, when it is born, sediments, or dies out. I note what certain authors happen to do, at points at which they happen to use the term 'sublime', and in ways which resonate with the treatise on the sublime. I hope that juxtapositions such as my own here may be a good way to accredit discussion of Longinus and the seventeenth century, may bring out well the rapid role-changes of the Longinian sublime, its plurality of associations — ranging, as noted, from the everyday to the ineffable.[72] Certainly these role-changes seem peculiarly appropriate to the study of a period which has been characterized in the last few years both — there being no contradiction here — as the 'age of suspicion' and as the 'age of experience'.[73]

One by-product of this study and others is the dulling of the hard contours of the 'Cartesian' abstractable self.[74] Critics have in the past tended, massively, to associate the seventeenth century with the inward-looking, world-excluding Cartesian self whose 'emergence' is, throughout Foucault's œuvre, the fundamental epistemological split which defines the passage into modernity.[75] Janet Varner Gunn, writing on 'classical autobiography' in the Cartesian tradition, states that 'the price exacted for the self's access to itself is very high: nothing less than the world, from which the subject must remove itself in order to think'.[76] Descartes rejects, in other words, the 'livre du monde'.[77] A contrast with Montaigne has often been thought instructive at this point. If Montaigne, according to Charles Taylor, identifies 'the individual in his or her unrepeatable difference', Cartesianism 'gives us a science of the subject in its general essence'.[78] 'Les *Essais*', confirms Antoine Compagnon, 'sont contraires à l'éthique classique de l'écriture et radicalement incompatibles avec elle', because this latter 'éthique' posits an idea of the subject 'qui transcende le livre; comme *res cogitans*, comme idée claire et distincte, il en est idéalement absent.'[79] But now reified definitions of this purely inward-looking *res cogitans* are an inaccurate stand-in for the theory of Descartes, as Michael Moriarty has argued in powerful terms: '[Descartes's] conception of selfhood is richer and more complicated than the conventional criticisms acknowledge, and it does not erect the self, or subject, into a secure position of self-mastery.'[80] And arguments about the extent to which the *res cogitans* defines an immediately powerful epistemic shift are therefore even more friable. This, I hope, will be borne out in what follows. The intermingling found in Longinian theory between our cognitive systems and those of others, between identification and identity, is, I argue, fascinating to Boileau, Pascal, and Corneille.[81]

We are dealing here with what we may call phenomenological approaches to literature which look at relationships described and assigned importance between human subjects and texts. The writing I consider gives us an opening onto the certainties and the uncertainties from which creative thinking accrues. For Longinus, as for the other writers with whom I am concerned, 'un livre écrit, mais non lu, n'existe pas pleinement. Il ne possède qu'une demi-existence'.[82] The activity of reading, like the activity of listening, depends upon the provocation and participation of (confusingly) different parties: 'Ce lecteur', writes Barthes, 'il faut que je le cherche (que je le "drague"), *sans savoir où il est*.'[83] I elide here the different socio-political contexts of these twentieth-century comments and their differing portrayals of power. But these modern authors may make familiar to us the kinds of response with which — in ways and to ends which are again very different — we are broadly concerned, as we consider Longinus's starting point that an agile writer can meet an active reader and create a propensity for the sublime.

These texts reflect, then, upon the endless modalities of convergence in human relations; and an understanding of this, gleaned via intimate critical readings sparked off in each case by the terms of the Longinian sublime, can help us to modify our understanding of early modern French literature.

Notes to Introduction

1. Throughout, I shall follow convention in referring to the anonymous author of *On the Sublime*, or *Peri hypsous*, as 'Longinus' rather than 'Pseudo-Longinus'. The genitive 'hypsous' turns to 'hypsos' when the term occurs outside the title.

2. Nicolas Boileau-Despréaux, *Œuvres complètes*, ed. by Antoine Adam and Françoise Escal (Paris: Gallimard, 1966), p. 550.

3. *On the Sublime*, 9.13. References in English will be to that edition of Longinus in which the translation of W. Hamilton Fyfe is revised by Donald Russell: *Aristotle, 'Poetics', Longinus, 'On the Sublime', Demetrius, 'On Style'*, Loeb Classical Library, 199 (Cambridge, MA: Harvard University Press, 1995). I shall also on occasion draw comparisons with the translation of G. M. A. Grube: *Longinus On Great Writing (On the Sublime)* (Indianapolis: Hackett, 1991).

4. Marc Fumaroli, *Héros et orateurs: rhétorique et dramaturgie cornéliennes* (Geneva: Droz, 1990), p. 345.

5. John Logan, 'Longinus and the Sublime', in *The Cambridge History of Literary Criticism*, III: *The Renaissance*, ed. by G. Norton (Cambridge: Cambridge University Press, 1999), pp. 529–39 (p. 539); Baldine Saint Girons, 'Avant-propos', in Edmund Burke, *Recherche philosophique sur l'origine de nos idées du sublime et du beau* (Paris: Vrin, 1973), p. 17.

6. On this, see the introduction to *On the Sublime* in *Aristotle, 'Poetics', Longinus, 'On the Sublime', Demetrius, 'On Style'*, pp. 145–58, and John M. Crossett and James A. Arieti, *The Dating of Longinus* (University Park: Department of Classics at Pennsylvania State University, 1975).

7. See Muret's mention of this in his commentary of Catullus, *Catullus et in eum commentarius M. Antonii Mureti* (Venice: Paulus Manutius, 1554), pp. 56–57. Muret thanks Manutius for encouraging him to undertake the translation. For useful detail about the various editions of *Peri hypsous*, see Bernard Weinberg, 'Translations and Commentaries of Longinus, *On the Sublime*, to 1600: A Bibliography', *Modern Philology*, 47 (1950), 145–51, and Jules Brody, *Boileau and Longinus* (Geneva: Droz, 1958), pp. 9–11. I sum up their findings in the following list of editions before Boileau:
   • Francesco Robortello (Basle: Jean Oporin, 1554), Greek text with Latin notes
   • Paulus Manutius (Venice: Paulus Manutius, 1555), Greek text
   • Domenico Pizzimenti (Naples: Scotus, 1566), Latin translation (*Dionysii Longini rhetoris praestantissimi Liber de grandi orationis genere, Dominico Pizimentio Vibonensis interprete*)
   • Franciscus Portus (Geneva: Jean Crespin, 1569), Greek text

- Petrus Paganus (Venice: Vincentius Valgrisius, 1572), Greek text with Latin translation (*Dionysii Longini de Sublimi dicendi genere liber a Petro Pagano latinitate donatus*)
- Gabriele de Petra (Geneva: J. Tournai, 1612), Greek text with Latin translation and notes (*Dyonisii Longini Liber de grandi sive sublimi genere orationis, latine redditus, et ad oram notationibus aliquot illustratus a Gab. de Petra*)
- Gerard Langbaine (Oxford: G. Webb, 1636), Greek text with Petra's translation and notes
- Niccolò Pinelli (Padua: G. Crivellari, 1639), Italian translation (*Dell'altezza del dire*)
- Giuseppe Aromatari (Venice: Salicata, 1643), Petra's translation
- Carolus Manolesius (Bologna: ev. Ducciae, 1644), Greek text with the three translations of Petra, Pizzimenti, and Paganus
- John Hall (Oxford: Roger Daniel for Francis Eaglefield, 1652), English translation (*Dionysius Longinus of the Height of Eloquence*)
- Tanneguy Le Fèvre (Saumur: J. Lenerius, 1663), Greek text with Petra's translation and Le Fèvre's own notes

8. Francesco Robortello, *In librum Aristotelis De arte poetica explicationes* (Florence: L. Torrentinus, 1548). In 1556, Henri Estienne published an edition of Anacreon containing the whole of the ode by Sappho conveyed only in Longinus's treatise: *Anacreontis et aliorum lyricorum aliquot pöetarum odæ. In easdem Henr. Stephani Observationes Eædem Latinæ* (Paris: G. Morel & R. Estienne, 1556), p. 69.

9. The editions in the libraries correspond to those published in 1554, 1569, 1612, and 1644. See Pseudo-Longin, *De la sublimité du discours: traduction inédite du XVIIᵉ siècle*, ed. by Emma Gilby (Paris: Éditions Comp'Act, forthcoming 2006), which looks into the debate (unresolved) surrounding authorship here, and gives a transcription, analysis, and annotation of the translation in question. The manuscript is found in Paris, Bibliothèque nationale de France (hereafter BnF), fonds italien, 2028 (catalogued as 'Recueil d'Extraits en diverses langues'), and contains, amidst much note-taking from volumes in Italian (hence its place in the fonds italien) and Latin, a version of Longinus entitled 'De la sublimité du discours'. My edition of this translation supplements a 1960s article by Bernard Weinberg: 'Une traduction française du "Sublime" de Longin vers 1645', *Modern Philology*, 59 (1961–62), 159–201. Weinberg supposes that the anonymous translation is by Mazarin, but it is difficult to conceive of Mazarin translating Longinus, bearing in mind not least that his translation would have been into a language that was not his mother tongue and undertaken in the interstices of his management of France's fiscal difficulties and war with Spain.

10. Fumaroli, *Héros et orateurs*, p. 345. Montaigne has connections with Marc-Antoine Muret, who taught him at the Collège de Guyenne in Bordeaux, is likely to have lectured him in Paris (see Roger Trinquet, *La Jeunesse de Montaigne: ses origines familiales, son enfance et ses études* (Paris: Nizet, 1972), pp. 611–12), and met him again at a party in Rome where they discussed Amyot's translation of Plutarch (see Montaigne, *Journal de voyage en Italie*, ed. by M. Rat (Paris: Garnier, 1955), p. 115). For loose hypotheses concerning Montaigne and Longinus, see Dorothy Gabe Coleman, 'Montaigne and Longinus', *Bibliothèque d'humanisme et de renaissance*, 47 (1985), 405–13; John Logan, 'Montaigne et Longin: une nouvelle hypothèse', *RHLF*, 83 (1983), 354–70. See also David L. Sedley, 'Sublimity and Skepticism in Montaigne', *PMLA*, 113 (1998), 1079–92.

11. Fumaroli, *Héros et orateurs*, p. 346.

12. On this, see Henry Phillips, *Church and Culture in Seventeenth-Century France* (Cambridge: Cambridge University Press, 1997).

13. Marc Fumaroli, *L'Âge de l'éloquence: rhétorique et 'res literaria' de la Renaissance au seuil de l'époque classique* (Paris: Albin Michel, 1994; orig. publ. Paris: Droz, 1980), p. 286.

14. See also *Héros et orateurs*: 'En interprétant dans le contexte théologique de la Réforme catholique le traité du rhéteur hellénistique, les rhéteurs jésuites avaient trouvé un moyen de lancer un pont entre littérature et vie religieuse, songeant d'abord à la prédication, mais aussi à la littérature catholique de combat en général' (p. 346).

15. Marc Fumaroli, 'Rhétorique d'école et rhétorique adulte: remarques sur la réception européenne du traité "Du Sublime" au XVIe et au XVIIe siècle', *RHLF*, 86 (1986), 33–51 (p. 36).

16. Fumaroli, *Héros et orateurs*, p. 384.

17. Fumaroli, 'Rhétorique d'école', p. 39.

18. *Boileau and Longinus*, p. 15.

19. Sophie Hache, *La Langue du ciel: le sublime en France au XVIIe siècle* (Paris: Champion, 2000).

20. François Ogier, *Apologie pour Monsieur de Balzac*, ed. by Jean Jehasse (Saint-Étienne: Publications de l'Université de Saint-Étienne, 1977), first published 1627, p. 75, and *Socrate chrestien par le Sr de Balzac; & autres oeuvres du mesme autheur* (Paris: Augustin Courbé, 1652), pp. 273–74. The notion that the *Apologie* was collaborative has at its origin Tallemant des Réaux's chapter on Balzac: 'Ogier le predicateur, son amy, entreprit de faire son *Apologie*. Il y en avoit desjà cinq ou six feuilles d'imprimées; Gomberville m'a dit qu'il les avoit, quand Balzac, arrivant icy, ne trouva point cela à sa fantaisie: il refit tout le discours, et ne se servit que de la matiere. Cela n'avoit garde de ne pas réussir, car Ogier est fort capable de choisir bien ses materiaux, et Balzac de faire fort bien le discours; aussi est-ce une des plus belles pieces que nous ayons.' Gédéon Tallemant des Réaux, *Historiettes*, ed. by Antoine Adam (Paris: Gallimard, 1961), II, 44. Tallemant later recounts Ogier's reaction on being asked to draw up Balzac's epitaph: '"Je m'en garderay bien," dit-il, "j'aurois peur qu'il ne se l'attribuast encore." Il disoit cela à cause de l'*Apologie*.' (p. 56)

21. Pierre Costar, *Defense des ouvrages de Monsieur de Voiture, à Monsieur de Balzac* (Paris: Courbé, 1653), p. 22.

22. Pierre Costar, *Suite de la Defense* (Paris: Courbé, 1655), p. 275.

23. Ibid., p. 276.

24. Marc Fumaroli, 'Pascal et la tradition rhétorique gallicane', in *Méthodes chez Pascal: actes du colloque tenu à Clermont-Ferrand, 10–13 juin 1976* (Paris: Presses universitaires de France, 1979), pp. 359–72 (p. 370).

25. Fumaroli, 'Rhétorique d'école', p. 50.

26. Georges Forestier, *Essai de génétique théâtrale: Corneille à l'œuvre*, 2nd edn (Geneva: Droz, 2004), p. 275.

27. Terence Cave, *Pré-histoires: textes troublés au seuil de la modernité* (Geneva: Droz, 1999), p. 177.

28. Stephen Hinds, *Allusion and Intertext* (Cambridge: Cambridge University Press, 1998), p. 18.

29. D. A. West and A. J. Woodman, eds, *Creative Imitation and Latin Literature* (Cambridge: Cambridge University Press, 1979), p. 179, quoted in Hinds, *Allusion*, p. 19.

30. Cave, *Pré-histoires*, p. 15.

31. For one of the most ambitious surveys, see Baldine Saint Girons, *Fiat lux: une philosophie du sublime* (Paris: Quai Voltaire, 1993); for one of the briefest, see Alain Michel, 'Rhétorique et poétique: la théorie du sublime de Platon aux modernes', *Revue des Études Latines*, 54 (1976), 278–307.

32. Edmund Burke, *A Philosophical Enquiry into the Origin of our Idea of the Sublime and the Beautiful* (Oxford: Oxford University Press, 1990), first published 1756.

33. Immanuel Kant, *Observations on the Feeling of the Beautiful and the Sublime*, trans. by John T. Goldthwait (Berkeley: University of California Press, 1991), first published 1757, and Book II of the *Critique of Judgement*, trans. by James Creed Meredith (Oxford: Oxford University Press, 1991), first published 1790.

34. Jean-François Lyotard, 'L'Instant, Newman', in *L'Inhumain: causeries sur le temps* (Paris: Galilée, 1988), pp. 89–99 (p. 91).

35. Slavoj Žižek has more recently rewritten Kantian concepts of the sublime: 'The Sublime is [...] the paradox of an object which, in the very field of representation, provides a view, in a negative way, of the dimension of what is unrepresentable.' *The Sublime Object of Ideology* (London: Verso, 1989), p. 202.

36. Thomas Weiskel, *The Romantic Sublime: Studies in the Structure and Psychology of Transcendence* (Baltimore: Johns Hopkins University Press, 1976), p. 11.

37. Suzanne Guerlac, *The Impersonal Sublime: Hugo, Baudelaire, Lautréamont* (Stanford, CA: Stanford University Press, 1990), p. 194.

38. Paul de Man, 'Phenomenality and Materiality in Kant', in *The Textual Sublime and its Differences*, ed. by H. J. Silverman and G. E. Aylesworth (Albany, NY: SUNY Press, 1990), pp. 87–108 (p. 105). See Richard Scholar, *The Je-Ne-Sais-Quoi in Early Modern Europe: Encounters with a Certain Something* (Oxford: Oxford University Press, 2005), p. 11.

39. Weiskel, *The Romantic Sublime*, p. 6.

40. On the close relationship between sublimity and scepticism, see in particular Sedley, 'Sublimity and Skepticism in Montaigne'.

41. Louis Marin, 'Le Sublime dans les années 1670: un je ne sais quoi?', *Papers on French Seventeenth-Century Literature*, 25 (1986), 185–201 (p. 186).
42. Jean-Luc Nancy, 'Le Sublime offrande', in Du Sublime, ed. by Jean-François Courtine (Paris: Belin, 1988), pp. 37–75 (p. 60).
43. In his massively influential article 'Meaning and Understanding in the History of Ideas' (*History and Theory*, 8 (1969), 3–53), Skinner anatomizes the different ways in which conceptual paradigms, when applied without sufficient thought for the linguistic context of particular illocutionary speech acts (what an author, 'in writing at the time he did write for an audience he intended to address, could in practice have been intending to communicate by the utterance of this given utterance', p. 49), can result in historical absurdity. He characterizes such absurdity as the 'mythology of doctrines', the 'mythology of coherence', the 'mythology of prolepsis', and the 'mythology of parochialism'.
44. Samuel H. Monk, *The Sublime: A Study of Critical Theories in XVIII-Century England* (Ann Arbor: University of Michigan Press, 1960), pp. 32, 6.
45. Louis Marin, 'On the Sublime, Infinity, Je Ne Sais Quoi', in *A New History of French Literature*, ed. by Denis Hollier (Cambridge, MA: Harvard University Press, 1989), pp. 340–45 (p. 343).
46. Forestier, *Essai de génétique théâtrale*, p. 292.
47. René Bray, *La Formation de la doctrine classique* (Paris: Hachette, 1927).
48. Aristotle, *Nicomachean Ethics*, trans. by H. Rackham, Loeb Classical Library, 73 (Cambridge, MA: Harvard University Press, 1990), Book VI, Chapter 4, subsection 1.
49. *The 'Art' of Rhetoric*, trans. by J. H. Freese, Loeb Classical Library, 193 (Cambridge, MA: Harvard University Press, 1994), 1356b.
50. Monk, *The Sublime*, p. 29.
51. Théodore Litman, *Le Sublime en France, 1660–1714* (Paris: Nizet, 1971), p. 71.
52. Nicolas Boileau-Despréaux, *Dissertation sur la Joconde, Arrest Burlesque, Traité du sublime,* ed. by Charles-H. Boudhors (Paris: Les Belles Lettres, 1966), p. 155.
53. Gilles Declercq, 'Topique de l'ineffable dans l'esthétique classique: rhétorique et sublime', *XVIIᵉ siècle*, no. 207 (April–June 2000), 199–220.
54. Declercq cites Monk approvingly: 'De l'aveu même de la critique anglaise, Boileau a contribué à l'émergence d'une théorie moderne du génie créateur.' 'Topique de l'ineffable', p. 203.
55. Marc Fumaroli, 'Apprends ma confidente, apprends à me connaître: les *Mémoires* de Retz et le traité *Du Sublime*', *Versants*, no. 1 (1981), 27–56 (p. 34).
56. *La Langue du ciel*, p. 395.
57. See Hache, *La Langue du ciel*, and Nicholas Cronk, *The Classical Sublime: French Neoclassicism and the Language of Literature* (Charlottesville: Rookwood Press, 2002).
58. Antoine Arnauld and Pierre Nicole, *La Logique ou l'art de penser*, ed. by Charles Jourdain (Paris: Gallimard, 1992), p. 31.
59. Thomas M. Carr, *Descartes and the Resilience of Rhetoric* (Carbondale and Edwardsville: Southern Illinois University Press, 1990), pp. 62–87 (p. 68).
60. Hache, *La Langue du ciel*, p. 21.
61. Jean Racine, *Œuvres complètes*, ed. by Luc Estaing (Paris: Éditions du Seuil, 1962), p. 266. Racine uses the term 'sublime' to make it qualify 'vertu' and mean 'great', 'high', 'superlative' in *La Thébaïde ou les frères ennemis*, line 139, and *Iphigénie en Aulide*, line 1665.
62. *Œuvres complètes*, p. 318.
63. *La Langue du ciel*, p. 80.
64. 'Lettres et opuscules spirituelles, XXVI', in François de Salignac de la Mothe-Fénelon, *Œuvres*, ed. by J. Le Brun, 2 vols (Paris: Gallimard, 1983–97), I, 684; Louis-Isaac Le Maistre de Sacy, Préface, *La Genese traduite en François, avec l'explication du sens litteral & du sens spirituel* (Paris: Lambert Roulland, 1682), unpaginated; Jacques-Bénigne Bossuet, 'Dissertio de Psalmis', in *Liber Psalmorum* (Lyons: Anisson, Posuel, and Rigaud, 1691), p. xliv.
65. Bossuet makes a biting reference to the Ciceronian sublime in his *Discours sur l'histoire universelle* (Paris: Garnier-Flammarion, 1966): 'Qu'ont gagné les philosophes avec leurs discours pompeux, avec leur style sublime, avec leurs raisonnements si artificieusement arrangés?' (Part II, Chapter 25, p. 292).
66. Antoine Arnauld, *Réflexions sur l'Eloquence des Predicateurs* (Paris: Florentin and Pierre Delaune, 1695), p. 16.

67. This is identification in 'ordinary parlance', and does not necessarily imply a Freudian assimilation of other people's attributes, or any other specifically psychoanalytical understanding (see Malcolm Bowie, *Lacan* (London: Fontana, 1991), p. 30). In *Sexuality and the Reading Encounter*, Emma Wilson notes (and troubles) this distinction when she aims 'to test, and indeed contest, the differences between the notion of identification used in its fullest psychoanalytic sense, and the notion of identification used more commonly with relation to reading a text or viewing a film where we speak of the possibility of "identifying" with a specific character, emotion, or spectatorial position'. *Sexuality and the Reading Encounter: Identity and Desire in Proust, Duras, Tournier, and Cixous* (Oxford: Clarendon Press, 1996), p. 5.

68. Corneille, *Writings on the Theatre*, ed. by H. T. Barnwell (Oxford: Blackwell, 1965), p. 38; Pascal, *Pensées*, ed. by Gérard Ferreyrolles (Paris: Livre de Poche, 2000), fragment S306; Longinus 1.2 (anonymous translation). See Chapters 2–4, 5–7, 8–9 respectively.

69. Neil Kenny, *The Uses of Curiosity in Early Modern France and Europe* (Oxford: Oxford University Press, 2004), pp. 2, 24.

70. Neil Kenny, *Curiosity in Early Modern Europe: Word Histories* (Wiesbaden: Harrassowitz, 1998), p. 26.

71. Scholar, *The Je-Ne-Sais-Quoi*, p. 57. This, in a way, brings his approach closer, he says, citing Kenny, to the mentalist assumptions of the early modern thinkers he discusses: concepts exist, here, in the mind before they pass into language (p. 57).

72. To speak of role-change and plurality is not — as should by now be clear — to espouse a standard deconstructive rigour here in rigorously pointing out the vacillations of a language that can never be rigorous. We might note that even Christopher Ricks, pathologically hostile to such, suggests in an essay on metaphor that 'the phenomenon of metaphor's intractability can itself be drawn upon'. Ricks continues: 'We might compare its not being possible to come up with satisfactory terms for the components or constitution of metaphor with other cases, such as the enduring and valuable unsatisfactoriness of our terms of the numinous or for the sexual, or our inability even to say satisfactorily what *kind* of distinction is the prose/poetry distinction, and our inability to find a satisfactory term for what, within a long poem, may unsatisfactorily have to be called a stanza, when it is no such thing, or a verse paragraph, likewise.' *Allusion to the Poets* (Oxford: Oxford University Press, 2002), p. 257.

73. Michael Moriarty's *Early Modern French Thought: The Age of Suspicion* (Oxford: Oxford University Press, 2003) traces a 'radical critical perspective on the spontaneous interpretation of human experience: an attitude of suspicion followed through no less rigorously by the early modern writers [Descartes, Pascal, Malebranche] than by the modern trinity [Marx, Freud, Nietzsche]' (p. 2); Richard Scholar writes that 'one might do worse than talk of this as "an age of experience", a category which reflects the fact that the rise to prominence of the *je-ne-sais-quoi* coincides with that of first-person experience as an object of fascination, suspicion, reflection and debate among thinkers and writers' (*The Je-Ne-Sais-Quoi*, p. 14).

74. Particularly influential here is the first of Terence Cave's two-volume *Pré-histoires*.

75. Self-reflexivity comes, in Foucault's account, with the modern production of subjects of power; with the habits and practices of self-control that individuals on the threshold of the modern age were increasingly forced to adopt. The emblem of these practices is the 'aveu', or confession. 'En Grèce', writes Foucault, 'la vérité et le sexe se liaient dans la forme de la pédagogie, par la transmission, corps à corps, d'un savoir précieux; le sexe servait de support aux initiations de la connaissance. Pour nous, c'est dans l'aveu que se lient la vérité et le sexe, par l'expression obligatoire et exhaustive d'un secret individuel.' Michel Foucault, *Histoire de la sexualité*, I: *La Volonté de savoir* (Paris: Gallimard, 1976), p. 82.

76. Janet Varner Gunn, *Autobiography: Toward a Poetics of Experience* (Philadelphia: University of Pennsylvania Press, 1982), p. 7

77. Descartes's reference to the 'livre du monde' comes in the *Discours de la méthode*: 'Mais après que j'eus employé quelques années à étudier ainsi dans le livre du monde et à tâcher d'acquérir quelque expérience, je pris un jour résolution d'étudier ainsi en moi-même, et d'employer toutes les forces de mon esprit à choisir les chemins que je devais suivre. Ce qui me réussit beaucoup mieux, ce me semble, que si je ne me fusse jamais éloigné, ni de mon pays, ne de mes livres.' *Discours de la méthode*, ed. by Geneviève Rodis-Lewis (Paris: Garnier-Flammarion, 1966), p. 39.

78. Charles Taylor, *Sources of the Self: The Making of the Modern Identity* (Cambridge: Cambridge University Press, 1989), p. 182.

79. Antoine Compagnon, *La Seconde Main, ou le travail de la citation* (Paris: Éditions du Seuil, 1979), p. 311.

80. *Early Modern French Thought*, p. 99.

81. The thesis on which this book is based was entitled 'Sublimity and Selfhood in Seventeenth-Century French Literature', and in it I expressed the hope that the self-evidently modern and English status of the term 'selfhood' would be enough to suggest that I was not 'reading it back' onto seventeenth-century French literature in an unproblematic way. It is possible to maintain, of course, that 'the self' exists in a form which is so complex and culturally specific that to speak of it at all is to espouse a silly kind of essentialism. One sometimes gets the impression that, once the true dependence of the individual upon his or her social context is pointed out, notions of selfhood, inwardness, and subjectivity evaporate together into naïve nothingness. This is a usefully labour-saving idea. I distance myself from any notion that 'selfhood' might refer to something infallible, complete, or grounded, while maintaining the idea that one can, without lapsing into historical absurdity, speak of there being, in the seventeenth century as at other times, aspects of selfhood or identity available to understanding and interrogation.

82. Michel Tournier, *Le Vol du vampire: notes de lecture* (Paris: Gallimard, 1983), p. 12.

83. Roland Barthes, *Le Plaisir du texte* (Paris: Éditions du Seuil, 1973), p. 11. Emma Wilson sets Tournier and Barthes in context in *Sexuality and the Reading Encounter*. She sums up her finely nuanced analyses in the form of the suggestion that texts can 'testify at once to the freedom of the reader *and* to the formative power of the reading encounter' (p. 6).

❖

CHAPTER 1

Longinus

The methodically minded have sought to rebuild an argument from the fragmentary remains of *Peri hypsous*. Elder Olson writes that 'a careful consideration of the direction and method of argument and of the assumptions involved in the critical judgments affords excellent ground for some restoration of the lacunae, at least to the extent of reconstructing the argument'.[1] But Longinus's extant sentences are wayward and his hypotheses flexible. So in spite of certain tactical reconstructions, it remains, in Neil Hertz's words, 'remarkably easy to lose one's way' in *Peri hypsous*.[2] Longinus's choice of examples, as Hertz suggests, seems particularly unruly: 'One quotation will suggest another but not necessarily because each illustrates the rhetorical topic at issue: both might, but the effective links between them seem at once flimsier and subtler than that' (p. 581). 'Longinus skates', writes Anne Carson, 'from Homer to Demosthenes to Moses to Sappho on blades of pure bravado.'[3] *Peri hypsous* is a text in which critical models are pervaded by variable inflations and perceptions. Let us consider, though, the most basic premise of *Peri hypsous*: the fact that language moves. This, like all basic premises, at once simplifies and intimates complexity, and I shall explore it in this chapter. One aim here will be to show that analyses of *Peri hypsous* which bring the text back to a single stylistic feature or moral aim fail. Another will be to look at how Longinus's *hypsos*, though ineffable, has a continuing relationship with the ways in which we make sense of the world and the people in it.

Hypsos

Longinus writes about language which touches us so successfully that we feel 'as if we had ourselves produced what we had heard'.[4] He calls this experience of identification 'hypsos'. 'Hypsos', we are told, 'shatters everything like a bolt of lightning and reveals the full power of the speaker at a single stroke' (1.4). Liddell and Scott's primary definition of the term is 'height'; they also have, citing Longinus, 'sublimity, grandeur'.[5] Etymologically, the term 'hypsos' and its relations

> ne sont que le sémitique 'ouf', *voler*, *s'élever*, et tous probablement qu'une belle onomatopée tirée du *soufflement*, *ronflement* ou *sifflement* que fait entendre l'air *froissé*, *foulé*, battu par l'aile ou tout autre corps. Ou du cri, du son *up*, *hup*, *houp*, que fait entendre toute bouche humaine lorsqu'il s'agit de lever, de soulever un fardeau de bas en haut, en comprimant subitement avec les lèvres une forte expiration de l'haleine.[6]

The English term 'sublimity' derives from the Latin 'sub-limen', or 'aloft, raised high', with the prefix denoting movement upwards and 'limen' meaning literally a doorstep, but indicating any form of metaphorical threshold.[7] Given the long-standing historical association of Longinus and the term 'sublime', the problem of finding a satisfactory English translation of 'hypsos' is not posed as often as it might be. As Grube notes: 'The English translators and editors seem to be agreed that "sublime" is an unsatisfactory translation of ὕψος, but they continue to use it; few of them give any clear idea of what Longinus is writing about.'[8] He questions the validity even of the metaphor of elevation:

> Longinus is trying to answer the question, what makes great writing, or, if we want to preserve the metaphor, how do writers reach those sudden heights which we all recognise as great? But we cannot keep the metaphor, for words such as 'elevation', which do, are the kind of technical term he avoided, and are in any case unsuitable. (p. 360)

In his own translation, Grube opts for the title *On Great Writing*, with *On the Sublime* in brackets.

One frequent confusion, as my introduction has already indicated, is between Longinian 'hypsos' and the 'genus grande' or 'genus sublime' by which rhetorical theory in the tradition of Cicero and Quintilian designates elevated diction (this is what Grube means by 'the kind of technical term [Longinus] avoided')[9] If Cicero's discourse is as powerful, in *Peri hypsous*, as 'a widespread conflagration, rolling around and devouring all around it', sublime words such as those of Demosthenes may by contrast be 'compared to a flash of lightning or a thunderbolt' (12.4). The language of both writers is obdurately and unstoppably strong; but sublimity is characterized by the suddenness, and so often also the simplicity, with which it enmeshes the listener or reader in its arousal of emotion.[10]

This distinction is fundamental. Boileau expresses it well at the beginning of the preface to his translation:

> Il faut donc sçavoir que par Sublime, Longin n'entend pas ce que les Orateurs appellent le stile sublime: mais cet extraordinaire et ce merveilleux qui frape dans le discours, et qui fait qu'un ouvrage enleve, ravit, transporte. Le stile sublime veut toujours de grands mots; mais le Sublime se peut trouver dans une seule pensée, dans une seule figure, dans un seul tour de paroles.[11]

But, as Boileau notes, sublimity of language and simplicity of language are not the same phenomenon: 'le Sublime *se peut* trouver dans une seule pensée' (my emphasis), but is not always found thus. Indeed, one chapter of *Peri hypsous* is devoted to sublime instances of periphrasis: 'that periphrasis can contribute to the sublime, no one, I fancy, would question' (28.1). Clearly, though, some of the instances of sublimity cited by Longinus are in the 'plain style'. One important example he gives is a version of the passage near the beginning of Genesis generally known as the *Fiat lux*: 'God said — what? "let there be light", and there was light, "let there be earth", and there was earth' (9.9). This passage, so Longinus's theory goes, gives the reader an absolute and immediate understanding of the qualities of the divine being portrayed by the author. Thus the utterance is not *just* great, noble, or elevated (although it may be seen to be all of these things too). It is sublime:

characterized by 'hypsos' because of its author's successful communication. The fact that God's power is communicated (or that the communicator is inspired by God) is secondary here. The analogy in *Peri hypsous* is with Homer's depiction of Poseidon (9.8).

If Longinus differentiates himself from such rhetors as Cicero in his definition of the sublime, he also nominates a move away from Caecilius of Caleacte, of whose 'little treatise on the Sublime' we are told that 'it appeared to us to fall below the level of the subject' (1.1). What kind of adequacy, then, does Longinus claim for himself? Caecilius 'endeavoured by a thousand instances to demonstrate the nature of the sublime', but stopped short of covering those key points that would permit us as readers to 'reach the goal ourselves' (1.1; Grube translates this latter phrase as 'make it ours', p. 3). Longinus seeks to facilitate a circuitry of participation and possession. In Longinus, the reader becomes the guarantor of the text's quality. If we cannot 'make it ours', it has failed. Longinus confuses any hierarchical relation between the writer and the receiver of text, creating a phenomenology of reading which fuses the features of the text and the reader's reaction to them, stresses the action brought about in response to language.

It follows that several critics have noted, with Richard Macksey, that 'Longinus variously associates [the sublime] with the inspired author, the "excited" text itself, and the impact transmitted to the audience'.[12] Olson, for example, writes similarly that, in distinguishing his own work from that of the canonical Greek rhetors, Longinus 'introduces the triad of terms — author, work and audience — which constitutes the fundamental framework of his argument'.[13] Sublimity cannot be attributed to any single one of these poles. As Olson continues, Longinus uses 'a reaction of the audience to define a fault or virtue of a work, a quality of the work to illustrate a faculty of the author', with the result that, in the sublime moment, 'we know ourselves to be moved to ecstasy by a literary work produced by a human agent' (p. 238). Longinus gives us to understand that 'hypsos' is best defined as a movement, and not merely a movement upwards (as one might expect from a term often translated as 'height'), but also horizontally, towards others. Sublime elevation is, importantly, only elevation inasmuch as it is elevation towards another human being.

But what kind of intermittent fault would cause the sublime to short-circuit? Authorial defects which would preclude the sublime include the spectre of plenitude that is bombast or tumidity: 'Tumours', we are told, 'are bad things whether in books or bodies' (3.3). They include puerility: 'the exact opposite of grandeur', 'an idea born in the classroom, whose overelaboration ends in frigid failure' (3.4). And they include false sentiment ('what Theodorus used to call the pseudo-bacchanalian'): 'emotion misplaced and pointless where none is needed', or 'unrestrained where restraint is required' (3.5). The refrain that Longinus modulates with these examples points to sublimity as the experience of encounter: as a trans-actional moment. The sublime cannot survive indifference catalysed by boredom or confusion.

To write sublimely about heroic adventure, then, an author must seem to participate fully in the dangers portrayed in his or her text. Euripides joins

Phaethon in his chariot ('Would you not say that the writer's soul is aboard the car, and takes wing to share the horses' peril?', 15.4), and in the *Iliad* Homer enters into the fray at Troy: 'The battle is blown along by the force of Homer's writing, and he himself "stormily raves, as the spear-wielding War-god, or Fire, the destroyer"' (9.11).[14] In a further example taken from the *Iliad* in 10.6, Homer 'has tortured his language into conformity with the impending disaster, magnificently figured the disaster by the compression of his language, and almost stamped on the diction the precise form of the danger'. It is clear that, as Suzanne Guerlac states, sublimity 'can only be presented in action, through and as an act of enunciation'.[15] And logically, sublimity is a function of 'the place, the manner, the circumstances, the motive' of the utterance: when Demosthenes swears an oath upon his ancestors, it is his particular statement, rather than 'the swearing of an oath', which is sublime (16.3).

Lawrence Kerslake has condensed the triangle of identification that is the sublime into two points of contact: 'Although [Longinus] deals, in the treatise, with the relationship between author and work, and with the relationship between audience and work, the most important aspect of the triad is the communication between author and audience.'[16] This, however, is to negate the care that Longinus takes to specify the intermediary role of discourse. It is vital that the means to the sublime should be discourse; it is worth noting that our anonymous seventeenth-century translator's version is entitled 'De la sublimité du discours', and Boileau is accurate in defining the sublime in his preface as an encounter with 'l'excellence et la souveraine perfection *du discours*'.[17]

Music, for instance, has undoubted emotive power. We read at 39.1 that 'men find in melody not only a natural instrument of persuasion and pleasure, but also a marvellous instrument of grandeur and emotion'. But Longinus deals with this emotive power in a way that intimates suspicion of it. A 'variety of sounds' or 'harmonious blending' is 'only a bastard counterfeit of persuasion' (39.3). The sublime is more forceful than persuasion ('our persuasions are usually under our own control, while these things exercise an irresistible power and mastery, and get the better of every listener', 1.4), but instrumental music is persuasion's illegitimate offspring, a 'bastard counterfeit'. Music is like persuasion, but is not quite as well founded, just as persuasion is like sublimity, but is not quite there. As George B. Walsh states when glossing this passage, 'Although illegitimate children certainly resemble their fathers, nothing comes from such resemblance — no wealth or power or prestige; it may be real but it does not count.'[18] The pathos of music is a poor relation, destined to insignificance. Only words 'reach not only [man's] ears but his very soul' (39.3). Similarly, nature can present us with powerfully affecting phenomena. In Chapter 35, Longinus contrasts 'small streams, clear and useful as they are' with 'the Nile, the Danube, the Rhine and above all the Ocean', and 'the little fire we kindle for ourselves' with 'the craters of Etna in eruption' (35.4). But his point here concerns the force of the unusual: 'On all such matters *I would say only this*, that what is useful or necessary is easily obtained by man; it is always the unusual which wins our wonder' (35.4, my emphases).[19] Music and powerful natural phenomena are analogies for, rather than examples of, the sublime, which pertains to discourse, is a 'specifically human product'[20] — one that can none the less, of course, make forceful use of metaphors and analogies sourced from the natural world.

Longinus repeatedly finds ways to rehearse and re-stress the cognition that accompanies emotion in the sublime. There is a cognitive dimension in the production of the sublime (obtaining 'a clear knowledge and appreciation of what is really sublime [...] is not an easy thing to grasp: judgement in literature is the ultimate fruit of ripe experience', 6.1), as well as in the sublime moment itself (with our identification, our understanding that it is 'as if we had ourselves produced the very thing we had heard', 7.2), and of course in the sublime moment's subsequent theorization, which may then, Longinus hopes, go on to equate to further production ('it is perhaps not impossible that a true discernment in such matters may be achieved from some such considerations as the following', 6.1).

The sublime, then, is not just an ecstatic loss of cognition. Demosthenes' sublime oath in Chapter 16 inculcates 'the lesson that "in the wildest rite" you must stay sober' (16.4). Throughout, we engage with the very category of cogent self-expression which sublime experience might be thought to annihilate in its ineffability. But nor is the sublime reducible to the gaining of a voice through ecstasy: what Hertz characterizes as 'the sublime turn'.[21] Hertz analyses the sublime in terms of a competition between self-expression, on the one hand, and that ineffable experience which would overwhelm the self on the other. Self-expression in the face of ineffable experience, subjectivity found in ecstasy, is 'the sublime turn'. But this generalizes in a way that does not do justice to the endlessly different voices and subject positions involved.

In sum, then, the sublime is a result of an author coming into cognitive contact with a reader who can identify with that author via discourse. One statement needs to be considered closely here: 'Elsewhere I have written something like this, "Sublimity is the echo of a noble mind"' (9.2).[22] Longinus is often understood by this to be saying that noble (elevated) souls always generate sublime speech, that sublimity is a quality that can inhere in an author alone. Thus, Guerlac states that Longinus 'declare[s] tautologically that sublimity comes from sublimity': 'What we learn from the "five genuine sources" of the sublime is less "how to reach the goal ourselves" than that the Longinian sublime appears to be simultaneously ends and means towards itself.'[23] And Macksey supposes that Longinus 'asks the paradoxical question of how we can "make ourselves capable" of great thoughts and feelings'.[24] Walsh sums up the contradiction: 'According to one view [contained within the treatise], language is an expressive medium that embodies the speaker's spirit, or at least emanates from it directly. [...] According to the other view, language is a medium of reference and description, unlike and separate from the spiritual experiences it is sometimes asked to represent.'[25]

There are indeed contradictory emphases here, but there are two principal responses to these comments. First, echoes are, precisely, reverberations and resonances, rather than thoughts. Even silence, and Longinus gives the example of the silence of Ajax in the Summoning of the Ghosts, has reverberative, communicative force; and the sublimity of this example is to be equated with this force, rather than with Ajax's (nonetheless undoubted) greatness. Secondly, 'nobility' is presented, in *Peri hypsous*, as intrinsic to humankind and therefore as universal: 'nature has judged man a creature of no mean or ignoble quality' (35.2). All human souls are the opposite of mean and ignoble: 'the whole universe is not enough to satisfy the speculative intelligence of human thought' (35.3). The 'nobility' to which Longinus is referring when he says that 'sublimity is the echo of a noble mind' is a quality available to everyone. As Kerslake notes, 'Our intrinsic nobility (35.2–4) makes possible both the production of the sublime and our response to it.'[26] But nobility (greatness, grandeur) only makes possible — is not synonymous with — the sublime communication and identification theorized by Longinus. Thus in Homer, grandeur is only what is left in old age: 'In the *Odyssey* one may liken Homer to the setting sun; the grandeur remains without the intensity' (9.13).

'Images drawn from real life'

Which texts, then, do produce sublime encounters? With the *Odyssey*, we are told, no longer 'does [Homer] preserve the sustained energy of the great *Iliad* lays, the consistent sublimity which never sinks into flatness, the flood of moving incidents in quick succession, the versatile rapidity and actuality, dense with images drawn from real life'. The sublime has its origin and source in the myriad details of 'real life'. In the *Odyssey*, which does 'sink into flatness' (and an explanatory analogy is drawn from the natural world: 'it is rather as though the Ocean had retreated into itself and lay quiet within its own confines', 9.13), we are told that 'the mythical element prevails over the real' (9.14). When the 'real' is subdued, sublimity is subtly deflected:

> Writing in the heyday of his genius [Homer] made the whole piece lively with dramatic action, whereas in the *Odyssey* narrative predominates, the characteristic of old age. [...] In great writers and poets, declining emotional power passes into character portrayals. (9.13–15)

This passage is reminiscent of Aristotle's subordination of character portrayals to action in the *Poetics*:

> Tragedy is mimesis not of persons but of action and a life. [...] It is not in order to provide mimesis of character that the agents act; rather, their characters are included for the sake of their actions.[27]

Characters exist to force us to grapple with action and interaction. Demosthenes is sublime when, leaping 'at once into further asyndeta and anaphoras', he makes us grapple with a man's grappling: '"By his manner, his looks, his voice, when he strikes with insult, when he strikes like an enemy, when he strikes with his knuckles, when he strikes you like a slave"' (20.2).[28] And it is worth noting here also that when music is characterized, in *Peri hypsous*, as a 'bastard counterfeit', it is opposed to 'energēmata gnēsia', 'genuine activities' (39.3). Sublimity is 'energēma', an action, activity, operation. It comes with writing which closes down any tranquillizing distance between narration and event.

The one example taken from the *Odyssey* in Longinus's Chapter 9 is chosen to show that the dramatic interrelationships which were the catalyst for the *Iliad* are merely footnoted in this later text:

> In fact the *Odyssey* is simply an epilogue to the *Iliad*:

> 'There then Ajax lies, great warrior; there lies Achilles;
> There, too, Patroclus lies, the peer of the gods in counsel;
> There, too, my own dear son.' (9.12)[29]

The *Iliad* has created a variegated and voluminous configuration of encounters and relationships. These catalyse the encounter with which Longinus is concerned: the sublime. What we perceive in Longinus is this: the sublime encounter can be theorized by Longinus in terms of the encounters that precede it. And language which uses encounters as its material, its building blocks, frequently precipitates the sublime. The sublime encounter that is language's impossible referent is dependent, here, upon writing which itself makes encounters its referent. 'Watch this spillage, which moves from the man who hits, to the words of Demosthenes describing him, to the judges hearing these words, to Longinus analyzing the whole process, to me recalling Longinus's discussion of it and finally to you reading my account.'[30]

Another of Longinus's key examples of a sublime writer is Sappho. The ode he transmits through his work reads as follows:

> He seems to me equal to the gods that man
> whoever he is who opposite you
> sits and listens close
> to your sweet speaking

> and lovely laughing — oh it
> puts the heart in my chest on wings
> for when I look at you, a moment, then no speaking
> is left in me

> no: tongue breaks, and thin
> fire is racing under skin and in eyes no sight and drumming
> fills ears

> and cold sweat holds me and shaking
> grips me all, greener than grass
> I am and dead — or almost
> I seem to me.[31]

Introducing his citation of this ode, Longinus writes:

> There are, in every situation, a number of features which combine to make up the texture of events. To select the most vital of these and to relate them to one another to form a unified whole is an essential cause of great writing. (Grube 10.3 p. 17)

Sappho both selects details successfully and presses them into close relationship. The forms of knowledge she conveys are drawn forth from observation and experience; they are combined without local support from anything other than these: 'She feels contradictory sensations, freezes, burns, raves, reasons, so that she displays not a single emotion, but a whole congeries of emotions' (10.3). And thus she successfully communicates her own ecstatic state.

Neil Hertz calls this simultaneous ecstasy and communication a good example of the 'sublime turn': 'a turning away from near-annihilation, from being "under death" to being out from under death'.[32] He writes that 'Longinus admires the poem because when it becomes "like a living creature" and "finds its voice" it speaks of a moment of self-estrangement in language that captures the disorganized quality of the experience'. Sappho's choppy grammatical structures convey the experience they point to, in a 'shift from Sappho-as-victimized-body to Sappho-as-poetic-force' (p. 585). This shift, he suggests, is the defining shift that takes place in the sublime moment (Hertz illustrates this with examples taken from Wordsworth: the latter's 'my mind turned round | as with the might of waters', p. 584, and 'weak, as is a breaking wave', p. 585). In a reading inspired by Hertz, Suzanne Guerlac writes: 'On the level of the *énoncé* [Sappho's poem] figures the *destinataire* of the sublime enunciation. If the "effect of genius" or sublimity is to "transport the audience outside themselves", this transport is figured by Sappho, "clearly beside herself with love".[33] Sappho identifies with another; the reader identifies, sublimely, with Sappho. Both author and reader are 'beside themselves', lose their own identities in a near-fatal moment of passion, yet gain the insights of irreducible experience in a 'sublime turn'.

Some critics have contested the appropriateness of this vocabulary of domination and passivity in studies of Sappho, because 'what emerges as "I" is neither subject nor object, but somewhere inbetween, perhaps — alive and almost dead, dead and almost alive, neither dead nor alive, both dead and alive'.[34] The sublime moment cannot be recuperated either in terms of a controlling agent, or in terms of an entirely passive or annihilated subject. On a more basic level, Sappho's ode to Longinus takes as its mainstay not a domination–passivity dichotomy, but rather a series of encounters. Sappho's object of passion is not an isolated woman but a woman in conversation —

> your sweet speaking
> and lovely laughing — oh it
> puts the heart in my chest on wings

— and a woman in conversation with a randomly presented man —

> that man
> whoever he is who opposite you
> sits and listens close.

This woman's encounter is the source of Sappho's own. What is phenomenalized here is not a grounded and centred subjectivity (either opposed to or found in ecstasy), but the formative role played by endlessly receding encounters. The text encourages our identification with the speaker's subject position because it is itself about interaction (this is different from saying that it dominates us because it is itself about domination). The text shows that the speaking subject is defined by multiple encounters with others, others who are themselves defined by encounters, and, in Longinus's treatise, it is particularly productive of the sublime encounter that is 'hypsos'.

Illustrating the sublimity of Alexander, a man 'of high spirit' who exemplifies 'those whose ideas are weighty', Longinus refers to Alexander's anecdotal answer to Parmenio (9.4). The anecdote in question (which is mentioned but not filled out in the text as six pages are lost at this point) runs as follows: Darius offered Alexander territory and one of his daughters in marriage; Parmenio said 'If I were Alexander, I should have accepted', and Alexander replied, 'If I were Parmenio, so should I'. There is nothing particularly morally uplifting or noble about this anecdote. This does not prevent Longinus from citing it as 'a splendid remark'. Clearly, inasmuch as Alexander is great, it is because he enables us to identify with his own response, to see his point with an extraordinary (and humorous) degree of acuity. It is easy to project into his subject position because the whole anecdote is about the 'if I were' of projection into different subject positions. Once again, sublime discourse brings an awareness of other people into play.

Longinus, throughout, engages with populated texts and our responses to these. Thus the domain of the ethical irrupts within *Peri hypsous*. This does not mean that *Peri hypsous* establishes within its own chapters principles by which we ought to live. Russell writes that 'it would be an exaggeration, but not a total falsehood, to say that περι ὕψους is a moral protreptic in the guise of literary criticism'.[35] His point is that '[Longinus's] ideal writer — the figure corresponding in a sense to the Socrates of the *Apology* or the Demosthenes of *de corona* — must be morally mature, superior to material considerations, and mentally big enough to grasp big ideas' (p. 85). But we have seen that Longinus does not consider 'big ideas' independently of their communication. Only in this sense does his treatise have a moral thrust, a 'must': it 'must show us how and by what means we may reach the goal ourselves' (1.1).

Claiming that Longinus 'introduces the assumption that the sublime is a function of the individual *phusis*', Macksey then comments that Longinus 'somewhat surprisingly does not get around to suggesting the context in which this *hupsos* may actually prove "useful" nor the sort of people who may benefit from his "methods"'.[36] But it is not necessarily surprising that Longinus does not provide a separate 'pragmatics' of the sublime. It is not the case that sublimity enables us, through its effects, to raise our natures to a certain pitch of moral elevation which can subsequently be useful; rather, sublimity is in itself defined as a movement, an elevation, towards an author via a text. Texts that blur the borders between existence and writing are more likely to have this effect, and in so doing they also force an awareness of the complexities of existence upon the reader. Sublimity carries its functionality along with it; it is not an elevated state that can be separated from its 'usefulness'.

The moral aspect of Longinus's message concerns, then, not so much how we can make ourselves capable of noble thoughts and feelings as how we are defined by the encounters we make (read, written, and lived). This understanding is useful to readers inasmuch as they are future writers, but also inasmuch as they are, quite simply, readers who respond to texts and people who respond to the world: they are forced by Longinus to contemplate the place of other people, and therefore contingency, in existence. The sublime encounter is also 'images drawn from real life' (9.13).

Contingency and the Cosmic

So a necessarily shifting identification provides the gravitational pull of Longinus's text: the experience of the sublime can only be given the kind of theoretical or argumentative linearity that defers to the dynamic of encounter. The thrust of the final chapter, which condemns 'the idleness in which all but a few of us pass our lives, only exerting ourselves or showing any enterprise for the sake of getting praise or pleasure out of it, never from the honourable and admirable motive of doing good to the world' (44.11), is that idleness precludes movement, and in particular a movement towards others. Charles P. Segal, though, offers a Platonic reading of this contempt for human idleness: he writes of 'the general idealism of Longinus, in which he follows in the steps of his "hero" Plato; both attack vehemently the materialism of the world'.[37] Longinus, in this last chapter, sets about 'removing the basis of *hypsos* from the ordinary world of men and bringing it into universal, cosmic and teleological significance' (p. 136).

Posing the question of whether Longinus's frequent mentions of Plato really entail loyalty to him and approbation of Platonic idealism, critics have often answered, with Segal, in the affirmative. D. C. Innes sees Plato's defence of mimesis in the *Ion* as congenial to the Longinian schema:

> In 13.1–3 Longinus [...] evokes the creative power of mimesis in his own imitation of Plato's magnetic chain of inspiration in *Ion* 533d, inspiration which like that of frenzied corybants or bacchants moves from Muse to poet (Homer) to rhapsode to audience.

In the *Ion*, Plato develops the notion of poetic frenzy as divine madness. The simile of the magnet with a chain of iron rings parallels poetic creation and the performance of the rhapsode: the Muse is the magnet who transmits her power to the poet, who passes it on to the rhapsode or actor, who in turn exercises the power of possession over the audience.[38] Talent is nothing without the Muse, without the poetry of divine madness, as the *Phaedrus* confirms:

> There is a third form of possession or madness, of which the Muses are the source. This seizes a tender, virgin soul and stimulates it to rapt passionate expression, especially in lyric poetry, glorifying the countless mighty deeds of ancient times for the instruction of posterity. But if any man come to the gates of poetry without the madness of the Muses, persuaded that skill alone will make him a good poet, then shall he and his works of sanity with him be brought to nought by the poetry of madness, and behold, their place is nowhere to be found.[39]

Longinian sublimity is likened to this 'rapt passionate expression' whose aim is to 'glorify' nobility for the sake of stimulating future generations to impressive achievement. But as we have seen, Longinian 'hypsos' is not, overall, to be equated entirely with nobility, nor with an artless possession or madness. This takes us away from the model of the *Phaedrus*. Moreover, the question of Longinus's affiliation to Plato is all the harder to evaluate given that Plato's own theory is so famously tensile and malleable.

For a view of poetry which differs from that of the *Ion*, we may turn, of course, to Plato's *Republic*, where the good city is defined by the elimination of the proliferating emotions provoked by poetry: emotions that inevitably provide a radical distraction from the deliberation or reasoning through which virtue is attained. The best kind of person, we are given to understand, is the philosopher. The philosopher's activities (if deliberation and reasoning can be classified as activities in Plato) are intrinsically superior to all others, given that they are concerned with the unchanging, immortal, and true. They deal with the form of the good, that which makes all things intelligible: 'It's goodness which gives the things we know their truth and makes it possible for people to have knowledge.'[40] The conflation of objects and their representations that is mimesis is, therefore, profoundly suspicious: poets have no place in these systemic elaborations. The only activities permitted serve to prepare the best life for its contemplative striving towards the unchanging, immortal, non-perspectival, good Truth.[41]

Seeking to reconcile Longinus with this aspect of Plato's thought is difficult, given that Longinus's experience of 'hypsos' magnifies the mimetic effect that Plato seems to recognize and vilify in his *Republic*. Russell has sought to attempt a reconciliation, in spite of noting that the 'centrality of the proposition that ὕψος is closely linked with pathos, emotional tension' is 'irrelevant to, or even at variance with, the need to defend Plato'.[42] This is because, maintaining a parallel between 'hypsos' and '"cosmic" feeling' (p. 82), he sees defending Plato as 'clearly a conspicuous theme in the whole' (p. 74). He suggests that Longinus's statement, seemingly going against the grain of the rest of the text, that 'πάθος is not a necessary element of ὕψος, since this clearly occurs in literature without it' (8.2) is motivated by the 'need to defend Plato' (p. 75). But Longinus's point in stating that 'hypsos' does not always possess an element of pathos (translated by Hamilton Fyfe and revised by Russell as follows: 'many sublime passages are quite without emotion') seems to be that the affecting or striking does not have to spring from self-evidently affecting or striking subject matter: his example here is Homer's description of the Aloades trying futilely to pile Mount Pelion upon Mount Ossa upon Mount Olympus in order to wage war upon the Olympian gods (8.2). Homer, exaggeratedly, daringly (these are the terms of *Peri hypsous*), says 'And they would have done it as well' (8.2). This statement, says Longinus, is sublime. And once again, the idea that the sublime can be aligned with the 'cosmic' is only a very loose one. The sublime, though universally affecting, mutates endlessly.

Whether Plato is attacking or defending the poets, he holds that the emotions induced by poetry are entirely non-cognitive.[43] But in Longinus, as we have seen, sublimity always has a cognitive dimension. It is not a state that can be distinguished from the particular cognitive structures of its participants. And the fact that the sublime is theorized in terms of the particular human relationships which go to make it up implies in itself a major distancing from Plato. A commonplace of Socratic theory that the best kind of person is 'pre-eminently capable of providing himself with a good life entirely from his own resources, and is absolutely the last person to need anyone or anything else'.[44] The dynamic of Longinus's text is in no way comparable to this expurgation of difference.

In the sublime moment as in the texts that provoke it, the borders between the outside world and fictional reworkings of it are smudged. At no stage of

Peri hypsous does Longinus allow for divisions between existence and text. The sublime is simultaneously empirical experience, the self-awareness that comes with this experience, and the further awareness that this self-knowledge is dependent upon communication. Discourse which provokes 'hypsos' is often discourse about human relations, and the moral thrust, the 'must' of the treatise on the sublime — as in 'the author must first define his subject, and secondly, though this is really more important, he must show us how and by what means we may reach the goal ourselves' (1.1) — needs to be understood accordingly. Longinus has often been understood to be stating that a moral improvement comes as a separate consequence of the sublime moment: aspiring towards sublimity is supposed to make us better people, and only those successful in being good can achieve it. But because the variables of human communication and interrelationships play a constituent part in his presentation of the sublime, Longinus cannot espouse a simplistic association of sublimity with the morally elevated or noble. The morality of *Peri hypsous* is a morality of flexibility (the judgement that we define ourselves through our encounters with other people), and defines (rather than comes as a separate consequence of) sublime experience. What I want to take away from this chapter for use in those which follow is the conceptual cluster provided for us by Longinus: sublime knowledge through encounter, and elevation through communication. This, as I shall argue in what follows, fascinates certain authors in seventeenth-century France.

Notes to Chapter 1

1. Elder Olson, 'The Argument of Longinus' *On the Sublime*', in *Critics and Criticism Ancient and Modern*, ed. by R. S. Crane (Chicago: University of Chicago Press, 1952), pp. 232–59 (p. 240).
2. Neil Hertz, 'A Reading of Longinus', *Critical Inquiry*, 9 (1983), 579–96 (p. 580). This article first appeared in *Poétique*, 15 (1973), translated into French by Jean-Michel Rabaté.
3. Anne Carson, '(Essay with Rhapsody): On the Sublime in Longinus and Antonioni', in *Decreation: Poetry, Essays, Opera* (New York: Knopf, 2005), pp. 43–51 (p. 45). Carson's brief essay-rhapsody, published in 2005 as work on this book was drawing to a close, gives voice beautifully to my preoccupations here; I am grateful to Katherine Ibbett for making sure that I encountered it when I did.
4. *On the Sublime*, 7.2.
5. *Greek–English Lexicon*, revised by Henry Stuart Jones and Roderick McKenzie (Oxford: Oxford University Press, 1968).
6. Étienne de Campos Leyza, *Analyse étymologique des racines de la langue grecque* (Bordeaux: Émile Crugy, 1874).
7. The *OED* has 'sublime' as a verb, the equivalent of 'to sublimate', meaning to cause to change state, 'to subject (a substance) to the action of heat in a vessel so as to convert it into vapour'.
8. G. M. A. Grube, 'Notes on the ΠΕΡΙ ΥΨΟΥΣ', *American Journal of Philology*, 78 (1957), 355–74 (p. 355).
9. The 'genera dicendi' were formulated notably in the *Ad Herennium*, in Cicero's *Orator*, and in Quintilian's *Institutio oratoria*. On this, see *'Longinus' On the Sublime*, ed. by D. A. Russell (Oxford: Clarendon Press, 1964), pp. xxxiv–xxxvii.
10. The categories of listener and reader smudge together in the Greek 'akroōmenos' (see *On the Sublime*, 1.4); in what follows, I often use 'reader' as an abbreviation of 'listener or reader'.
11. *Œuvres complètes*, ed. by Antoine Adam and Françoise Escal (Paris: Gallimard, 1966), p. 338.
12. Richard Macksey, 'Longinus Reconsidered', *MLN*, 108 (1993), 913–34 (p. 916).
13. Olson, 'The Argument of Longinus' *On the Sublime*', p. 238.
14. The reference is to the *Iliad*, Book xv, line 605.

15. Suzanne Guerlac, 'Longinus and the Subject of the Sublime', *New Literary History*, 16 (1985), 275–90 (p. 279).

16. Lawrence Kerslake, 'Longinus', in *Essays on the Sublime: Analyses of French Writings on the Sublime from Boileau to La Harpe* (Berne: Peter Lang, 2000), pp. 25–40 (p. 40).

17. *Œuvres complètes*, p. 341 (my emphases). For a wider discussion of these translators, see Chapter 8. Georges Forestier homes in straight away on the importance of discourse for Longinus — 'Certes Longin ne traite que du sublime dans le discours (oratoire ou poétique)' — although, as I noted in my Introduction, I would otherwise question the brevity and sufficiency of his résumé of Longinus: 'Le sublime est le ravissement vers la grandeur par la violence de la beauté. Il suffit de lire le traité *Du sublime* de Longin pour s'en convaincre.' *Essai de génétique théâtrale: Corneille à l'œuvre*, 2nd edn (Geneva: Droz, 2004), p. 275. See the following chapters on Corneille.

18. George B. Walsh, 'Sublime Method: Longinus on Language and Imitation', *Classical Antiquity*, 7 (1988), 252–69 (p. 254).

19. As Kerslake notes, 'These references to grandeur in nature furnish an authority in Longinus's text itself for later theories that find instances of the sublime in the natural world. But if we pay strict attention to what the treatise says, we realize that Longinus's own position does not accord with such an interpretation.' *Essays on the Sublime*, p. 39.

20. Ibid., p. 40. Kerslake is rightly careful not to criticize or to undermine the fruitfulness of later writers who, responding to the force of Longinus's language here, go on to make theories out of the sublimity of the natural world itself. By the same token, certain critics have brought Poussin's depictions of tempests, floods, and storms into line with Longinus's treatise. This has been in the interests of arguing that, like the reception of Longinus's discussion of sublime response, these depictions should be seen as a constituent part of classicism. See Louis Marin, *Sublime Poussin* (Paris: Éditions du Seuil, 1995) (which includes several articles on the subject, among them 'Le Sublime dans les années 1670: un je-ne-sais-quoi?', originally published in *Papers on French Seventeenth-Century Literature*, 25 (1986), 185–201), and Clélia Nau, *Le Temps du sublime: Longin et le paysage poussinien* (Rennes: Presses universitaires de Rennes, 2005). 'Le classicisme pouvait', writes Nau, citing in particular Paul Bénichou and his *Morales du grand siècle*, 'trouver à s'allier avec le sublime, quelle que conflictuelle que soit cette alliance, quel que problématique soit cet appariement. Ce dont l'oeuvre de Poussin est la plus parfaite illustration. Il y a chez lui une aspiration à l'ordre, à la mesure, à la raison (au sens du *logos* grec), qui fait de lui un classique. Mais il y a aussi, simultanément, et pourrait-on dire, contradictoirement, chez lui une fascination pour le désordre.' *Le Temps du sublime*, p. 314.

21. 'A Reading of Longinus', p. 584.

22. ' "Sublimity is the echo of a great mind — as I believe I have written somewhere else" (9.2), says Longinus, echoing gently.' Carson, '(Essay with Rhapsody)', p. 49.

23. 'Longinus and the Subject of the Sublime', p. 277.

24. 'Longinus Reconsidered', p. 919.

25. 'Sublime Method', p. 259.

26. *Essays on the Sublime*, p. 29.

27. Aristotle, *Poetics*, trans. by Stephen Halliwell, in *Aristotle, 'Poetics', Longinus, 'On the Sublime', Demetrius, 'On Style'*, Loeb Classical Library, 199 (Cambridge, MA: Harvard University Press, 1995), 1450a15.

28. Longinus's example is from Demosthenes, *Oration*, 21.72.

29. The reference is to the *Odyssey*, III. 109–11.

30. Carson, '(Essay with Rhapsody)', p. 46.

31. This is the translation of Anne Carson, in ' "Just for the Thrill": Sycophantizing Aristotle's *Poetics*', *Arion*, 1.1 (1990), 142–54 (pp. 148–49). This translation has since been reprinted with others of Sappho by Carson in *If Not, Winter: Fragments of Sappho* (London: Virago, 2002). Longinus's treatise is the only source of this ode, known as 'fragment 31'.

32. 'A Reading of Longinus', p. 584.

33. 'Longinus and the Subject of the Sublime', p. 282.

34. See Yopie Prins, 'Sappho's Afterlife in Translation', in *Re-reading Sappho: Reception and Transmission*, ed. by Ellen Green (Berkeley: University of California Press, 1996), pp. 36–67 (p. 41). Prins gives a fascinating reading of various translations of Sappho's ode: 'Hall introduces

Sappho as a lyric subject within a legacy of Petrarchan fragmentation, Philips translates Sappho into the past tense as a posthumous lyric subject, Hewitt inscribes Sappho onto a suffering body that does not speak, and Barnard locates Sappho's voice in the moment of its interruption. Sappho survives as a text never quite sublimated into voice: a corpus used for, and ab-used by, translation' (p. 66). For commentary on early modern translations of Sappho, see Pseudo-Longin, *De la sublimité du discours: traduction inédite du XVIIe siècle*, ed. by Emma Gilby (Paris: Éditions Comp'Act, forthcoming 2006).

35. D. A. Russell, 'Longinus Revisited', *Mnemosyne*, 34 (1981), 72–86 (p. 85).

36. 'Longinus Reconsidered', p. 916.

37. Charles P. Segal, *ΎΨΟΣ and the Problem of Cultural Decline in the De Sublimitate'*, *Harvard Studies in Classical Philology*, 64 (1959), 121–46 (p. 137).

38. '[The Muse] first makes men inspired, and then through these inspired ones others share in the enthusiasm, and a chain is formed, for the epic poets, all the good ones, have their excellence, not from art, but are inspired, possessed, and thus they utter all these admirable poems.' Plato, *Ion*, trans. by Lane Cooper, 533d–e, in *Plato: The Collected Dialogues*, ed. by Edith Hamilton and Huntingdon Cairns (Princeton: Princeton University Press, 1961).

39. *Phaedrus*, trans. by R. Hackforth, 245a, ibid.

40. Plato, *Republic*, trans. by Robin Waterfield (Oxford: Oxford University Press, 1993), 508e.

41. As Julia Annas shows, Plato oscillates between a view of poetry as important and dangerous on the one hand and merely trivial on the other. In the arguments in Book x of the *Republic*, we 'get the odd spectacle of Plato arguing passionately for the banishment of poetry because of its danger to moral life, on the basis of arguments that show (if they succeeded) that poetry is so trivial that it has no moral significance at all'. *An Introduction to Plato's Republic* (Oxford: Oxford University Press, 1981), p. 342.

42. 'Longinus Revisited', p. 74.

43. Charles H. Kahn aligns the *Ion* with the later Plato in this regard: 'We notice that this conception [Socrates' conception of poetry in the *Ion*] gives a non-cognitive explanation for the achievement of the poet as well as that of the rhapsode, and thus undermines any claim for the poet's thought (*dianoia*) to make an intellectual contribution to education.' *Plato and the Socratic Dialogue: The Philosophical Use of a Literary Form* (Cambridge: Cambridge University Press, 1996), p. 105.

44. Plato, *Republic*, 387e.

CHAPTER 2

❖

The Sublime and the Tragic

Corneille, writes Pierre-Daniel Huet, 'n'avait de complaisance que pour les règles qu'il s'était faites, méprisant toutes les autres, et ne les apercevant même pas'.[1] This is not, of course, the case. Corneille's dramatic theory defines itself by the analytic work it performs on Aristotle. He might claim to ignore what the intervening centuries have produced in terms of commentary: 'Je m'assure que beaucoup de mes lecteurs [...] ne seront pas fâchés que je donne à des productions nouvelles le temps qu'il m'eût fallu consumer à des remarques sur celles des autres siècles.'[2] But the *Poetics* acts as a nexus within a network of Cornelian preferences and rejections, and the way in which the categories of poetics and ethics intertwine in Aristotle is mirrored in the structure of Corneille's own interrogations. This is what made Corneille such an emblematic target for those critics who sought to grant their own poetics the status of an official and so ethically sufficient doctrine. What is of interest to me here is a very particular way in which Corneille expresses, in response to these critics, the originality of his own rich theoretical assemblage. He forges, in his *Discours de la tragédie et des moyens de la traiter selon le vraisemblable ou le nécessaire*, 'une tragédie d'un genre peut-être plus sublime que les trois qu'Aristote avoue'.[3] Corneille's rewriting of Aristotle is perpetrated, in other words, in distinctly Longinian terms.

   We might note briefly to start with that Corneille justifies his explication of Aristotle on the basis of his own experience of its success:

> Ce n'est pas démentir Aristote que de l'expliquer ainsi favorablement, pour trouver [...] une espèce de nouvelle tragédie plus belle que les trois qu'il recommande [...] Je pense être bien fondé sur l'expérience. (pp. 40–41)

And like that of Longinus, for whom precepts can always defer to 'the fruit of ripe experience' (6.1), Corneille's theory is constructed in sustained defiance of any desire for theoretical regulation: 'Trouvons quelque modification à la rigueur de ces règles du philosophe, ou du moins quelque favorable interprétation, pour n'être pas obligés de condamner beaucoup de poèmes que nous avons vu réussir sur nos théâtres' (p. 36). Neither writer, in other words, is afraid to advocate a certain 'violence à l'ordre commun des choses' (p. 60) if it means that a flexible reception theory is allowed to develop and flourish: 'Il est de beaux sujets où on ne la [cette sorte de violence] peut éviter, et un Auteur scrupuleux se priverait d'une belle occasion de gloire, et le Public de beaucoup de satisfaction, s'il n'osait s'enhardir à les mettre sur le Théâtre' (p. 60).[4] It is easy to see, in the light of these general comparisons, that the poetics of Longinus provides Corneille with tools sufficient to the task of chipping away at the edifice of academic censorship. We may consider in more detail, however, the ways in which Corneille's engagements with Aristotle and with a very Longinian sublime can be seen as synchronic and as mutually defining.

Aristotelian Theory

'The poet should create the pleasure which comes from pity and fear through mimesis.'[5] When early modern authors take it upon themselves to comment upon Aristotle's *Poetics*, their conception of what the tragic poet 'should do' shifts, as we shall see, not only from one text to another but within texts, within paragraphs, sometimes seemingly within sentences. But all agree that the (ancient) controversy surrounding the ethical orientation of tragedy has its foundation in this pity-fear composite, in the fact that the spectator, when spectating, is carried along with the action presented on stage, experiencing a degree of fellow-feeling. The first question we are likely to ask, in considering Corneille's interpretation of Aristotle, concerns the nature of the pity and fear which Aristotle himself accommodates. I shall analyse this, and the related issue of the distance that Aristotle puts, in this regard, between himself and Plato, before moving on to Corneille's own *Discours*.

Tragic response, then, is described in Aristotle as a pity which is yoked to fear. Pity objectifies the suffering of another and acknowledges the significance of this suffering: its transformative action, its modification of the life of the sufferer. Aristotle insists that, for pity to be brought about, the suffering in question has to be undeserved, or at least entirely disproportionate to any fault committed by the tragic hero: 'Let pity then be a kind of pain excited by the sight of evil, deadly or painful, which befalls one who does not deserve it.'[6] Pity, as a cognitive awareness of the undeserved, is an awareness of the vertiginous human possibilities for pain: 'All that men fear in regard to themselves excites their pity when others are the victims.'[7] If undeserved, the suffering in question may equally be visited upon people other than the immediate sufferer; the pitier is in no sense immune. But though undeserved, this suffering also has to be shown to be brought about by a recognizably causal chain of events. The pity-fear composite is precluded by complete arbitrariness. If misfortune is seen as too improbable, the spectator will not fear, will not see the events affecting the sufferer as also potentially bearing down upon him or her. Thus the causal mechanisms of necessity and probability are essential to Aristotelian tragedy. They are presupposed in the fundamentally important categories of peripeteia or reversal ('when things come about contrary to expectation but because of one another') and of anagnorisis or recognition, when the tragic hero is brought to understand how things have come about.[8] 'These elements [reversal and recognition]', we read, 'should emerge from the very structure of the plot' (1452a18).

As our initial quotation from the *Poetics* also illustrated, the pity-fear which comes with mimesis is, equally, pleasure. This is because 'we enjoy contemplating the most precise images of things whose actual sight is painful to us' (1448b9). We enjoy the act of contemplation because of the satisfying deduction and reasoning it brings with it: 'people enjoy looking at images, because through contemplating

THE SUBLIME AND THE TRAGIC　　37

them it comes about that they understand and infer what each element means, for instance that "this person is so-and-so"' (1448b14). Tragic pleasure is understanding and inference. If it is difficult, here, to make any distinction between emotion and reasoning, this is because the intermingling of these two categories provides a gravitational centre for much of Aristotle's thought (and not least for the opening premise of the *Metaphysics*: 'All men naturally desire knowledge').[9]

In his *Rhetoric*, Aristotle instructs a young orator how knowingly to produce emotive effects in his audience by making them believe certain things. If particular beliefs were not generally sufficient for particular emotions, then this enterprise would be an invalid one.[10] Emotions can be sought out, solicited, and made to perform by cognitive procedures, and the ensuing emotional experience is both cognitive and emotional in tenor. Emotions are defined, in the *Rhetoric*, by the nature of the beliefs that produce them; if the beliefs change, so do the emotions. It follows that the pity-fear of mimesis can be entirely consonant with the cognitive aspects of recognition and identification. It is in this context that the important term 'catharsis' comes into play: 'The function of tragedy is through pity and fear to accomplish the catharsis of emotions of that kind.'[11] I shall return to the question of Corneille's interpretation of this term. Meanwhile, and to quote Stephen Halliwell,

> It had better be said at once that we do not really know what Aristotle meant in this context by katharsis. We can be moderately confident only that it offers a response to the Platonic view that tragedy arouses emotions which ought, for the sake of general psychological and moral well-being, to be kept in check.[12]

To get some sense of the luxuriantly many-layered status and function of Aristotelian emotions we need, as Halliwell suggests, to return to Plato. Plato, of course, had argued that the genre of tragedy must be eliminated from the good city because of its provocative tendency towards emotiveness. As we saw in the last chapter, emotions in Plato are not in any sense to be associated here with cognitive value, reasoning. One ramification of making an independent intellect the seat of virtue is that goodness cannot be deflected by any external circumstance. A good person has nothing to fear from the contingencies of human existence, as Socrates points out to his jury: 'You too, gentlemen of the jury, must look forward to death with confidence, and fix your minds on this one belief, which is certain: that nothing can harm a good man either in life or after death, and his fortunes are not a matter of indifference to the gods.'[13] Pity and fear, according to this Platonic angle of vision, are both shameful and pointless. Pity is directed either at good people, whose goodness remains intact whatever life may throw at them, and so who do not require pitying, or alternatively at bad people, who, being bad, deserve their own misfortune. All human activity should go towards pursuing the beauty of form, making all human relationships non-specific and interchangeable.[14]

Aristotle, faced with this, coerces Plato's fixities into movement:

> Tragedy is a mimesis not of persons but of action and a life. And happiness [eudaimonia] and unhappiness consist in action, and the goal is a certain kind of action, not a qualitative state: it is in virtue of their characters that people have certain qualities, but through their actions that they are happy or the reverse. (*Poetics*, 1450a15–20)

As Halliwell notes, 'Aristotle's views on this matter connect a conception of drama with a conception of life: both, in the philosopher's mind, fundamentally concern activity rather than static qualities.'[15] Thus the external ricochets back from neglect in Plato to consideration in Aristotle. In the *Nicomachean Ethics*, 'no one would choose to live without friends, but possessing all other good things' (VIII. I. I). The perfect virtue for Aristotle is not internal deliberation, but an externally oriented justice:

> Justice then in this sense is perfect Virtue, though with a qualification, namely that it is displayed towards others [pros heteron]. This is why Justice is often thought to be the chief of the virtues, and more sublime [thaumaston] 'or than the evening or the morning star' [...] There are many who can practise virtue in their own private affairs but cannot do so in their relations with another [pros heteron].[16] (V. I. 15)

In the last chapter, I argued against the view that the Longinian sublime can be defined as a loosely Platonic 'transcendence', assimilated to the vast panoply of the theory of forms. I brought into question the exclusive relevance of Platonist paradigms of perfection for the Longinian sublime. This, I noted, is concerned with a search for perfection in form only inasmuch as this perfection defers to the messiness and the infinite flexibility of human encounters — read about, written about, lived through (in any order). Texts that acknowledge human encounters, and readers who are open to such texts, can come together in moments of 'hypsos', or some kind of identification. Each sublime encounter is different, contingent upon what the reader brings to it. This troubles the Platonic dynamic of anamnesis (a loss of worldly identity in a union with the transcendental) in its intermingling of cognition and external-dependent emotion. By contrast with Plato, Aristotle's readily permutable investigations place enormous emphasis on the usefulness of emotions which have identification with other people as the condition for their existence. Longinus can be read in a way that brings his thought close to (some aspects of) Plato's, but he can also be read in a way that brings him closer to a concern with the identifications of the *Poetics*. This is worth bearing in mind in an analysis of Corneille's use of the term 'sublime'.

'Le plus sublime et le plus touchant'

When Corneille comes to engage with Aristotle, contemplating 'une tragédie d'un genre peut-être plus sublime que les trois qu'Aristote avoue' (p. 40), he has just established a hierarchy of tragedy with, at its pinnacle, 'tragédies parfaites' which he also defines using the term 'sublime': as 'du genre le plus sublime et le plus touchant' (p. 38). Failing to attain sublime perfection does not deprive other tragedies of technical perfection; these, 'pourvu qu'elles soient régulières à cela près, ne laissent pas d'être parfaites en leur genre, bien qu'elles demeurent dans un rang moins élevé' (p. 39). This move away from considerations of technicality is of itself, as I noted at the beginning of this chapter, and as most commentators have perceived, a Longinian move.[17] But Corneille goes into more detail regarding his conception of sublime perfection in tragedy. This 'consiste bien à exciter de la pitié et de la crainte par le moyen d'un premier acteur' (p. 36); it is also expressly linked to proximity, to liaison: 'c'est donc un grand avantage, pour exciter la commisération, que la proximité du sang et les liaisons d'amour ou d'amitié entre le persécutant et le persécuté, le poursuivant et le poursuivi; mais il y a quelque apparence que cette condition [...] ne regarde que les tragédies parfaites' (p. 38).

Corneille's mention of 'commisération' might lead us to go around the loop of seventeenth-century catharsis: an edifice of extreme and contradiction-ridden density, and one which has at its disposal numerous verbs of intellectual operation. In Dacier's 1692 reading of Aristotelian catharsis, identification turns inwards, self-consumes, habituating the pitying spectator to pity and thereby catalysing subsequent inurement and indifference.[18] This insulation is characterized by Dacier as a 'juste modération': '[La tragédie] les excite [les passions] en nous mettant devant les yeux les malheurs, que nos semblables se sont attirez par des fautes involontaires, et elle les purge, en nous rendant ces mêmes malheurs familiers, car elle nous apprend par là de ne les pas trop craindre, et à n'en etre pas trop touchez quand ils arrivent veritablement' (pp. 78–79). In Rapin too, 'elle [la Tragedie] instruit l'esprit par les sens, et [...] rectifie les passions par les passions mesmes, en calmant par leur émotion le trouble qu'elles excitent dans le coeur'.[19]

These moralizing readings had been anticipated by Scudéry in his *Apologie du théâtre*, citing the case of Orestes pursued by the Eumenides: 'Est-il une ame assez sanguinaire, pour ne fremir point à l'aspect de ce chatiment? Et qui pour s'exempter d'un semblable, ne quite sa cruelle inclination?'[20] And they are signalled at the beginning of *De la tragédie* by Corneille:

> La pitié d'un malheur où nous voyons tomber nos semblables, nous porte à la crainte d'un pareil pour nous; cette crainte au désir de l'éviter; et ce désir à purger, modifier, rectifier et même déraciner en nous la passion qui plonge à nos yeux dans ce malheur les personnes que nous plaignons, par cette raison commune, mais naturelle et indubitable, que pour éviter l'effet il faut retrancher la cause. (p. 29)

But Corneille expresses fundamental doubts about this expurgation or rectification: 'Si la purgation des passions se fait dans la tragédie, je tiens qu'elle doit se faire de la manière que je l'explique; mais je doute si elle s'y fait jamais' (p. 32). He goes on to call as witnesses the spectators of *Le Cid*: 'ils peuvent en demander compte au secret de leur coeur, et repasser sur ce qui les a touchés au théâtre, pour reconnaître s'ils en sont venus par là jusqu'à cette crainte réfléchie, et si elle a rectifié en eux la passion qui a causé la disgrâce qu'ils ont plainte' (p. 32). The provocation of a passionate 'commisération' in Corneille, then, does not entail its own subsequent self-consumption.[21] Passions are not 'purged' — expunged, evacuated — in Corneille's theory. The point of 'commisération' has to be sought elsewhere.

We are helped in our analysis of Cornelian 'commisération' if we consider that, in positing a sublime 'tragédie parfaite', in ennobling 'une espèce de tragédie plus belle que les trois qu'il [Aristote] recommande', Corneille formulates an important upheaval of Aristotle's tragic taxonomy. The three kinds of tragedy admitted by Aristotle are, in Corneille's words, the following:

1. 'On connaît celui qu'on veut perdre, et on le fait périr en effet.'
2. 'On le fait périr sans le connaître, et on le reconnaît avec déplaisir.'

3. 'On est prêt de faire périr un de ses proches sans le connaître, et qu'on le reconnaît assez tôt pour le sauver.' (p. 39)

Aristotle's text reads as follows:

First, the action can occur as in the early poets who made the agents act in knowledge and cognisance (as Euripides made Medea kill her children). Alternatively, the agents can commit the terrible deed, but do so in ignorance, then subsequently recognise the relationship, as with Sophocles' Œdipus [...]. This leaves a third possibility, when the person is on the point of unwittingly committing something irremediable, but recognises it before doing so. These are the only patterns; either the action is or is not executed, and by agents who either know or do not know its nature.[22]

A fourth category is rejected by Aristotle: 'ceux qui connaissent, entreprennent et n'achèvent pas' (p. 39): 'Of these, the worst is for someone to be about to act knowingly, and yet not to do so: this is both repugnant and untragic (since it lacks suffering)' (1453b). This is the category singled out for interest by Corneille, who notes that 'si cette condamnation n'était modifiée, elle s'étendrait un peu loin, et envelopperait non seulement *le Cid*, mais *Cinna*, *Rodogune*, *Héraclius* et *Nicomède*' (p. 39). He modulates his interest in this category, however, by excluding from it cases in which the 'n'achèvent pas' specification is linked to 'un simple changement de volonté' on the part of the protagonists, 'sans aucun événement notable qui les y oblige, et sans aucun manque de pouvoir de leur part' (pp. 39–40). On the other hand,

Quand ils [ceux qui connaissent la personne qu'ils veulent perdre] y font de leur côté tout ce qu'ils peuvent, et qu'ils sont empêchés d'en venir à l'effet par quelque puissance supérieure, ou par quelque changement de fortune qui les fait périr eux-mêmes, ou les réduit sous le pouvoir de ceux qu'ils voulaient perdre, il est hors de doute que cela fait une tragédie d'un genre peut-être plus sublime que les trois qu'Aristote avoue. (p. 40)

Sublimity is granted to tragedy when the external (the uncontrollable, the uncertain) provides striking dramatic events in the form of 'quelque puissance supérieure' or 'quelque changement de fortune'. Corneille harks back at this point to some of his earlier comments on 'dénouement' in comedy, where he again denounces a 'simple changement de volonté' (p. 11, as p. 39), saying that a father's sudden acceptance of his son's or daughter's marriage plans should come about only through a comparably surprising 'événement notable' or 'changement de fortune' (taken literally in this case): 'Comme si l'amant de sa fille lui sauvait la vie en quelque rencontre où il fût prêt d'être assassiné par ses ennemis, ou que par quelque accident inespéré il fût reconnu pour être de plus grande condition, et mieux dans la fortune qu'il ne parassait' (p. 11). Returning to the five sublime tragedies listed — *le Cid*, *Cinna*, *Rodogune*, *Héraclius*, and *Nicomède* — Corneille then discusses the characters Chimène, Cinna, Cléopâtre, Phocas, and Prusias. All 'connaissent les personnes qu'ils veulent perdre' (this is the case with Phocas, who knows that he must kill Héraclius even if he does not know to whom the identity corresponds). All are prevented by 'quelque puissance supérieure' or 'quelque changement de fortune'.

So sublimity in tragedy is born, for Corneille, both from the encounters made by 'ceux qui connaissent la personne qu'ils veulent perdre' and from the contingencies and the plural possibilities of those encounters. The combination of knowledge, contingency and combat throws up exponentially multiplied possibilities for tragic emotion on the part of the audience: 'Mais lorsqu'on agit à visage découvert, et qu'on sait à qui on en veut, le combat des passions contre la nature, ou du devoir contre l'amour, occupe la meilleure partie du poème, et de là naissent les grandes et fortes émotions qui renouvellent à tous moments et redoublent la commisération' (p. 41). This 'commisération', broadly synonymous with compassion (the *Dictionnaire de l'Académie française* has 'commiseration' down as 'compassion, pitié, mouvement de l'ame qui est touchée de la misere, du malheur d'autrui'), is, then, run together interestingly with Corneille's comments on being 'empêchés'. 'Commisération' seems to approach, here, something like identification through an acknowledgement of the truth about limited human potential: a sense that the actions which make up a life or which are prevented within it, defining an identity in either case, are born out of contingent encounters with 'quelque puissance supérieure' or 'quelque changement de fortune'. We may note the repetition of the indefinite adjective, with the sustained note of variability it gives. Corneille's 'commisération', like his use of the term 'sublime', finds itself resident within this variability. It is not to be straightforwardly corralled into 'admiration' (though this too, as wonder, amazement, astonishment, is a valid and desirable tragic response), as indeed the disjunctions of Corneille's *Examen* of *Nicomède* make clear: 'La fermeté des grands coeurs, qui *n'excite que* de l'admiration dans l'âme du spectateur, est *quelquefois aussi agréable que* la compassion que notre art nous ordonne d'y produire par la représentation des spectateurs' (my emphases).[23] The term 'sublime', we have seen, does not seek to describe, and is not adequately described, by 'la fermeté des grands coeurs', but spans the curtailments imposed upon characters, and the configurations in which they find themselves. Corneille's sublime attaches itself to Cinna, who has undertaken but not achieved, rather than to his great emperor Auguste.[24]

Sublime Cognition

Corneille, in his attribution of sublimity to certain kinds of tragedy, shifts importance onto situations that facilitate 'émotions qui renouvellent à tous moments' (p. 41) and away from from a single moment of intensely concentrated pathos (reversal-recognition). He makes the case for plays in which tragic action is 'à visage découvert' (p. 41), rather than bound to a single ravishingly powerful move from ignorance to knowledge. A knowledge-from-ignorance dynamic is not allowed to come to rest in the *Discours* here; instead, a restless knowledge (that of Chimène, for example, or Cinna, or Cléopâtre) finds modulation, sometimes violently, in its encounters with other people. A cross-cutting engagement with others, rather than a single coming-to-recognition, is theorized as producing ongoing 'commisération'.

We can return here to Corneille's insistence, as a condition for sublimity in tragedy, on 'liaisons d'amour et d'amitié', on 'la proximité du sang'. What these relationships have in common is the uniqueness of the bond they establish: these are relationships which, once formed, are irreplaceable, non-exchangeable. They are by definition, of course, particularly vulnerable to change; to external pressures, to death or displacement, to a 'changement de fortune', or to being 'réduit sous le pouvoir' of another. These kinds of bonds, first, can be seen as specifically preferable in tragedy only if Corneille seeks to espouse this vulnerability. Further, these bonds — no matter how unique each instantiation of them, or how noble the particular case on show — are also banal, trivial, common. Each spectator has 'liaisons d'amour et d'amitié', knows 'la proximité du sang'. So Corneille's preference can be expressed as sublime only if sublimity is understood as bearing upon our perception of the mutable, complex, and heterogeneous material of human life, and of the differing demands thus commonly made upon us. Corneille uses the term sublime, here, in a way that bears no relation (precisely because it is concerned with relations) to an absolute notion of 'grandeur'.[25]

This reading may also be seen to shift away from an understanding that 'Corneille advertises his preference for plots in which acts are performed in full knowledge of the circumstances', that the 'à visage découvert' specification 'certainly illustrates the extent to which Corneille's critical language attempts to excise what is covert or hidden, what is not the object of conscious knowledge'.[26] Such statements oppose 'conscious' and 'covert or hidden'. In the recognition scene, conscious and covert or hidden come together, clash, in a re-cognition of the hidden. Corneille is seen to excise the hidden as he is seen to reduce the importance of the recognition scene. But Corneille modulates the opposition between 'conscious' and 'covert', displaying a professional lack of interest in the clash between the two. He modulates this opposition, one might say, in much the same way that Lacan modulates Freud when, in one of the best known of his utterances, he rewrites the latter to state that 'l'inconscient, c'est le discours de l'Autre'.[27] Corneille opposes, as Lacan did in his *Écrits*, 'conscious' and (not merely 'hidden' but) 'external'.[28] In Corneille, we have seen that opposition to provide a plethora of dramatic possibilities, as the protagonist is exposed to a 'changement de fortune' or 'réduit sous le pouvoir' of an external force. Corneille gives us to understand that the characters on stage are bounded by a 'discours de l'Autre'; and while this discourse may be impressively great, it is its unknowable and unpredictable nature which does important work within the Cornelian theory I have been discussing.

Tragic effect for Corneille is not just produced, suggest his *Discours*, when ignorance comes into forceful contact with the hidden. Rather, it is produced when his own two preoccupying categories — the conscious and the external — combine. This dynamic blurs the need for the conscious and the hidden to combine in a single, ravishingly powerful recognition scene. Recognition scenes can be spun out in Corneille into a series of actions and encounters. The tragic effect produced, suggests Corneille, is sublime. It might (this, we saw, was Aristotle's point, in *Poetics*, 1453b) lack 'suffering' or (more closely to the Greek here) 'pathos' — might lack a concentrated moment of pitying-fearing. But it does promote a more diffuse identification where what is experienced on the part of the audience is an ongoing illumination regarding our human situation and the contingencies of it.[29] Human possibilities are defined and limited through the fact that we have no permanent purchase upon the encounters we make. In Corneille's theory, as in that of Longinus, sublime discourse is discourse about human relations.

At the same time as Corneille was developing these ideas in his theoretical discourses (in other words, during the period of silence which followed the failure of the 1651 *Pertharite*), he was also working on *Œdipe*, commissioned by Fouquet (who had presented Corneille with a choice of subject matter) and first performed in 1659. In the next chapter, I shall suggest that we can read Corneille's Longinian re-emphases through his treatment of the canonical figure of Oedipus. *Œdipe* was controversial, with D'Aubignac publishing caustic criticisms of the play in the form of his 1663 *Dissertation*. These criticisms seek out in particular Corneille's manipulation of 'vraisemblance', a term that also moulds our understanding of the kinds of events to which Corneille exposes his characters. And so my discussion of Corneille's 'sublime' and 'touchant', having hitherto made its connections with 'connaissance', will spill over into Corneille's theoretical discourses about truth, veracity, truthfulness, and verisimilitude as further conditions for the identification of the observer with the character on stage.

Notes to Chapter 2

1. Pierre-Daniel Huet, *Mémoires (1718)*, trans. by Charles Nisard, ed. by Philippe-Joseph Salazar (Toulouse: Klincksieck, 1993), p. 118.
2. Pierre Corneille, *Writings on the Theatre*, ed. by H. T. Barnwell (Oxford: Blackwell, 1965), p. 27. All future references to Corneille's *Discours* and *Examens* will be to this edition.
3. *Writings on the Theatre*, p. 40.
4. We can cite Boileau's ninth satire as testimony to Corneille's success in this regard: 'En vain contre le Cid un ministre se ligue | Tout Paris pour Chimène a les yeux de Rodrigue. | L'Académie en corps a beau le censurer, | Le public révolté s'obstine à l'admirer' (*Œuvres complètes*, ed. by Antoine Adam and Françoise Escal (Paris: Gallimard, 1966), p. 54).
5. Aristotle, *Poetics*, trans. by Stephen Halliwell, in *Aristotle, 'Poetics', Longinus, 'On the Sublime', Demetrius, 'On Style'*, Loeb Classical Library, 199 (Cambridge, MA: Harvard University Press, 1995), 1453b12.
6. *The 'Art' of Rhetoric*, trans. by J. H. Freese, Loeb Classical Library, 193 (Cambridge, MA: Harvard University Press, 1994), 1385b8.
7. *Politics*, trans. by H. Rackham, Loeb Classical Library, 264 (Cambridge, MA: Harvard University Press, 1932), 1386a13. See, on this, J. Jones: *On Aristotle and Greek Tragedy* (London: Chatto & Windus, 1962): 'One should hyphenate Aristotelian pity-and-fear because it is a mistake to think of pity in isolation and interpret it [...] in a spirit of Christian altruism' (p. 39).
8. *Poetics*, 1452a2.
9. Aristotle, *The Metaphysics*, trans. by Hugh Tredennick, Loeb Classical Library, 287 (Cambridge, MA: Harvard University Press, 1933), 980a22. For the intermingling of these two categories in seventeenth-century thought, see my article, 'Emotions and the Ethics of Response in Seventeenth-Century French Dramatic Theory', *Modern Philology*, forthcoming 2007. This article makes mention of the 'grandes et fortes émotions' that, as we shall see in a moment, Corneille seeks to produce.
10. Martha Nussbaum, 'Tragedy and Self-Sufficiency: Plato and Aristotle on Fear and Pity', *Oxford Studies in Ancient Philosophy*, 10 (1992), 107–60 (p. 133), and *The Fragility of Goodness: Luck and Ethics in Greek Tragedy and Philosophy*, 2nd edn (Cambridge: Cambridge University Press, 2001), Interlude 2, pp. 378–94.
11. *Poetics*, 1449b23.
12. Stephen Halliwell, *The 'Poetics' of Aristotle: Translation and Commentary* (London: Duckworth, 1987), pp. 89–90.

13. Plato, *Apology*, 41d, trans. by Hugh Tredennick, in Plato, *The Collected Dialogues*, ed. by Edith Hamilton and Huntingdon Cairns (Princeton: Princeton University Press, 1961).

14. 'If all possible means have been taken to make even what nature has made our own (idion) in some sense common property, I mean, if our eyes, ears and hands seem to see, hear, act, in the common service; if moreover, we all approve and condemn in perfect unison and derive pleasure and pain from the same sources — in a word, when the institutions of a society make it most utterly one, that is a criterion of their excellence than which no truer or better will ever be found.' Plato, *Laws*, 739c–d, trans. by A. E. Taylor, in Plato, *The Collected Dialogues*.

15. *The 'Poetics' of Aristotle*, p. 94.

16. On the Aristotelian conception of the good life, see Nussbaum, *The Fragility of Goodness*. Nussbaum notes that Aristotle 'uses Platonic terminology in a deliberately anti-Platonic way: where Plato had insisted that no true value is a relational (*pros heteron*) item, Aristotle now insists that all true excellence of character has a relational nature' (p. 352). See also the application of the debate on 'moral luck', a term coined by Bernard Williams in the 1970s, to ancient philosophy: *Moral Luck: Philosophical Papers, 1973–1980* (Cambridge: Cambridge University Press, 1981).

17. 'It is worth noting that in this definition of "perfect" tragedy Corneille uses a very Longinian terminology (*sublime, élevé, beauté, éclat, pompe, magnificence*), and that his minimizing of regularity may stem from the same possible source.' Barnwell in Corneille*, Writings on the Theatre*, p. 226, n. 48. 'L'Introduction du terme de "sublime" signale que Corneille est bien en train de fonder une nouvelle échelle de valeur esthétique.' Bénédicte Louvat and Marc Escola, eds, *Corneille: Trois discours sur le poème dramatique* (Paris: Garnier-Flammarion, 1999), p. 177, n. 32.

18. *La Poétique d'Aristote*, trans. and ed. by André Dacier (Paris: Barbin, 1692). On seventeenth-century catharsis, see in particular Henry Phillips, *The Theatre and its Critics in Seventeenth-Century France* (Oxford : Oxford University Press, 1980); John D. Lyons, *Kingdom of Disorder: The Theory of Tragedy in Classical France* (West Lafayette, IN: Purdue University Press, 1999); Georges Forestier, 'Passions purgées ou passions épurées? Le problème de la *catharsis*', in *Passions tragiques et règles classiques* (Paris: Presses universitaires de France, 2003), pp. 141–54.

19. René Rapin, *Réflexions sur la poétique de ce temps, et sur les ouvrages des poetes anciens et modernes*, 2nd edn, rev. and enlarged (Paris: François Muguet, 1675), p. 113.

20. Georges de Scudéry, *L'Apologie du théâtre* (Paris: Augustin Courbé, 1639), p. 19.

21. An interesting exception comes with the reference made to mothers who may be watching Cléopâtre in *Rodogune*: 'Bien qu'elles ne soient pas capables d'une action si noire et si dénaturée, que celle de cette Reine de Syrie, elles ont en elles quelque teinture du principe qui l'y porta, et la vue de la juste punition qu'elle reçoit leur peut faire craindre, non pas un pareil malheur, mais une infortune proportionnée à ce qu'elles sont capables de commettre' (pp. 33–34).

22. *Poetics*, 1453b.

23. This is where I differ (I shall return to this difference) from Forestier in *Essai de génétique théâtrale: Corneille à l'œuvre*, 2nd edn (Geneva: Droz, 2004): 'La poétique de Corneille est une poétique de la grandeur, c'est-à-dire du sublime' (p. 277) (Forestier had earlier noted that: 'Le sublime est le ravissement vers la grandeur par la violence de la beauté. Il suffit de lire le traité *Du sublime* de Longin pour s'en convaincre', p. 275). Forestier makes much of sublimity as grandeur, violence, perfection, 'la perfection (esthétique) de la violence' (p. 275), 'la situation porteuse de violence qui lui paraît le comble du sublime' (p. 285), the sublimity of heroes who face these situations; all of this going to show that 'la tragédie cornélienne est le lieu de la rencontre entre la conception de la grandeur tragique et la conception de la perfection héroïque' (p. 328). Forestier is extending to a discussion of the sublime a line of thought that has been dominant in French criticism since the highly influential work of Paul Bénichou, who writes in his *Morales du grand siècle* of 'les concours de valeur entre les grands' as 'institution morale' ('Le héros cornélien' in *Les Morales du grand siècle* (Paris: Gallimard, 1948), pp. 15–67 (p. 27)). Bénichou writes that: 'Les spectateurs de *Cinna* ou de *Nicomède* ne sont pas seulement des spectateurs de théâtre; ils jouent en même temps leur partie comme compagnons des héros et témoins de leur gloire. Ils composent l'auditoire indispensable à ces créatures faites pour l'admiration, et dont la vie n'aurait aucun sens si elle n'affrontait victorieusement l'épreuve du jugement public' (p. 26). For a summary of Marc Fumaroli's thoughts on 'l'idéal héroïque', see 'L'Héroïsme de Corneille et

l'éthique de la magnamité' in *Héros et orateurs: rhétorique et dramaturgie cornéliennes* (Geneva: Droz, 1990), pp. 323–49.

24. I contrast my reading here with Forestier's attribution of sublimity to Auguste in *Cinna* ('le geste sublime du monarque', 'l'expression du sublime monarchique', *Essai de génétique théâtreale*, p. 306) and Polyeucte ('le sacrifice sublime du martyr', p. 306). We may note also his discussion in this context of 'constance' to Œdipe and to 'le véritable Héraclius' (pp. 259–60, p. 340).

25. We are not dealing with 'un dépassement de l'humaine condition' (*Essai de génétique théâtrale*, p. 306).

26. Terence Cave, *Recognitions* (Oxford: Oxford University Press, 1988), pp. 84, 100; the discussion of *Héraclius* and *Œdipe* on pp. 303–22 goes into more detail however about shades of covert and conscious. The question of recognition in *Héraclius* 'takes on the character of a tragic theme (all the more because it remains in a sense hypothetical, separated from the effective action)' (p. 306).

27. Jacques Lacan, *Écrits* (Paris: Éditions du Seuil, 1966), p. 379.

28. In Lacan, 'the message that is passed across the gap between the subject and the external Other passes inwardly too, for the supra-individual, social world is installed by language within the individual mind'. Malcolm Bowie, *Freud, Proust and Lacan: Theory as Fiction* (Cambridge: Cambridge University Press, 1987), p. 118.

29. It will by now be clear that this diffuse illumination differs from a 'ravissement absolu devant l'accomplissement, *in extremis*, de l'impossible' (Forestier, *Essai de génétique théâtrale*, p. 299), from 'le ravissement fondé sur la surprise absolue d'un événement qui se produit quand jusqu'au bout rien ne l'autorise à se produire' (p. 302), from 'un sentiment d'admiration émerveillée' (p. 311); we might also note that the Greek noun 'thaumaston', which Forestier brings up at this point ('l'effet de surprise', p. 308) because of its interest to dramatic theorists (it appears in Aristotle, as in *Peri hypsous*) has, in its verb form, self-reflexive connotations, just as is the case with 'wonder' in English (I wonder?). These self-reflexive connotations themselves trouble the very idea of 'ravissement absolu'. In any case, 'ravissement' and 'admiration émerveillée' as desired tragic responses require exploration and qualification of the kind I have sought to offer in this chapter.

CHAPTER 3

❖

Theatrical Controversy

Into Corneille's theoretical declarations, I have observed, is sewn the intensity of his rejection of the single recognition scene in favour of action 'à visage découvert' which produces 'grandes et fortes émotions qui renouvellent à tous moments et redoublent la commisération',[1] as well as his preference for — 'sublime', he says — plot structures in which characters 'connaissent, entreprennent et n'achèvent pas' (p. 39). The statements of rejection and preference are contemporaneous with Corneille's rewriting of the Oedipus myth. Corneille's views on acting 'à visage découvert', I shall suggest now, can be usefully cross-referenced to Oedipus: he who doesn't know, he whose solving of riddles prior to dramatic time only serves to plunge him deep into the dramatic space of the unknown.

Œdipe

The broad brushstrokes of Corneille's re-painting of Oedipus are as follows. Corneille opens his version of the play by introducing the characters Dircé, daughter of Laïus and Jocaste, and her lover Thésée, prince of Athens.[2] The love of Dircé and Thésée is frustrated by Œdipe, who, as Jocaste's second husband, has promised Dircé's hand to a certain Aemon. Œdipe, before arriving at Thebes, had left Corinth to travel in the hope of endorsing, in the manner of Hercules, the maxim that 'c'est loin de ses parents qu'un homme apprend à vivre' (Act I, scene 4, line 305).[3] The authority that he asserts over Dircé prompts her threat of suicide (II. 1. 503–04). When it becomes clear that the source of the plague devastating Thebes is the 'grand crime impuni' (II. 2. 605) that was the death of Laïus, Dircé supposes that she must be the guilty party, responsible because her birth prompted her father's fatal trip:

> L'amour qu'il me portait eut sur lui tel pouvoir
> Qu'il voulut sur mon sort faire parler l'oracle
> [...] Hélas! Sur le chemin il fut assassiné.[4] (II. 2. 646–47, 653)

Dircé resolves that her own death is both necessary for this reason and, given her seemingly impossible love for Thésée, desirable in any case.

Thésée himself, however, then puts himself forward as the abandoned son of Laïus and Jocaste in order to save Dircé (III. 5). His claim is rejected by Jocaste's (accurate here, although evidently unreliable given her relationship with Œdipe) 'voix du sang': 'Je ne sens point pour vous l'émotion du sang' (III. 5. 1103). Thésée calls to witness the elderly Phorbas, the servant whom Laïus and Jocaste had charged with removing their infant son and shackling him to the distant Mount Cythéron.[5] Phorbas confirms that he failed to fulfil his task, taking pity on the child and giving him to a passer-by, but also goes on to act as a much more powerfully dramatic catalyst, given that it was he who had been present in the king's côterie on the day of his death. Phorbas, although he had previously stated that the king had been killed by a group of brigands in order to hide the shame of the king's party's defeat by a single man, is thus able to identify Œdipe as the killer. But it is only when Iphicrate, an elderly statesman, arrives from Corinth and reveals to Œdipe his origins that the further charges of incest and parricide are brought upon Œdipe, who puts out his eyes (with his own hands, rather than with the Sophoclean brooch-pin) off-stage.[6]

Knowledge and ignorance, in this play, are manipulated and modified by Corneille. The *Oedipus Rex* of Sophocles grapples with the extreme ignorance of Oedipus's incest-patricide (we saw above, note 3, that this ignorance is, in Corneille's *Examen*, seen as improbably extreme). Given the frightening nature of the unknown quantity in question, Oedipus's coming to consciousness is proportionally violent, monumental; it is also, on any reading, linear. Aristotle stresses this linearity for his own purposes ('best of all is recognition ensuing from the events themselves, where the emotional impact comes from a probable sequence, as in Sophocles' *Oedipus*'), as does Freud: 'The action of the play consists of nothing other than the process of revealing, with cunning delays and ever-mounting excitement, that Oedipus himself is the murderer of Laius, but further, that he is the son of the murdered man and Jocasta.'[7]

In Corneille, however, a single extreme ignorance is shattered into multiple unknown quantities provided by multiple intersecting relationships: those of Dircé and Thésée, Dircé and Œdipe, Jocaste and Thésée, and so on. It is shattered into their attendant contingencies ('L'amertume de vivre, et n'être point à vous', IV. I. 1216), dependencies ('Rendez-vous cependant maître de tout mon sort', II. I. 503) and questionings ('Quoi? Vous seriez mon fils?', III. 5. 1083). Sophocles offers us a schema in which we are preoccupied with a single, monumental 'unknown', with that which is brought to the surface thanks to a 'probable sequence' and with 'ever mounting excitement'. Corneille replaces this schema with one in which relationships bring with them speculative extremities of unpredictability. A vertically oriented model of the unknown as plunging depth is replaced by a different, cross-cutting model of the unknown as the endless modalities of human relations.

One of Corneille's most specific modifications becomes particularly significant here. In Sophocles, the man who bore witness to Laius's death presents initially (as Phorbas does later in Corneille) a mendacious testimony as regards the number of people in the party responsible. As in Corneille, this is seen as fundamental:

> You said he spoke of *robbers* —
> That *robbers* killed him. If he still says *robbers*,
> It was not I; one is not more than one.
> But if he speaks of one lone wayfarer,
> There is no escape; the finger points to me.[8]

But in Sophocles, the importance attached to this particular testimony evaporates. Sophocles takes his audience from this to the unconnected statements from the Corinthian messenger that Polybus, the king of Corinth who had brought up Oedipus, is dead, that King Polybus was never Oedipus's father in the first place, that Oedipus had been taken from Mount Corinth as a damaged, dying baby and named precisely because of his ensuing weakness (the Greek *oidipous* meaning 'swollen foot'). This information is enough for Jocasta, 'white with terror'. Then it takes the arrival of the shepherd who had received the infant from her and Laius to bring Oedipus to blinding recognition — 'Alas! All out! All known, no more concealment!' (p. 58) — and the question of the 'lone wayfarer' dissipates and dissolves altogether in the face of the linear force of these developments.[9]

In Corneille, however, the question of Œdipe's 'rencontre en Phocide' (line 1438) is given much more theatrical time, dominating Act IV. Œdipe is positively identified as the lone wayfarer in Act IV, scene 4:

> ŒD.:   Mais ce furent brigands, dont le bras …
> JOC.:   C'est un conte
> Dont Phorbas au retour voulut cacher sa honte.
> Une main seule, hélas! fit ces funestes coups,
> Et par votre rapport, ils partirent de vous. (IV. 4. 1477–80)

This positive identification is important because, in getting the revelation of Œdipe's deed out of the way, it makes his current relationships seem increasingly proliferating and complex:

> J'ai tué le feu Roi jadis sans le connaître,
> Son fils qu'on croyait mort vient ici de renaître,
> Son peuple mutiné me voit avec horreur,
> Sa veuve mon épouse en est dans la fureur. (V. 2. 1677–81)

The second of Aristotle's categories of tragedy (in Corneille's paraphrase in the *Discours*, 'On le fait périr sans le connaître, et on le reconnaît avec déplaisir', p. 39) is perfectly encompassed within Œdipe's initial statement here ('J'ai tué le feu Roi jadis sans le connaître'), but three other acknowledgements pile exorbitantly upon the first. Then Œdipe's decision to act — to leave Thebes for his supposed fatherland, Corinth — is swiftly annulled by Iphicrate:

> Le repos à Corinthe en effet serait doux
> Mais il n'est plus de sceptre à Corinthe pour vous. (V. 2. 1687–88)

This sparks off ('Et qui suis-je, Iphicrate?', V. 2. 1701]) further questions and answers about Œdipe's now multiply converging relationships. Faced with the 'on le fait périr' and the 'on le reconnaît' of Aristotle's specification, Corneille splays out such simply expressed transitivity, and displays the glutinous impossibility of separating any cognition, self-knowledge or action from external relations, from 'rencontre' (the 'rencontre en Phocidé') and 'rapport'.

What, though, in all this, of the role of the gods? Mégare, a servant, serves to enunciate the standard alignment of the gods with an unknown and unknowable profundity at an early stage in the play:

> Nous ne savons pas bien comme agit l'autre monde,
> Il n'est point d'oeil perçant dans cette nuit profonde. (II. 2. 561–64)

In Mégare's portrayal, the gods are the out-of-reach, underground divinity that we would call the unconscious. There is a structurally expressed difference between this understanding and the utterance of Dircé which closes the play:

> Un autre ordre demain peut nous être donné.
> Allons voir cependant ce Prince infortuné,
> Pleurer auprès de lui notre destin funeste,
> Et remettons aux Dieux à disposer du reste. (v. 9. 2007–10)

It is significant that, by the end of Corneille's *Œdipe*, the 'unknown' represented by the actions of the gods is expressed, not in terms of a 'nuit profonde' to be 'pierced' by the human eye, but in terms of an order, a disposition to be grappled with. The gods express themselves, according to Dircé, in terms of those complexities of human encounter that have been our concern from the first scene of Corneille's version of the play. That which is unknown and inaccessible is not a 'nuit profonde', but the countless 'dispositions' in which we may find ourselves and those around us. The gods are inaccessible; and the miniature, pantographically reduced version of that inaccessibility turns out to be the unpredictability of human encounters. There is in Corneille, in other words, a confused coagulation of the 'psychological' and the environmental.

Midway between Mégare's and Dircé's differing conceptions of the gods comes Thésée's extraordinary speech damning an understanding of the divine as source and origin of all human action:

> Quoi? La nécessité des vertus et des vices
> D'un astre impérieux doit suivre les caprices
> Et Delphes, malgré nous, conduit nos actions
> Au plus bizarre effet de ses prédictions? (III. 5. 1149–52)

Thésée acknowledges, agitatedly, an understanding of the gods as a profoundly unknowable 'abîme' within the human ('N'enfonçons toutefois ni votre oeil ni le mien | Dans ce profond abîme où nous ne voyons rien', III. 5. 1171–72), only to submit this to brutal dismissal, reclaiming as his own a liberty of vision and movement: 'D'un tel aveuglement daignez me dispenser' (III. 5. 1167). But far from providing an unconditional advertisement for a joyously determinant human will, Thésée merely redefines the unpredictability previously attributed to the gods in human terms:

> Delphes a pu vous faire une fausse réponse,
> L'argent put inspirer la voix qui les prononce,
> [...] Et par tous les climats on n'a que trop d'exemples
> Qu'il est ainsi qu'ailleurs des méchants dans les temples.
> (III. 5. 1173–74, 1177–78)

And in her response to Thésée, Jocaste too displaces the unpredictability of the gods into the human plane:

> Attendons toutefois ce qu'en dira Phorbas:
> Autre que lui n'a vu ce malheureux trépas,

> Et de ce témoin seul dépend la connaissance
> Et de ce parricide et de votre naissance. (III. 5. 1191–94)

The necessity of Phorbas's testimony makes 'connaissance' not divine or 'profonde' but mortal and embodied; all the more so because Phorbas then defers ('tu dois le connaître', v. 3. 1750]) to the equally ambient authority of a second witness, Iphicrate. Corneille, in providing a chain of witnesses, cannot do otherwise than bind epistemology to the social world in which the chain has been forged.

Longinus sees a sublime 'sense of multitude' in Sophocles' depiction of Oedipus and Jocasta:

> Curse on the marriages
> That gave us birth and having given birth
> Flung forth the selfsame seed again and showed
> Fathers and sons and brothers all blood-kin,
> And brides and wives and mothers, all the shame
> Of all the foulest deeds that men have done. (23.3)[10]

'These all mean one person, Oedipus, and on the other side Jocasta,' he writes, 'but the expansion into the plural serves to make the misfortunes plural as well' (23.3). Corneille provides us with an object lesson in multiplying Sophoclean plurality. In displaying multiple relationships on stage, he pays dramatic tribute, in a much more striking way than his ancient models, to the endemic complexities of the social.[11]

'La différente route que j'ai prise', writes Corneille in his *Examen*, comparing himself to the 'grands génies' of the past, 'm'a empêché de me rencontrer avec eux.'[12] Corneille's chosen mode of rewriting *Oedipus* is an invigorating reaffirmation of the order of priorities he puts forward in his *Discours*. Corneille, who 'treats very gingerly the question of the horror of the play, its monstrous transgressions', who is worried that 'ce qui avait passé pour merveilleux en leurs siècles [ceux de Sophocle et de Sénèque] pourrait sembler horrible au nôtre',[13] displaces sensitivities from shock and awe into the powerful commiseration that comes with a discourse about human relations. It follows that Œdipe alone is not the prime source of tragic emotion: 'Le poème entier en excite [de la commisération] peut-être autant que *le Cid* ou que *Rodogune*; mais il en doit une partie à Dircé, et ce qu'elle en fait naître n'est qu'une pitié empruntée d'un épisode.'[14] Above all, we may say that *Œdipe* is a tribute to the enormity of other people, to 'la proximité du sang et les liaisons d'amour ou d'amitié entre le persécutant et le persécuté, le poursuivant et le poursuivi, celui qui fait souffrir et celui qui souffre' (p. 38). In *Œdipe*, the irrationalities of the 'voix du sang' are splintered into the complex human concerns of a 'proximité du sang', which is made even less epistemologically sound thanks to its imbrication with 'liaisons d'amour'. Corneille is fascinated, like the writers of another *Anti-Œdipe*, with the individual as 'groupuscule'.[15] *Œdipe* diverts *Oedipus* away from its clear course within the second of Aristotle's tragic models ('*On le fait périr sans le connaître, et on le reconnaît avec déplaisir*') and restocks the play with the preoccupations of the fourth ('*ceux qui connaissent, entreprennent et n'achèvent pas*'). Decisions, knowledge, enterprise — whether on the part of Dircé, Thésée, Œdipe, or Jocaste — are waylaid by a flux of intrusive encounters and events. The world does not provide us with observational evidence that we receive unproblematically, on the basis of which we decide how and what to 'entreprendre', but provides a constitutive and unreliable part of the 'entreprise' itself, inflecting its 'achèvement' and, moreover, making any kind of achievement or lack of it difficult to quantify. In other words, Œdipe is interested in all that which goes, as we saw in Chapter 2, to make up tragedies 'du genre le plus sublime et le plus touchant'.

D'Aubignac

We have seen that, simply put, Œdipe does not offer any easy moral message, because it confirms that unpredictability determines actions and whether they turn out well or not. While this is true of Sophocles' Oedipus too, with its plunging engagement with the dictates of the gods, the proximities established by Corneille, the encounters and relationships that define his version of the play, demand the close attention of the audience and turn an unfathomable unknown into a more complex unpredictability. It is precisely this which most disturbs the Abbé d'Aubignac.

D'Aubignac's criticisms of Œdipe target, predictably and precisely, Corneille's preoccupation with the fluctuations and unpredictabilities of human relations. 'A quoi bon', he writes, 'de faire voir au peuple, que ces têtes couronnées ne sont pas à l'abri de la mauvaise fortune?'[16] To impinge upon the rigidity of monarchical authority is, from D'Aubignac's point of view, to withdraw from the domain of the ethically sound: 'Ce n'est pas assez qu'un poète cherche les moyens de plaire, il faut encore qu'il enseigne les grandes vérités et principalement dans le Poème Dramatique' (p. 89). Royalty, the source and origin of all meaning, is beyond judgement (and we see here that a critical, Cornelian commiseration is beyond D'Aubignac): 'Il faut enseigner des choses qui maintiennent la société publique, qui servent à retenir les peuples dans leur devoir, et qui montrent toujours les Souverains comme des objets de vénération, environnés des vertus comme de la gloire' (p. 89).

Indeed, any suggestion that the body of 'la société publique' might comprise elements of hetereogeneity is condemned: 'Il n'y faut rien mêler qui sente le dérèglement des moeurs [...] il faut empêcher que les peuples s'imaginent d'être châtiés pour les crimes d'autrui sans être les premiers coupables' (pp. 89–90). The dangers presented by the weight of 'autrui', as they are given leverage by Corneille, are condemned by D'Aubignac. It is worth noting that Corneille's preference for characters who 'connaissent, entreprennent et n'achèvent pas' recurs in D'Aubignac at the level of the tiniest textual detail: characters

> s'interrompent à tout propos, se ferment la bouche l'un à l'autre en plusieurs occasions qui mériteraient bien que l'on sût tous leurs sentiments; ils commencent à dire plusieurs choses qu'ils *n'achèvent pas*, tant celui qui les écoute précipite sa réponse [...]. De faire jusqu'à vingt-quatre interruptions, si je les ai bien comptées, dans une même Pièce, comme en celle-ci, il n'est point d'homme raisonnable qui ne les condamne et qui ne les juge insupportables en lisant. (pp. 98–99, my emphases)

Some of D'Aubignac's most striking criticisms of Corneille, however, are rolled up in the concept of 'vraisemblance'. Much of the *Troisième dissertation* serves to denounce Œdipe as inappropriate (both improper and implausible) subject matter for a tragedy (D'Aubignac's comments in this regard reach a gratifying level of vindictiveness with the speculation that Corneille 'se devait souvenir que dans son *Pertharite* il avait fait d'un beau sujet un mauvais Poème, et penser qu'il lui serait plus malaisé de faire un bon Poème sur un méchant sujet', p. 88). It is worth considering, then, that Corneille's concept of 'vraisemblance' can also be seen to collaborate fully in the original critical discourse facilitated by his appropriation of the term 'sublime'.

Vraisemblance

It is of course a critical commonplace that, in his theoretical *Discours*, Corneille sets about directly challenging prevailing views of verisimilitude. As H. T. Barnwell writes:

> It can be shown without difficulty that in his critical self-justification Corneille stood apart from the majority of his contemporaries and, in particular, from Racine — hence the usual contrast between a Corneille rebelling against the literary orthodoxy of his day and claiming the right to create freely the original works of his imagination, and a Racine conforming to that orthodoxy and claiming to be the faithful follower and imitator of the great writers of antiquity.[17]

The prevailing views of verisimilitude at the time of Corneille's *Discours* tend towards Rapin's later statement that 'le vray-semblable est tout ce qui est conforme à l'opinion du public'.[18] 'L'opinion du public' stands for a generalized reasonableness; 'ces visions, ces enchantemens prodigieux sont semblables aux imaginations creuses d'un malade, et ils font pitié à ceux qui ont du sens: parce qu'ils n'ont aucune couleur de vray-semblance'.[19] Seventeenth-century texts make a series of confident associative journeys between 'vraisemblance' and that kind of 'sens' which, usually qualified as 'bon', equates to reason: in D'Aubignac's words, only the 'vraisemblable' could '*raisonnablement* fonder, soustenir, et terminer un Poëme dramatique' (my emphasis).[20]

Corneille's push beyond the 'vraisemblable' is evident from the first pages of the *Discours*:

> On est venu jusqu'à établir une maxime très fausse, qu'il faut que le sujet d'une tragédie soit vraisemblable: appliquant aussi aux conditions du sujet la moitié de ce qu'il [Aristote] a dit de la manière de le traiter. Ce n'est pas qu'on ne puisse faire une tragédie d'un sujet purement vraisemblable [...] mais les grands sujets qui remuent fortement les passions, et en opposent l'impétuosité aux lois du devoir, ou aux tendresses du sang, doivent toujours aller au-delà du vraisemblable. (pp. 1–2)

Corneille's important distinction here is between the subject matter of a tragedy and the manner in which it is treated: the 'sujet' can fall outside the realm of the generally 'vraisemblable' as long as a notion of 'vraisemblance' upholds its treatment. Corneille goes on to state that '[ces grands sujets] ne trouveraient aucune croyance parmi les auditeurs, s'ils n'étaient soutenus, ou par l'autorité de l'histoire qui persuade avec empire, ou par la préoccupation de l'opinion commune qui nous donne ces mêmes auditeurs déjà tous persuadés' (p. 2).

The originality of Corneille is generally seen to reside, here, in his positing of a 'vraisemblance' of 'l'histoire' as well as of 'opinion'. History can blur into myth ('story'; 'histoire' with a small 'h') given the common element of belief involved: 'Il n'est pas vraisemblable que Médée tue ses enfants, que Clytemnestre assassine son mari, qu'Oreste poignarde sa mère; mais l'histoire le dit, et la représentation de ces grands crimes ne trouve pas d'incrédules' (p. 2). But the fact that something has happened also automatically grants it believability. 'Le vrai' is a superior and faultless form of the possible, its possibility in no doubt. '*Quelquefois ce n'est pas le meilleur qu'elles se soient passées de la manière qu'il décrit; néanmoins elles se sont passées effectivement de cette manière*, et par conséquent il est hors de faute' (p. 50). This superior form of possibility extends to what Corneille calls the particular: 'le particulier est ce qu'a pu ou dû faire Alexandre, César, Alcibiade, compatible avec ce que l'histoire nous apprend de ces actions' (p. 55).

The unified, universalizing, univocal impulse against which Corneille pitted himself with his privileging of history can be seen in Jean Chapelain's 1623 preface to Marino's *Adone*. Chapelain cites approvingly those 'Anciens' who banned the specifics of history from their work and who, 'jugeant que la vérité des choses, supposé qu'elles dépendissent du hasard, nuisait par leurs fortuits et incertains événements à leur intention si louable, tous d'accord ont banni la vérité de leur Parnasse'.[21] This emphasis at the beginning of the century is also readily applicable towards its end in André Dacier's commentary on Aristotle: 'L'Histoire ne peut instruire qu'autant que les faits qu'elle raporte, luy en donnent l'occasion, &, comme ces faits sont particuliers, il arrive rarement qu'ils soient proportionnez à ceux qui les lisent, il n'y en a pas un entre mille à qui ils puissent convenir.'[22] René Rapin similarly disallows truth in tragedy on account of 'le meslange des conditions singulières, qui la composent': 'la vérité ne fait les choses que comme elles sont; & la vray-semblance les fait comme elles doivent être'.[23] This expression backs up very clearly Gérard Genette's observation of 'la liaison étroite et pour mieux dire l'amalgame entre les notions de vraisemblance et de bienséance, amalgame parfaitement représenté par l'ambiguïté bien connue (*obligation* et *probabilité*) du verbe devoir'.[24] And we need to contrast Rapin's injunction with the following statement in Corneille's *Discours*: 'Il ne les [les poèmes] faut pas pousser loin sans les appliquer au particulier; autrement c'est un lieu commun, qui ne manque jamais d'ennuyer l'auditeur, parce qu'il fait languir l'action' (pp. 4–5). We are reminded here of Aristotle's dictum that tragedy is 'a mimesis not of persons but of action and life' (*Poetics*, 1450a15).

John D. Lyons, commenting on the 'timeless, abstract quality that opponents of Corneille sought to establish in opposition to a tragedy of history, theoretically and practically founded on the concept of time', states that history is useful to Corneille because of the shock value of the 'singular, implausible historical event'.[25] It is useful because it is the record of 'broken patterns' (p. 98). In Corneille's theory, 'the nonverisimilar plot and the pleasure of the spectator are thus joined as Corneille proceeds to exemplify the pleasurable emotional turmoil caused by the nonverisimilar, criminal stories of Medea, Clytemnestra, and Orestes' (p. 138). It is certainly the case that the particular truth of history's broken patterns can be pleasurably shocking. More fundamentally, though, history itself is not the domain of truth claims:

> L'histoire est des choses qui passent, et qui succédant les unes aux autres n'ont que chacune un moment pour leur durée, dont il en échappe beaucoup à la connaissance de ceux qui l'écrivent. Aussi n'en peut-on montrer aucune qui contienne tout ce qui s'est passé dans les lieux dont elle parle, ni tout ce qu'ont fait ceux dont elle décrit la vie. (p. 56)

Corneille is radical in this denial of any stable relationship between present and past. The reader is confronted with a perpetual divergence between writing subject and the 'reality' or particularity of written history. No factual authority is granted even to those who have lived the life they seek to objectify: 'Je n'en excepte pas même les commentaires de César qui écrivait sa propre histoire, et devait la savoir tout entière' (p. 56). Corneille modifies the privileges that he had awarded history by protecting the structures of the 'particulière'. Instead, he becomes fascinated by what falls between the cracks of 'des choses qui passent': by the experiential interstices of history.

Importantly, Corneille makes a space for these interstices in his theories of 'vraisemblance' — and this is what will see me loop back to the sublime 'liaisons' and proximities, the dramatic desirability of a 'changement de fortune', which have been my concern throughout. The space Corneille makes here is the 'extraordinaire'. The category of 'vraisemblance extraordinaire' differs from all other structures of verisimilitude, 'pour n'aller point jusqu'au miracle, ni jusqu'à ces événements singuliers, qui servent de matière aux tragédies sanglantes par l'appui qu'ils ont ou de l'histoire, ou de l'opinion commune' (p. 57). Corneille quotes two Aristotelian examples of the 'extraordinaire': 'l'un d'un homme subtil et adroit qui se trouve trompé par un moins subtil que lui: l'autre d'un faible qui se bat contre un plus fort que lui, et en demeure victorieux' (p. 57).[26] In Aristotle, it is perhaps the case that 'this passage of the *Poetics* remains probably too contorted and textually corrupt to interpret clearly'.[27] In Corneille, however, these examples of the extraordinary hark back coherently to the unpredictability of human relations which defined the sublime 'tragédie parfaite', and to the 'commisération' thereby produced.

'Vraisemblance extraordinaire', in other words, is what is accepted as possible within the untidy realm of human interrelationships: it does not extend to Medea slaughtering her children, or to the miracles of God, but it does extend to all that comes under the remit of luck, chance, encounter. It corresponds to interrelationships as these determine the synchronicity which makes moments in time irreducible to the diachronic. The 'extraordinaire' allegorizes the interrelationships that make up the lives of each of the spectators watching. Their grasping of the allegory in question, and their grasping application of it to themselves, is the ineffable tragic effect that Corneille seeks to produce. In Corneille, even the most ravishing, breathtaking, shocking, or surprising moment must never preclude the association of the encounters portrayed on stage and the encounters which make up the lives of the audience:

> Il [le poète] peut bien choquer la vraisemblance particulière par quelque altération de l'histoire, mais non pas se dispenser de la générale, que rarement,

et pour des choses qui soient de la dernière beauté, et si brillantes, qu'elles éblouissent. Surtout il ne doit jamais les pousser au-delà de la vraisemblance extraordinaire.[28]

The ethical thrust of Corneille's writing is towards an applied understanding of the 'extraordinaire', the vulnerability of human relations.

As Barnwell comments, 'It has often been said that Corneille's heroes act in full knowledge of what they are doing and see their way forward in the clear light of day. This clarity of vision is supposed to be the mark of the "généreux".'[29] But as we have seen, Corneille's preference for characters who act 'à visage découvert' does not in any sense imply the hegemony of 'full knowledge' in his thought. It refers rather to characters' acute awareness of the force of the relationships which surround them, and to the transferred version of this awareness that is the spectators' 'commisération'. It is not that Corneille excises the unknown from his theatre, merely that the unknown takes the form of the unpredictable.

Barnwell writes further that 'the sense of fittingness and inevitability give rise to what Corneille suggested as a new tragic emotion, admiration: admiration on the aesthetic level for the coherence of the play as a work of art, but admiration too [...] at the spectacle of heroic and terrible deeds and at the revelation of an abiding moral order' (p. 248). But Corneille is preoccupied, in his *Discours*, with the way in which relationships, circumstances, intervene continually and changeably in the actions of characters: 'Mais quand ils y font de leur côté tout ce qu'ils peuvent, et qu'ils sont empêchés d'en venir à l'effet par quelque puissance supérieure, ou par quelque changement de fortune qui les fait périr eux-mêmes, ou les réduit sous le pouvoir de ceux qu'ils veulent perdre, il est hors de doute que cela fait une tragédie plus sublime que les trois qu'Aristote avoue'.[30] The lesson to be drawn from this which is most salient to morality, it seems, is that the complexities of circumstance can jemmy open an unbridgeable gap between intention and outcome.[31] What Corneille does with Oedipus, who 'ne fait que disputer le chemin en homme de coeur contre un inconnu qui l'attaque avec avantage' (*Writings on the Theatre*, p. 31), is, as we have seen, of particular interest to us here.

I have suggested that Corneille's promotion of 'vraisemblance extraordinaire' resonates powerfully with his theorization of sublime 'tragédies parfaites', as he uses the sublime, and the 'extraordinaire', as tools to say something about the precise and not remotely idealized topic of human interaction. And I hope now to illustrate further that we need to be wary of readings which equate the sublime and the highly regarded, understanding Corneille's characters as representing the great, and therefore as *being* sublime, by considering the way references to Corneille are marshalled and mediated by his seventeenth-century readers.

Notes to Chapter 3

1. Pierre Corneille, *Writings on the Theatre*, ed. by H. T. Barnwell (Oxford: Blackwell, 1965), p. 41.
2. In his *Examen*, Corneille writes that, until his version, 'l'amour n'ayant point de part en cette tragédie, elle était dénuée des principaux agréments qui sont en possession de gagner la voix publique'. *Writings on the Theatre*, p. 155.

3. Corneille, *Œdipe*, in *Œuvres complètes*, ed. by André Stegmann (Paris: Éditions du Seuil, 1963). In Sophocles, Oedipus encounters as a young man the tale 'of horror and misery: how I must marry my mother, | And become the parent of a misbegotten brood, | An offence to all mankind — and kill my father'. It is this which prompts him to leave: 'At this I fled away, putting the stars | Between me and Corinth, never to see home again.' *King Oedipus*, in Sophocles, *The Theban Plays*, trans. by E. F. Watling (London: Penguin, 1968), lines 792–96. Corneille is clearly perturbed by the following question: can Oedipus really flee Corinth for fear of the rumours regarding his future incest and patricide and not (immediately upon meeting Jocasta, or at least earlier on in dramatic time) connect these rumours to the oracle which led Laius and Jocasta to abandon their infant son? He writes, 'J'ai retranché le nombre des oracles qui pouvait être importun, et donner à Œdipe trop de soupçon de sa naissance.' *Writings on the Theatre*, p. 155.

4. See the *Examen*: 'J'ai rendu la réponse de Laïus, évoqué par Tirésie, assez obscure dans sa clarté apparente pour en faire une fausse application à cette princesse.' *Writings on the Theatre*, p. 155.

5. This witness, unnamed in Sophocles, is called Phorbas in Seneca's *Oedipus*.

6. In a display of self-righteous 'politesse' which befits the 'Examen' of a play commissioned by Fouquet, Corneille writes: 'Je reconnus que ce qui avait passé pour merveilleux en leurs siècles [ceux de Sophocle et de Sénèque] pourrait sembler horrible au nôtre; que cette éloquente et sérieuse description de la manière dont ce malheureux prince se crève les yeux, qui occupe tout leur cinquième acte, ferait soulever la délicatesse de nos dames, dont le dégoût attire aisément celui du reste de l'auditoire.' *Writings on the Theatre*, p. 155. On this, see Terence Cave, *Recognitions* (Oxford: Oxford University Press, 1988), pp. 101–03.

7. Aristotle, *Poetics*, 55a18. Sigmund Freud, *The Interpretation of Dreams* (New York: Avon, 1965), p. 295. Freud writes in an early letter, 'I have found, in my own case too, falling in love with the mother and jealousy of the father, and I now regard it as a universal event of early childhood [...] If this is so, we can understand the riveting power of *Œdipus Rex*, in spite of all the objections raised by reason against its presupposition of destiny.' 'Letter to Fliess', in *The Standard Edition of the Complete Psychological Works of Sigmund Freud*, trans. and ed. by James Strachey, 24 vols (London: Hogarth Press, 1953–74), I, 265. The Oedipus complex, whose desires are repressed into the unconscious, is defined by Freud as the crucial transitional moment of human development. It holds of course a similar degree of significance in Lacanian psychoanalysis, although the latter system of thought modifies Freud in a number of ways: the Oedipus complex is made to mark the move of a child into a relationship in which the authority that is the name-of-the-father is recognized, and the idea of a symbolic 'phallus' is introduced. Gilles Deleuze and Félix Guattari's *Capitalisme et schizophrénie*, I: *L'Anti-Œdipe* (Paris: Éditions de Minuit, 1972) does more detailed work on the intermingling of psychical structure described by psychoanalysis and social structure.

8. Sophocles, *The Theban Plays*, p. 49.

9. Jonathan Culler picks up on this to make the point that Sophocles privileges discursive forces as such over any given event narrated in discourse: 'The "whole action of the play" is the revelation of this awful deed (the killing of Laius), but we are never given the proof, the testimony of the eye-witness. Œdipus himself and all his readers are convinced of his guilt but our conviction does not come from the revelation of the deed. Instead of the revelation of a prior deed determining meaning, we could say that it is meaning, the convergence of meaning in the narrative discourse, that leads us to posit this deed as its appropriate manifestation.' *The Pursuit of Signs: Semiotics, Literature, Deconstruction* (London: Routledge, 1981), p. 174.

10. Longinus is quoting *Oedipus Tyrannus*, lines 1403–08.

11. *Writings on the Theatre*, p. 38. One might say that, in extending Aristotle's specifications concerning acceptable tragic patterns, Corneille also extends Aristotle's notion of what has come to be called, as I noted earlier, 'moral luck' or 'the fragility of goodness': the foreseeing of circumstances beyond one's own control, the need for responsiveness and flexibility. Bernard Williams, *Moral Luck: Philosophical Papers, 1973–1980* (Cambridge: Cambridge University Press, 1981); Martha Nussbaum, *The Fragility of Goodness: Luck and Ethics in Greek Tragedy and Philosophy*, 2nd edn (Cambridge: Cambridge University Press, 2001).

12. *Writings on the Theatre*, p. 155.

13. Cave, *Recognitions*, p. 101; *Writings on the Theatre*, p. 155.

14. Ibid., p. 41.

15. 'Chacun est un groupuscule et doit vivre ainsi', write Deleuze and Guattari in *L'Anti-Œdipe* (p. 434). Deleuze and Guattari's extended attack on the Freudian Oedipus complex as transcendental signifier (and also on the textbook reifying of the writings of Lacan, 'lui qui fut le premier au contraire à schizophréniser le champ analytique', p. 435) privileges triumphantly the work of D. H. Lawrence, concerned as it is with the borders of society and the individual mind: 'Lawrence s'en prend à la pauvreté des images identiques immuables, rôles figuratifs qui sont autant de garrots sur le flux de sexualité: "fiancée, maîtresse, femme, mère" — on dirait aussi bien "homosexuels, hétérosexuels", etc. — , tous ces rôles sont distribués par le triangle œdipien, père-mère-moi, un moi représentatif étant supposé se définir en fonction des représentations père-mère, par fixation, régression, assomption, sublimation, et tout ça sous quelle règle?' (p. 420). They argue passionately that the truly productive psychological insights of the twentieth century are those of authors (in the following quotation, Henry Miller and R. D. Laing in combination with Lawrence) who 'ont su le montrer profondément: assurément, ni l'homme ni la femme ne sont des personnalités bien définies — mais des vibrations, des flux, des schizes et des "noeuds"' (p. 434).

16. L'Abbé d'Aubignac, 'Troisième dissertation concernant le poème dramatique', in *Dissertations contre Corneille*, ed. by N. Hammond and M. Hawcroft (Exeter: University of Exeter Press, 1995), p. 89.

17. H. T. Barnwell, *The Tragic Drama of Corneille and Racine: An Old Parallel Revisited* (Oxford: Oxford University Press, 1982), p. 72.

18. René Rapin, *Réflexions sur la poétique de ce temps, et sur les ouvrages des poetes anciens et modernes*, 2nd edn, rev. and enlarged (Paris: François Muguet, 1675), p. 34.

19. Ibid., p. 35.

20. Abbé d'Aubignac, *La Pratique du théâtre*, ed. by P. Martino (Geneva: Slatkine Reprints, 1996; orig. publ. Paris: Antoine de Sommaville, 1657), p. 77.

21. Jean Chapelain, *Opuscules critiques*, ed. by Alfred C. Hunter (Paris: Droz, 1936), p. 87.

22. *La Poétique d'Aristote*, trans. and ed. by André Dacier (Paris: Barbin, 1692), p. 131.

23. *Réflexions*, p. 36.

24. Gérard Genette, 'Vraisemblance et motivation', in *Figures II* (Paris: Éditions du Seuil, 1969), pp. 71–101 (p. 72).

25. John D. Lyons, *Kingdom of Disorder: The Theory of Tragedy in Classical France* (West Lafayette, IN: Purdue University Press, 1999), pp. 97, 100. For more on history in Corneille, see Lyons, *The Tragedy of Origins: Pierre Corneille and Historical Perspective* (Stanford: Stanford University Press, 1946).

26. 'In reversals and simple structures of events, poets aim for what they want by means of the awesome: this is tragic and arouses fellow-feeling. This occurs when an adroit but wicked person is deceived (like Sisyphus), or a brave but unjust person is worsted.' *Poetics*, 1456a18–23.

27. Stephen Halliwell, *The 'Poetics' of Aristotle: Translation and Commentary* (London: Duckworth, 1987), p. 152.

28. *Writings on the Theatre*, p. 59. This goes against Forestier's comment: 'Ces événements qui servent de matière à la tragédie sont si exceptionnels — et sur le plan anthropologique et sur le plan statistique — qu'ils ne sont même pas justiciables de la vraisemblance extraordinaire.' Georges Forestier, *Essai de génétique théâtrale: Corneille à l'œuvre*, 2nd edn (Geneva: Droz, 2004), p. 288.

29. *The Tragic Drama of Corneille and Racine*, p. 248.

30. *Writings on the Theatre*, p. 40.

31. My reading of Corneille's *Discours* abstracts them from the 'awe' seen in the following reading as being essential to tragedy: 'When we have seen terrible things happening in the play, we understand, as we cannot always do in life, why they have happened; or if not so much as that, at least we see that they have not happened by chance, without any significance.' D. F. Kitto, quoted in Barnwell, *The Tragic Drama of Corneille and Racine*, p. 248. Barnwell's own comments on Corneille are dismissive and imply a lack of interest in some of the specificities of his rewriting which I have sought to examine here: 'It is significant that *Œdipus Rex*, which was, for Aristotle, the discovery-tragedy par excellence and perhaps the masterpiece of Greek theatre, comes in for a good deal of criticism from Corneille: it is, of course, obvious that he had no real understanding of either hamartia or catharsis and that he was, like all his contemporaries, hopelessly tangled up with moral and psychological concepts quite foreign to Greek drama.' *The Tragic Drama of Corneille and Racine*, p. 163.

CHAPTER 4

Corneille's Movements

Boileau, in a 1701 addition to the *Préface* to his translation of Longinus and in his *Réflexion X* (published posthumously in 1713 but composed around 1710), cites two examples from Corneille's theatre as being particularly successful in embodying the sublime. When the play *Horace* has le vieil Horace enjoining Julie to 'pleure[r] le deshonneur de toute nostre race', and when she spits out her defensive response, 'que vouliez-vous qu'il fist contre trois', the sublime is, for Boileau, unambiguously embodied in old man's answer: 'Qu'il mourust.'[1] 'Voilà des termes fort simples', writes Boileau:

> Cependant il n'y a personne qui ne sente la grandeur qu'il y a dans ces trois syllabes, Qu'il mourust. Sentiment d'autant plus sublime qu'il est simple et naturel, et que par là on voit que ce Heros parle du fond du coeur, et dans les transports d'une colere vraiment Romaine. (p. 548)

Similarly significant for Boileau is Médée's response to the despairing 'que vous reste-t-il' of her *confidente*: 'Moy, dis-je, & c'est assez.'[2] The forcefulness of this statement moves Boileau to the following interrogation:

> Peut-on nier qu'il n'y ait du Sublime, et du Sublime le plus relevé dans ce monosyllabe Moy? Qu'est-ce donc qui frappe dans ce passage, sinon la fierté audacieuse de cette Magicienne, et la confiance qu'elle a dans son Art? (p. 549)

These examples are renowned. As Georges Forestier notes, 'Depuis Boileau s'est développé un véritable lieu commun de la sublimité de l'esprit et des pensées de Corneille qui peuvent s'exprimer dans des vers sublimes, et qui sont prononcés par des personnages eux-mêmes sublimes de magnanimité.'[3] Certainly, the current critical association of Corneille and sublimity is powerful enough for the most recent monograph on the seventeenth-century sublime to state confidently that Corneille 'peut ainsi apparaître comme le seul auteur français véritablement sublime'.[4]

'Le sublime cornélien'

Such statements as this of Hache revolve around the view, already discussed in the context of critical readings of Corneille's *Discours*,[5] that Corneille's 'admirable' characters move in the domain of the sublime as a result of their propensity to induce 'admiration' in the audience. 'Le sublime cornélien', writes Paul Bénichou, 'naît [...] d'un mouvement particulier par lequel l'impulsion humaine, sans se nier ni se condamner, s'élève au-dessus de la nécessité.'[6] The sublime is a 'sublime de la liberté': 'Dans le cas de Cléopâtre, il ne faut pas dire que la force de la volonté engendre le sublime, abstraction faite du bien et du mal; c'est plutôt le mépris du bien et du mal qui est sublime, dès lors que l'ambition, l'orgueil, la haine de la médiocrité et de la dépendance, en sont le principe.'[7] Sublimity is opposed to 'médiocrité' and 'dépendance' and concomitantly equated to greatness. The direction taken by Bénichou's study has been followed, it seems, by most critics since.

Another major critical point of reference in this regard is Fumaroli's article 'L'Héroïsme cornélien et l'éthique de la magnanimité': 'S'il y a chez Corneille un sublime de la magnanimité héroïque, franchissant les normes du grand style tragique à l'instant même où la grande âme, emportée par un "nescio quid", franchit les limites de la nature humaine, il y a aussi le sublime inverse de la grandeur d'âme incontrôlée.'[8] Similarly, Baldine Saint Girons takes Corneille's comment on Cleopatra in the *Discours* ('en même temps qu'on déteste ses actions, on admire la source dont elles partent') and describes this as a 'formule essentielle, puisqu'elle assure l'indifférence relative de l'effet par rapport au principe et qu'elle légitime le mouvement de la sublimation, indépendamment des fins qu'il se donne'.[9] Saint Girons's comments make sublimity 'sublimation' (in scientific terms a change from solid to vapour; metaphorically any move upwards; in psychoanalytical terms the diversion towards higher aims of energy derived from an instinct that is denied gratification).[10] And Saint Girons, like the other critics cited, makes the point that 'l'admiration ne concerne pas seulement l'extraordinaire vitalité de Cléopâtre et la somme d'énergie qu'elle met en jeu, mais une force qui est déjà morale dans son principe: celle d'une volonté dont la tension, ici pervertie par un mauvais usage, aurait pu se déployer vers les sommets de la moralité' (p. 421).

This modern criticism, while it goes about a dissociation of Cornelian 'admiration' from normatively ethical debates about what it is for something to be admirably virtuous, does still force the sublime along smooth channels of impressive greatness.[11] One consequence of this is that seemingly any Cornelian character, or verse, can be described as 'sublime'. Hence Bénichou: 'Camille défie Horace vainqueur, Émilie défie Auguste tout-puissant. [...] C'était là tout le sublime du fameux "qu'il mourût", cent fois répété par Corneille sous diverses formes. C'était l'idée, constamment reprise, d'une mort éclatante ou d'un glorieux supplice' (p. 31). Fumaroli makes a similar move: 'Outre le "Qu'il mourût" du vieil Horace', he states, 'Boileau aurait pu citer bien d'autres exemples': 'le "Je suis maître de moi comme de l'Univers" d'Auguste, le "A la mort" ? — "Non, à la gloire" de Polyeucte' (p. 348).

It seems noteworthy, however, that Boileau did not cite these examples; and what I shall suggest now is that the kind of commodious critical language which states that he might have done rides roughshod over the interest of his comments. Here, as elsewhere in this study, we need to go further than the notion that sublimity equates to a non-specific 'greatness'. We need to bear in mind, beyond the comments already made about Corneille's own appropriation of the term 'sublime', the basic fact that 'greatness', in Longinus, only ever accompanies an interest in successful communication. I have already looked, then, at the kinds of tragedy described by Corneille as 'sublime', showing that he seeks to promote theatrical identification by means of an investigation into disparate and unpredictable human encounters. I shall now argue that the strong lines of relation that seventeenth-century authors establish in order to bind Longinus and Corneille have relevant lessons to teach us in our consideration of Boileau's subsequent singling out of the latter.

Seventeenth-Century Readings

'Vive donc notre vieil ami Corneille!' exclaims Madame de Sévigné to her daughter in 1672: 'Pardonnons-lui de méchants vers, en faveur des divines et sublimes beautés qui nous transportent: ce sont des traits de maître qui sont inimitables.'[12] Sévigné's vocabulary here, pinning down an understanding of sublimity as that 'transport' which summons the mind to ecstasy and steamrollers any consideration of technical or rhetorical detail, has as its specific intertext Boileau's translation of Longinus, and most obviously the celebrated passage in Chapter 1: '[Le sublime] ne persuade pas proprement, mais il ravit, il transporte, et produit en nous une certaine admiration mêlée d'étonnement et de surprise, qui est toute autre chose que de plaire seulement, ou de persuader' (p. 341). Indeed Sévigné's letter illustrates, usefully, that knowledge of this translation had entered the wider critical domain before its publication in 1674: 'Despréaux en dit encore plus que moi' (p. 459). Her comments come in the context of a comparison between Corneille and Racine in which the latter is reproached because his *Bajazet* contains 'des choses agréables', but 'rien de parfaitement beau, rien qui enlève, point de ces tirades de Corneille qui font frissonner'. The 'frisson', then, is the test which, delimiting and enshrining the sublime, establishes the superiority of Corneille as dramatist: 'Ma fille, gardons-nous bien de lui comparer Racine, *sentons-en* la différence' (p. 459, my emphasis).[13]

The hierarchy that Mme de Sévigné sets up in order to subjugate Racine to Corneille is explored and then maintained throughout the latter decades of the seventeenth century by Saint-Evremond, who states similarly that 'Racine doit avoir plus de réputation qu'aucun autre, après Corneille'.[14] Saint-Evremond's preference too is built, as we read in the *Jugement sur quelques auteurs françois*, around 'la sublimité du discours':

> Corneille se fait admirer par l'expression d'une grandeur d'âme héroïque, par la force des passions, par la sublimité du discours; Racine trouve son mérite en des sentimens plus naturels, en des pensées plus nettes, dans une diction plus pure et plus facile. Le premier enleve l'ame; l'autre gagne l'esprit; celui-ci ne donne rien à censurer au Lecteur; celui-là ne laisse pas le Spectateur en état d'examiner.[15]

We find here, as well as 'l'expression d'une grandeur d'âme héroïque', the alignment of a 'sublimité du discours' with a writing which 'enleve l'ame' and 'ne laisse pas le Spectateur en état d'examiner'. This preoccupation is explored further in the 'dissertation' that Saint-Evremond devotes to Racine's tragedy *Alexandre le Grand*. Racine, here, finds himself unable to 'entrer dans l'interieur, et tirer du fond de ces grandes ames, comme fait Corneille, leurs plus secrets mouvements'.[16] Racine, by contrast, 'regarde à peine les simples dehors, peu curieux à bien remarquer ce qui paroist, peu profond à penetrer ce qui se cache' (p. 93). The movements of Corneille's investigations are set against the invitingly intelligible surface of Racine's plays. In the drama of competition that Saint-Evremond sustains, a superior dignity is granted to the way Corneille weaves into the imaginative fabric of his characters a sense of 'leurs plus secrets mouvements'. The fact that he makes these movements a source of fascination for the spectator is in turn the source of Saint-Evremond's admiring praise.

Saint-Evremond, we know, had by 1673 read Longinus, offering in his *Sur les traducteurs* a translation of *Peri hypsous* 9.10 which bears no relation to Boileau's:

> Ajax se trouvant, dit-il, dans un combat de nuit effroyable, ne demande pas à Jupiter qu'il le sauve du danger où il se rencontre; cela seroit indigne de luy. Il ne demande pas qu'il luy donne des forces surnaturelles pour vaincre avec seureté; il auroit trop peu de part à la victoire. Il demande seulement de la lumière, afin de pouvoir discerner les ennemis, et d'exercer contre eux sa propre vaillance: *Da lucem et videam.*[17]

What is at issue here is the 'vertu des grands hommes', a 'vertu' which, as Ajax illustrates, is human rather than divine: 'Personne n'a mieux entendu que Longin cette économie de l'assistance du ciel et de la vertu des grands hommes' (p. 111). Just as Longinus (like Homer) communicates this successfully, so too does Corneille; and this comes across well when Saint-Evremond articulates a distinction between Corneille's 'sublimité' and that of the playwrights of antiquity:

> J'avoüe que nous excellons aux ouvrages de Theatre; et je ne croirai point flatter Corneille, quand je donnerai l'avantage à beaucoup de ses tragédies sur celles de l'Antiquité. Je sçai que les anciens tragiques ont eu des admirateurs dans tous les temps, mais je ne sçai pas si cette sublimité dont on parle, est trop bien fondée.[18]

Saint-Evremond circles around, here, a 'sublimité dont on parle'. This he sees as inadequate first because it is an unreflective (because generally accepted) attribution of that greatness to playwrights with a reputation for being great; and secondly because such playwrights as Sophocles and Euripides did not have sufficient experience to get across either the 'majesté d'un grand roi' (p. 25) or, further, the human 'perturbations' that go along with it: 'Ou ils négligent les passions pour estre attachez à representer exactement ce qui se passe, ou ils font les discoureurs au milieu des perturbations mêmes, et vous disent des sentences, quand vous attendez du trouble et du désespoir' (p. 27). They were, says Saint-Evremond, 'de beaux esprits resserrez dans le ménage d'une petite République' (p. 25). Corneille, on the other hand, 'a crû que ce n'estoit pas assez de faire agir [les personnes], il est allé au fond de leur ame chercher le principe de leurs actions; il est descendu dans leur coeur pour y voir former les passions, et y découvrir ce qu'il y a de plus caché dans leurs mouvemens' (p. 27).[19]

'Cette sublimité dont on parle', that which is attributed to the Ancients, cannot be properly 'fondée' because it does not bear witness to, identify, or draw out these 'mouvemens'. A vital responsibility has been assumed by Corneille, according to Saint-Evremond: the rejection of a theatrical experience in which 'il manque à nos sentimens quelque chose d'assez profond' on the grounds that 'les passions à demy-touchées n'excitent en nos ames que des mouvemens imparfaits, qui ne sçavent ni les laisser dans leur assiette, ni les enlever hors d'elles-mêmes' (p. 31). What Saint-Evremond ordains, then, is a capacious 'sublime' which allows for the movements of the 'humain' as well as for 'grandeur' or 'majesté': ancient playwrights 's'elevoient quelquefois au sublime et au merveilleux; mais alors ils faisoient entrer tant de dieux et de déesses dans leurs tragédies, qu'on n'y reconnoissoit presque rien d'humain' (p. 25). Saint-Evremond is exploring the specifics of a Longinian identification: one in which 'transport' is not just a move towards grandeur, but is also coextensive with text that is 'dense with images drawn from real life' (*Peri hypsous*, 9.13): Corneille 'ne va point chercher dans les Cieux de quoi faire valoir ce qui est assez considerable sur la terre; il lui suffit de bien entrer dans les choses, et la pleine image qu'il en donne, fait la veritable impression qu'aiment à recevoir les personnes de bon sens' (pp. 25–26).

A 1666 letter makes it clear that Saint-Evremond's definition of Corneille's work as 'sublime' does not bear an exclusive or absolute relation to his, or his characters', 'grandeur d'âme'. 'Magnanimité', as we shall see, is not what Saint-Evremond is interested in. He asks his correspondent, Madame Bourneau, whether she might send him Racine's *Alexandre le Grand*:

> Je meurs de peur que ce ne soyent de beaux discours de morale, qui expriment mieux la magnanimité en général, que le véritable Alexandre, ou le vray Porus en particulier. A la réserve de Corneille, tous les autres Poëtes font leurs Héros des beaux sentimens qu'ils leur donnent à leur fantaisie et ne conçoivent pas bien ce que les Héros estoyent apparemment.[20]

What is systematically praised here is Corneille's practical work on particularity — 'le véritable Alexandre', 'le vray Porus' — and the working out of relevant theatrical dynamics. Too often, in Saint-Evremond's view, 'beaux sentimens' are supposed to be in themselves a mark of merit. But Corneille's talent is for engaging with the individual he portrays: 'Il ne trouve point cela dans son âme: il faut qu'il ayt le secret d'entrer dans celle des autres.'[21] This is the movement which makes Corneille sublime, which makes Saint-Evremond condemn any theatrical situation where 'l'Acteur, plus transporté que le Poëte, prête de la fureur et du desespoir à une agitation mediocre'.[22] It seems that both actors and writers can, as in Longinus, 'often behave as if they were drunk and give way to outbursts of emotion which the subject no longer warrants, but which are private to themselves and consequently tedious, so that to an audience which feels none of it their behaviour looks unseemly. And naturally so, for while they are in ecstasy, the audience is not' (3.5). Corneille's writing, in Saint-Evremond's reading of it, is not given to this self-centred kind of excess.

It is difficult, in the light of this discussion, to give credence to Litman's comments that 'ses goûts [de Saint-Evremond] répugnent à un sublime qui frappe et emporte l'âme', that 'son manque d'intérêt et son incompréhension totale de la théorie de la catharsis l'empêchent d'apprécier le sublime'.[23] Hache follows Litman's reading of Saint-Evremond's work as developing 'une virulente critique contre l'excessive admiration portée aux Anciens en général et à Longin en particulier'.[24] But Saint-Evremond shows a critical interest in Longinus, and applies this to Corneille.[25]

Saint-Evremond does not dismiss Ancient authors. It is simply necessary (Michael Moriarty bears in mind the social and material conditions which underlie this simple one) to have what Saint-Evremond calls 'le bon goust de l'Antiquité'.[26]

It is worth noting that when Corneille himself comes to write his *Examen* of *La Mort de Pompée* (1642), inspired by Lucan's *Pharsalia*, it is his capacity to 'joindre' his own mind and that of Lucan of which he is particularly proud: 'J'ai traduit de Lucain tout ce que j'y ai trouvé de propre à mon sujet [...], j'ai tâché pour le reste à entrer si bien dans sa manière de former ses pensées et de s'expliquer, que ce qu'il m'a fallu y joindre du mien sentît son génie.'[27] And in his 1644 *Au lecteur*, Corneille describes the way in which the act of reading Lucan 'm'a rendu si amoureux de la force de ses pensées et de la majesté de son raisonnement'.[28] But when Lucan's later translator, Brébeuf, comes to comment on Corneille's version of *Pharsalia*, he subtly misses Corneille's emphasis on communication:

> Surtout je ne me suis pas satisfait moi-même dans les sujets que M. de Corneille a traités, et ses nobles expressions étaient si présentes à mon esprit qu'elles n'étaient pas un médiocre empêchement aux miennes. Dans ce poème inimitable qu'il a fait de la Mort de Pompée, il a traduit avec tant de succès ou même rehaussé avec tant de force ce qu'il a emprunté de Lucain et il a porté si haut la vigueur de ses pensées et la majesté de son raisonnement qu'il est sans doute un peu malaisé de le suivre.[29]

In Brébeuf, force is made more forceful by being 'rehaussé' or 'porté si haut'. Saint-Evremond is of the opinion that Brébeuf has misunderstood 'force' entirely:

> La plupart des gens croient qu'il y a de la force où il n'y a que de la dureté, comme en beaucoup d'endroits de la *Pharsale* de Brébeuf; et quand un effort d'imagination a poussé la pensée trop loin, une chose forcée est prise assez souvent pour une chose qui a de la force.[30]

But Saint-Evremond's approbation of Corneille, his references to Corneille's 'sublimité du discours', have as their foundation a forceful capacity to enter into the mind of another, and to construct a chain of identification between author, text, and reader.

For La Bruyère too, Corneille provides the model example of a dramatist who is transported into other subject positions by the act of writing:

> [Corneille] est simple, timide, d'une ennuyeuse conversation; il prend un mot pour un autre, et il ne juge de la bonté de sa pièce que par l'argent qui lui en revient; il ne sait pas la réciter, ni lire son écriture. Laissez-le s'élever par la composition: il n'est pas au-dessous d'Auguste, de Pompée, de Nicomède, d'Héraclius; il est roi, et un grand roi; il est politique, il est philosophe; il entreprend de faire parler des héros, de les faire agir.[31]

Corneille's 'grandeur' is defined in terms of moral elevation only in circumstances in which the fact of the elevation defers to the fact of identification: 'il est roi, et un grand roi; il est politique, il est philosophe'. Boileau's comments on Moses' *Fiat lux* in his *Réflexion X* (written around 1710), echo interestingly, as I shall discuss in more detail in Chapter 8, La Bruyère's appreciation of Corneille's ability to 'faire parler', to 'faire agir': 'ce grand Prophete n'ignorant pas que le meilleur moyen de faire connoistre les Personnages qu'on introduit, c'est de les faire agir; il met d'abord

Dieu en action, et le fait parler' (p. 551). And one other vital intertext for Boileau's critical reflections is, as I shall explain, Bouhours's *La Manière de bien penser dans les ouvrages d'esprit* (1687).

A procession of examples moves through these dialogues to suggest that, for Bouhours too, Corneille's work is enshrined in the testable definitions provided by Longinus. One key example given is taken from *Horace*, where Philinte states, after having cited Lucan:

> J'aime encore mieux ce que Corneille fait dire au vieil Horace, aprés que le dernier de ses fils eût tué les trois Curiaces, dont la soeur estoit sa belle-fille, & dont l'un devoit estre son gendre:
>
> > *Rome triomphe d'Albe, & c'est assez pour nous:*
> > *Tous nos maux à ce prix doivent nous estre doux.*
>
> La noblesse, le sublime est là sans enflure, ajouta Eudoxe, et Longin lui-même serait content de Corneille. [...] Selon ce grand Maistre du sublime c'est un défaut dans la Tragédie, qui est naturellement pompeuse & magnifique, que de s'enfler mal-à-propos.[32]

The sublime is the 'à propos', and the 'à propos', in its reciprocally experienced fittingness, rejects vehemently all that is 'enflure' and self-consciously bombastic magnificence. Bouhours's comments on the 'mal-à-propos' go back to Longinus 3.5, and Boileau's translation of this:

> On voit tres-souvent des Orateurs, qui comme s'ils estoient yvres, se laissent emporter à des passions qui ne conviennent point à leur sujet, mais qui leur sont propres; [...] ils se rendent à la fin odieux et insupportables. Car c'est ce qui arrive necessairement à ceux qui s'emportent et se debattent mal-à-propos devant des gens qui ne sont point du tout émûs. (pp. 344–45)

But another of Bouhours's examples sends influence ricocheting back to a receptive Boileau:

> Le vieil Horace apprenant que le troisiéme de ses fils qui restoit aprés la mort des autres tuez par les Curiaces, avoit pris la fuite, s'emporte contre luy, & dit à Julie Dame Romaine:
>
> > *Pleurez le deshonneur de toute nostre race.*
> > *Que vouliez-vous qu'il fist contre trois,*
>
> Replique Julie? *Qu'il mourust*, répond le pere d'Horace. Ce *qu'il mourust* exprime la générosité Romaine d'une maniere vive & touchante, qui frappe l'esprit, & émeut le coeur en mesme temps. (p. 174)

This, as we have seen, is precisely the example Boileau uses in his later *Réflexions* and 1701 *Préface*. The 'générosité Romaine' is only as important as the humanity of the 'maniere vive & touchante' in which it is expressed. The reader both identifies with and is moved by Horace, so Bouhours suggests, and this simultaneous self-identity and motion excludes a notion of grandeur which can be separated from an identificatory force: 'N'y a-t-il pas bien de la force', asks Bouhours, '& de la grandeur dans ce seul mot-là?' (p. 175). And we encounter in this dialogue an explicitly Longinian move from the notion that certain kinds of writing 'portent la conviction avec elles, entraisnent comme par force nostre jugement, remuënt nos passions, & nous laissent l'éguillon dans l'ame' (p. 173) to a more humane aggregation of knowledge and affectivity, 'esprit' and 'coeur', in the 'Qu'il mourust' example. The verbs 'frapper' and 'émouvoir' invite a chiastic application to either 'l'esprit' or 'le coeur' as Bouhours theorizes, 'en mesme temps', reflection as reaction and reaction as reflection. This is elevation through communication, and sublimity, as in Longinus, is not a state or quality that can be distinguished from the cognitive structures of the reader.

Literary criticism has tended to forget that Boileau's extensive citation of Corneille in the 1701 *Préface* and the later *Réflexions critiques* is built on the solid seventeenth-century foundations I have pointed to here. One of Boileau's main aims, in citing the 'qu'il mourust', is to illustrate that the Longinian definition of sublime discourse bears no relation to the Ciceronian 'sublime style' (indeed, as we shall see in Chapter 8, his *Réflexion X* is written in express response to Huet's misunderstanding of Longinus's sublime simplicity). But he also wants to make the same point as the other seventeenth-century authors cited about Corneille's transporting, rather than simply moral, force as a writer. Moral circumlocutions — about the fact of le vieil Horace's impressiveness or the fact of Médée's pride — do not represent the only operational procedure here. Like the other authors I have discussed, Boileau is interested in Corneille's ability to see into and communicate: '*par là on voit* que ce Heros parle du fond du coeur'; '*qu'est-ce donc qui frappe* dans ce passage, sinon la fierté audacieuse de cette Magicienne' (pp. 548, 549, my emphases). And Boileau might be seen to signal the debt that his own example from *Horace* owes to Bouhours in his 1701 *Préface*:

> Il m'a paru qu'il ne seroit peut-estre pas mauvais, pour mieux faire connoistre ce que Longin entend par ce mot de Sublime, de joindre encore ici au passage que j'ay rapporté de la Bible quelque autre exemple pris d'ailleurs. En voici un qui s'est presenté assez heureusement à ma memoire. (p. 339)

Boileau's statement may be seen to be untrammelled and unsupported, at this initial stage, by *Horace* itself: it is not just the extract from *Horace* that Boileau has found 'présenté [...] à [s]a mémoire', but its status as example. Boileau turns his comments on a prior seventeenth-century association of Corneille and Longinus as well as on Corneille's plays.

Within the important and insistent seventeenth-century association of the sublime with Corneille's work, we find not just the heroism of Corneille's characters — and nor is that just accompanied by the heroism of Corneille himself. Rather, we find his ability to project into different subject positions, enabling his audience to do the same. Sublimity does not map in any direct way onto a 'grandeur d'âme'; and this also confirms the point — I return here to the ground covered in Chapter 2 — that theoretical writings can, just as much as plays or characters, emerge as instructive and interesting in an analysis of Corneille and sublimity. Indeed, when La Bruyère writes about Corneille's 'esprit sublime' — 'ce qu'il y a eu en [Corneille] de plus éminent, c'est l'esprit, qu'il avait sublime, auquel il a été redevable de certains vers, les plus heureux qu'on ait jamais lus ailleurs, de la conduite de son théâtre, qu'il a quelquefois hasardée contre les règles des anciens, et enfin de ses dénouements' — this sublimity has as its stake the 'conduite de son théâtre' and the structure of his 'dénouements' as much as his 'vers'.[33] Corneille notes that his three theoretical *Discours* 'ont plus coûté que n'auraient fait trois pièces de théâtre', and John D. Lyons has remarked in this context that Corneille 'is the author who sees theory, in its modern form, as an aesthetic object in its own right and not solely as an instrument for the composition of tragedy'.[34]

I have explored, then, in these chapters, Corneille's theorization, using the term 'sublime', of the kinds of text which produce 'grandes et fortes émotions' and which can enable him and his audience to transport themselves into the position of the characters on stage. Looking beyond Corneille's critical interest in 'grandeur', I have shown that he can also be seen to work with the complex Longinian constellation of sublimity, knowledge, and encounter (encounters with texts and encounters within them), staking out certain of his own most important and controversial theoretical positions within this constellation, and rearranging them in the contemporaneous *Œdipe*. D'Aubignac's criticisms of *Œdipe*, as well as the concerns of *Œdipe* itself, hark back exactingly to these key preoccupations of Corneille's discourses on theatre — degrees of 'connaissance', diffuse 'liaisons', the ordinariness of the 'extraordinaire'. And just as Corneille thinks hard about what it takes and means to be transported by what one hears or reads, so too do those critics — Saint-Evremond, Bouhours, Boileau — who call him sublime, and quote him. 'The passionate moment echoes from soul to soul. Each controls it temporarily. Each enjoys it quote by quote.'[35]

Notes to Chapter 4

1. *Horace*, Act III, scene 5, lines 1021–22.
2. *Médée*, I. 4. 320–21.
3. Georges Forestier, *Essai de génétique théâtrale: Corneille à l'œuvre*, 2nd edn (Geneva: Droz, 2004), p. 273.
4. Sophie Hache, *La Langue du ciel: le sublime en France au XVIIe siècle* (Paris: Champion, 2000), p. 321.
5. See Chapter 2 for notes on Forestier's reading in particular.
6. Paul Bénichou, *Morales du grand siècle* (Paris: Gallimard, 1948), p. 31.
7. Ibid., pp. 31, 35.
8. Marc Fumaroli, 'L'Héroïsme cornélien et l'éthique de la magnanimité', in *Héros et orateurs: rhétorique et dramaturgie cornéliennes* (Geneva: Droz, 1990), pp. 323–49 (p. 348).
9. Pierre Corneille, *Writings on the Theatre*, ed. by H. T. Barnwell (Oxford: Blackwell, 1965), p. 14; Baldine Saint Girons, *Fiat lux: une philosophie du sublime* (Paris: Quai Voltaire, 1993), p. 421.
10. For a psychoanalytical definition of sublimation, see Jean Laplanche and J.-B. Pontalis, *Vocabulaire de la psychanalyse* (Paris: Presses universitaires de France, 1967), who give the following example: 'La pulsion [sexuelle] est dite sublimée dans la mesure où elle est dérivée vers un nouveau but non sexuel et où elle vise des objets socialement valorisés.'
11. For eighteenth-century readings which do equate the sublime, the admirable, and the normatively virtuous, see the examples of Silvain and Jaucourt. Silvain writes of Médée's 'moi' that 'Ce moi a beaucoup de force, j'en conviens; mais il ne me paroît pourtant pas sublime, parce qu'après tout, il ne présente que Médée; c'est-à-dire, une femme couverte de mille crimes. La grande idée qu'elle paroît avoir d'elle-même ne change pas celle que les autres ont, & qu'ils en doivent avoir' (François Silvain, *Traité du sublime*, à M. Despreaux (Geneva: Slatkine, 1971; orig. publ. Paris: Pierre Prault, 1732), p. 61). And Jaucourt writes that 'Les sentiments sont sublimes

quand fondés sur une vraie vertu, ils paroissent être presque au-dessus de la condition humaine & qu'ils font voir, comme l'a dit Séneque, dans la foiblesse de l'humanité, la constance d'un Dieu [...] mais cette Médée est une méchante femme dont on a pris soin de me faire connoître tous les crimes. [...] Je sais que M. Despréaux, suivi par plusieurs critiques, semble faire consister le sublime de la réponse de Médée, dans le seul monosyllabe moi; mais j'ose être d'un avis contraire'. Louis de Jaucourt, under 'sublime' in *Encyclopédie ou Dictionnaire raisonné des sciences, des arts ou des métiers*, ed. by Denis Diderot and Jean Le Rond D'Alembert (Neufchastel: Samuel Faulche, 1765), pp. 566–70 (pp. 569–70).

12. Mme de Sévigné, 16 March 1672, in *Correspondance*, ed. by R. Duchêne, 3 vols (Paris: Gallimard, 1972–78), I, 459.

13. On the comparison between Corneille and Racine, see also Sévigné's letter of 15 January 1672: 'Pour ce qui est des belles comédies de Corneille, elles sont autant au-dessus de celles de Racine que celles de Racine sont au-dessus de toutes les autres. Croyez que jamais rien n'approchera (je ne dis pas surpassera) des divins endroits de Corneille. Il nous lut l'autre jour une comédie chez M. de La Rochefoucauld, qui fait souvenir de la Reine-Mère [Pulchérie]. Cependant je voudrais, ma bonne, que vous fussiez avec moi après dîner, vous ne vous seriez point ennuyée; vous auriez peut-être pleuré une petite larme, puisque j'en ai pleuré plus que vingt' (ibid., I, 417).

14. 'Lettre au Comte de Lionne', March/April 1668, in *Lettres de Saint-Evremond*, ed. by René Ternois, 2 vols (Paris: Didier, 1967–68), I, 134–41 (p. 141).

15. 'Jugement sur quelques auteurs françois', in *Œuvres en prose*, ed. by René Ternois, 4 vols (Paris: Didier, 1962–69), IV, 343–45 (pp. 343–44).

16. 'Dissertation sur le grand Alexandre', ibid., II (1965), 84–102 (p. 92).

17. 'Quelques réflexions sur nos traducteurs', ibid., III (1966), 100–17 (pp. 111–12). On this, see H. T. Barnwell, 'Saint-Evremond et la tragédie classique', *XVIIᵉ siècle*, no. 57 (January–March 1962), 24–42 (pp. 33–34). As Barnwell suggests, likely sources for Saint-Evremond, who is probably citing Longinus from memory and certainly freely, are Gabriele de Petra's Latin text (published in Geneva in 1612, in Oxford in 1636, and in Tanneguy Le Fèvre's Saumur edition in 1663) or John Hall's English translation (published in 1652). Barnwell is unaware of the translation of Longinus signalled by Bernard Weinberg in 'Une traduction française du "Sublime" de Longin vers 1645' (*Modern Philology*, 59 (1961–62), 159–201) and which I have subsequently edited; Saint-Evremond's text is not taken from the latter. Barnwell's article makes, although loosely, some points which will correspond to my arguments here: that 'les Discours et les autres écrits critiques [de Corneille] ont probablement joué un rôle tout aussi important que ses tragédies dans la formation des idées de Saint-Evremond sur ce genre' (p. 31), and that 'une certaine notion du sublime est sous-jacente aux préférences de Saint-Evremond en ce qui concerne l'histoire et la tragédie' (p. 40).

18. 'Sur les tragédies', in *Œuvres en prose*, III, 24–31 (p. 24).

19. As H. T. Barnwell puts it here, 'Ces héros, ces empereurs pourraient bien être, littéralement, extraordinaire; mais il n'étaient que des hommes. [...] Saint-Evremond demande donc que l'histoire soit un exposé de la vie des héros, héros pénétrés cependant d'une grandeur purement humaine, hommes qui, en agissant et en parlant, révèlent leur humanité et leur grandeur.' 'Saint-Evremond et la tragédie classique', p. 26.

20. 'Lettre à Mme Bourneau', in *Œuvres en prose*, II, 76–82 (p. 76).

21. Ibid., p. 77.

22. 'Sur les tragédies', p. 30.

23. Théodore Litman, *Le Sublime en France, 1660–1714* (Paris: Nizet, 1971), pp. 146, 147.

24. *La Langue du ciel*, p. 240.

25. Lawrence Kerslake says that Saint-Evremond is 'not rejecting the sublime as such, but is correcting what he considers to be a misapplication of the concept when it is used to characterize "le merveilleux" in ancient literature'. *Essays on the Sublime: Analyses of French Writings on the Sublime from Boileau to La Harpe* (Berne: Peter Lang, 2000), p. 442.

26. 'Dissertation sur le grand Alexandre', p. 90; Michael Moriarty, *Taste and Ideology in Seventeenth-Century France* (Cambridge: Cambridge University Press, 1988), pp. 106–19. 'French culture', for Saint-Evremond, 'is menaced with the same fate as that of Rome, which throve under the late Republic — with its proliferation of great men, men of action who were intellectuals, intellectuals who were men of action — and decayed under the emperors' (pp. 118–19).

27. *Writings on the Theatre*, p. 124.
28. Ibid., p. 182. Huet writes in his *Mémoires* that 'parfois je frémissais d'horreur, lorsqu'il [Corneille] me confessait ingénument, quoique avec une sorte de honte, qu'il préférait Lucain à Virgile'. Pierre-Daniel Huet, *Mémoires* (1718), trans. by Charles Nisard, ed. by Philippe-Joseph Salazar (Toulouse: Klincksieck, 1993), p. 118.
29. Georges de Brébeuf, *La Pharsale de Lucain* (Paris: A. de Sommaville, 1665), *Avertissement*, unpaginated.
30. 'Lettre à Mme Bourneau', p. 77.
31. Jean de La Bruyère, 'Des jugements', in *Les Caractères ou les mœurs de ce siècle*, ed. by Robert Pignarre (Paris: Garnier-Flammarion, 1965), p. 314.
32. Dominique Bouhours, *La Manière de bien penser dans les ouvrages d'esprit* (Brighton: Sussex Reprints, 1917; orig. publ. Paris: Michel Brunet, 1715), pp. 374–75.
33. La Bruyère, *Les Caractères*, p. 95.
34. Corneille, 'Lettre à l'Abbé de Pure', 25 August 1660, in *Œuvres complètes*, p. 860, in which Corneille also writes that 'quand cela paraîtra, je ne doute point qu'il ne donne matière aux critiques' (p. 859), and John D. Lyons, *Kingdom of Disorder: The Theory of Tragedy in Classical France* (West Lafayette, IN: Purdue University Press, 1999), p. 16.
35. Anne Carson, '(Essay with Rhapsody): On the Sublime in Longinus and Antonioni', in *Decreation: Poetry, Essays, Opera* (New York: Knopf, 2005), pp. 43–51 (p. 46).

CHAPTER 5

❖

Pascalian 'Connaissance'

Pascal's writing works at the limits of what it is possible to know. His theology is one of the fall and the redemption, of perfect knowledge made imperfect, of the incarnational presence of God in Christ, of God-given insight broken down into a network of difficult human epistemologies. The divine and the fallen coexist in the Christianity Pascal seeks to communicate, and the outstanding simplicity of this fact belies the complexity of the truths behind it: 'La foi embrasse plusieurs vérités qui semblent se contredire' (S614/L733).[1] Pascal's overarching impulse is to counter those who neglect to explore such truths: 'La source de toutes les hérésies est l'exclusion de quelques-unes de ces vérités.'

Fragment S614/L733 continues as follows: 'D'ordinaire il arrive que, ne pouvant concevoir le rapport de deux vérités opposées et croyant que l'aveu de l'une enferme l'exclusion de l'autre, ils [les hérétiques] s'attachent à l'une, ils excluent l'autre.' Heretics, it seems, are not cast out by orthodoxy, but render themselves heterodox, split themselves off, by a refusal or incapacity to see the whole picture. The word 'heresy' itself comes from the Greek 'hairesis', meaning a 'particular opinion', and in Pascal particularity appears to come across as blindness. The movement with which he is concerned is a movement towards integration. Pascal acknowledges the powerfully inclusive possibilities of metanoia, spiritual conversion or reorientation. God may, through an efficacious grace, reveal his divine veracity to humankind, the human and the divine may become as one, and the metaphysical truth offered by the Christian religion may be integrated as an affective reality into the course of lived human experience. In Pascal's writing of it, this kind of personal revelation brings 'certitude, certitude, sentiment, joie, paix' (S742/L913).[2] Which does not alter the fact that this emphatic 'certitude, certitude' is complexly restated, too, in Pascal; and this restating will provide my subject matter in the following chapters.

Of course, 'Dieu seul peut mettre [les vérités divines] dans l'âme, et par la manière qu'il lui plaît.'[3] But Pascal hopes to make his readers aware, at least, of these 'vérités divines'. He hopes, as I said in the Introduction to this book, to place the reading of his work in some undecidable and metaphorical relationship to religious certainty. And Pascal, in my reading, vociferous about ineffability, also participates fully in an account of knowledge through human interaction. Such terms as 'sublime', 'connaissance', and 'expérience' insert this kind of account into his text. Pascal makes the writing of spiritual possibility accompany an investigation into the hard details of human experience. The centrality of the incarnation for Pascal — the co-

presence in Christ of two natures, divine and human, permanent and transient,[4] —
enfolds this commentary. 'Hors de là [knowing God in and through Christ] et sans
l'Écriture, sans le péché originel, sans médiateur nécessaire, promis et arrivé, on ne
peut prouver absolument Dieu, ni enseigner ni bonne doctrine, ni bonne morale'
(S221/L189). Pascal is endlessly interested in mediations between human behaviour,
religious doctrine, and truth. He also knows that Scripture's proof of God through
Christ, whose future coming was revealed to and prophesied by generations of Jews
(S9/L390), will not carry immediate weight with his unbelieving readers. We shall
be looking in what follows at, as he beautifully puts it, 'un balancement douteux
entre la vérité et la volupté'.[5]

'Certitude, certitude'

It has often been noted that Pascal's 'certitude, certitude' has structural affinities with
the Longinian sublime: a moment of absolute insight, concurrent with the arousal
of intense emotional experience, which in the treatise *Peri hypsous* is produced by
identification with another person via that person's written or spoken text. Both
Pascal's 'certitude' and Longinus's sublime have an enduring force. 'Eternellement en
joie pour un jour d'exercice sur la terre', reads Pascal's 'mémorial'; 'the memory of
it is stubborn and indelible', ordains Longinus of the experience of sublimity (7.3).[6]
This force is not only enduring but entirely overwhelming. The sublime exercises
'an irresistible power and mastery' (1.4); in Boileau's translation, it 'ne persuade pas
proprement mais il ravit, il transporte' (p. 341). 'Ô ce discours me transporte, me
ravit etc', pronounces the speaker in Pascal's wager fragment (S690/L418), subject
to the ecstasy which, as the Greek 'ek-stasis', is a 'dis-placement', a move away
from a previous lack of belief. 'The effect of the discourse on Pascal's represented
listener', writes Richard Lockwood, 'is a sensation of wonder, of being carried
away to another place, overwhelmed and delighted, a position that also exceeds
representation, can be represented only by an ellipsis, "etc".'[7] The same critic writes
of the verb 'admirer' (to wonder at, be amazed or astonished) that 'in Pascal it is
clearly to be connected to the sublime, and like the sublime carries with it the
sense of being overwhelmed, "ravi", lifted out of oneself, "transporté"' (p. 281,
n. 18). In my Introduction, we saw Louis Marin (Lockwood's major influence)
aligning Pascal and Kant on the basis of a common concern with 'the infinite': 'More
than a century before Immanuel Kant's *Critique of Judgment* (1796), Pascal describes
the mind's encounter with the infinite in terms that announce the sublime.'[8]

We may expand upon the link forged by critics between Longinus and Pascal.
Marc Fumaroli, in this context, analyses the putative simplicity of Pascal's rhetoric.
He clearly has in mind the dictum of fragment S671/L513, 'la vraie éloquence se
moque de l'éloquence', along with Longinus's frequent association of sublimity
with an unadorned language possessing the power to move. Fumaroli uses Pascal
to argue for the place of a 'rhétorique gallicane' in seventeenth-century French
writing, a rhetoric he defines as forceful because pared down, fashioned 'dans la
polémique incessante contre la "sophistique jésuite" et ultramontaine'.[9] Hence his
description of Pascal's language:

> plus de médiation commode, plus de glissement insensible sur un terrain qui ne
> se dérobe jamais sous nos pas, et que balisent les pots à fleur de la Compagnie,
> mais des principes que seul la Grâce imméritée pourrait nous faire franchir,
> d'un trait. Pour initier à cet univers troué d'abîmes, seuls conviennent les éclairs
> du style coupé. (p. 364)

It is Fumaroli's conclusion which is of most relevance, and which I therefore cite
here in full:

> Telles qu'elles nous sont parvenues, telles qu'elles apparurent dès leur publication
> sous une forme pourtant affadie, les *Pensées* demeurent le *Traité du sublime* de
> la prose française classique. Par leur dédain pour la 'rhétorique' scolaire ou
> pédante, par leur manière souverainement 'adulte' de poser les problèmes de
> l'éloquence, par leur refus de dissocier la forme de la pensée, par le caractère à
> la fois sombre et fulminant, biblique et sénéquien de celles-ci, Pascal y actualise
> les plus hautes leçons du Pseudo-Longin, et de son héritier chrétien, le saint
> Augustin des *Confessions* et de la *Doctrina christiana*. (p. 370)

Pascal's writing is seen as 'sublime' inasmuch as, espousing precision and mocking
the prolix, it embodies both brevity and cogency and integrates these into pure
force. The 'plus hautes leçons de Longin' are seen to emanate from those sections
of the *Traité du sublime* which state that rhetorical simplicity can have emotive
force, and which draw parallels with the language of the Bible to prove this
point. Fumaroli limits his discussion of the sublime to the domain of the stunning
rhetorical effectiveness of the simple.[10] He has an interest in tempering certain
accounts of seventeenth-century literature — those that see 'classicism' as an entity
of a profoundly Aristotelian stripe — with this 'fulminant' yet simple discourse
which speaks directly to the heart.

Sophie Hache follows Fumaroli in defining a sublime dynamic as the fashioning
of a simple rhetoric with a power to move, observing 'l'acceptation grandissante du
primat de la simplicité sur toute autre valeur' and displaying a continued interest
in 'des axes d'étude qui pourraient être fructueux dans une approche des points
de rencontre entre baroque et classicisme'.[11] But Hache is troubled by Pascal. 'Les
Pensées de Pascal', she writes, 'devraient constituer aux yeux des contemporains à la
fois une véritable adaptation du traité de Longin à la rhétorique française grâce à ses
développements sur l'éloquence, mais aussi un modèle de la prose apte à stupéfier et
"ravir" l'âme du lecteur' (p. 396). In fact, 'dans les ouvrages d'éloquence que nous
avons pu dépouiller, Pascal n'est jamais cité comme exemple du sublime' (p. 396).

Hache is interested, however, in the section of *De l'esprit géométrique* entitled 'De
l'art de persuader'. Here, Pascal attunes himself to, in order to criticize, elevated
language:

> Ce n'est pas dans les choses extraordinaires et bizarres que l'on trouve de
> l'excellence de quelque genre que ce soit. On s'élève pour y arriver, et on s'en
> éloigne: il faut le plus souvent s'abaisser. [...] Et l'une des raisons principales qui
> éloignent autant ceux qui entrent dans ces connaissances du véritable chemin
> qu'ils doivent suivre est l'imagination qu'on prend d'abord que les bonnes
> choses sont inaccessibles, en leur donnant le nom de grandes, hautes, élevées,
> sublimes. Cela perd tout. Je voudrais les nommer basses, communes, familières,
> ces noms-là leur conviennent mieux.[12]

'Je hais ces mots d'enflure', is Pascal's uncompromising conclusion. Hache's gloss on this passage reads as follows: 'La langue la plus banale, la plus quotidienne, les mots les plus usés, sont les mieux à même porter vers le sublime, au sens longinien du terme' (p. 102).

This passage will provide my first foray into the reading of Pascal, who does not in fact use the term 'sublime' in the Longinian sense here. He uses it, precisely and very critically, in the 'Ciceronian' sense, which is to say in the sense of a 'mot d'enflure'. His criticism of an understanding of 'enflure' as sublimity may itself be (is, often) seen as Longinian, but that is not to say that this passage gestures towards simplicity of language. Pascal is talking, here, about knowledge, 'ces connaissances du véritable chemin', and means of obtaining knowledge. These 'connaissances' are of the humanly accessible variety, susceptible to 'l'art de persuader' and to discursive treatment in an essay: 'Je ne parle pas ici des vérités divines, que je n'aurais garde de faire tomber sous l'art de persuader, car elles sont infiniment au-dessus de la nature' (p. 413). Pascal takes for granted 'l'éloignement où nous sommes de consentir aux vérités de la religion chrétienne' (p. 414).

Once the embodiment of perfection, humankind is now fallen into sin. It is bound in its present existence, or fallen 'second' nature, to the confusion and disarray which original sin induced in a break from the 'first' nature which was given by God. At the point of sin, humankind dislocated itself from the divine by its disobedience and by a desire for independence. In the Augustinian tradition of Western thought, this has had lasting consequences for views on the human capacity to judge, to reason; as Henry Chadwick notes in his study of Augustine, 'Sin impels the mind towards external things, away from the contemplation of transcendent realities.'[13] Even when talking, in 'De l'art de persuader', about 'les vérités de notre [human, fallen] portée' (p. 414), Pascal makes the point 'que bien peu entrent [dans l'âme] par l'esprit' (p. 414). Famously, 'L'art de persuader consiste autant en celui d'agréer qu'en celui de convaincre, tant les hommes se gouvernent plus par caprice que par raison' (p. 416). But Pascal's subject here will be 'celui de convaincre', 'l'art de convaincre' (p. 416), and he knows that he can at least make with conviction the point that 'les bonnes choses' are not always 'inaccessibles'. 'L'art de convaincre' is reduced to foundational precepts and principles, 'règles' which, though few in kind, offer certainty (the same level of certainty as geometry): 'Tout l'art en est renfermé dans les seuls préceptes que nous avons dits. Ils suffisent seuls. Ils prouvent seuls' (p. 426).

So writing about the simple textures of this limited 'art de convaincre', its formulae and its shapes, Pascal notes that 'rien n'est plus commun que les bonnes choses: il n'est question de les discerner; et il est certain qu'elles sont toutes naturelles et à notre portée, et même connues de tout le monde. Mais on ne sait pas les distinguer' (p. 427). Pascal has himself sought here, scrupulously, to 'discerner' and 'distinguer' the methods and principles within human reach. Like a geometer, he proceeds from the simple to the complex. Pascal objects to the pedantry and syllogistic confusion surrounding 'les bonnes choses [...] à notre portée' (p. 427). 'Ce n'est pas *barbara* et *baralipton* qui forment le raisonnement', he says, nodding to the kind of vocabulary associated with syllogism (p. 428).[14] Syllogism proceeds from the general to the particular (all men are mortal; Socrates is a man; therefore Socrates is mortal); Pascal's procedure here is the opposite: he moves from particular principles to wider demonstrations.[15] It is correspondingly, and simply, the case for Pascal that 'les meilleurs livres sont ceux que ceux qui les lisent croient qu'ils auraient pu faire' (p. 427). We find here, as Mesnard puts it, 'le passage de la géométrie proprement dite aux réalités humaines' (p. 383). It is in this context that, as Pascal notes, 'l'une des raisons principales qui éloignent autant ceux qui entrent dans ces connaissances du véritable chemin qu'ils doivent suivre est l'imagination qu'on prend d'abord que les bonnes choses sont inaccessibles, en leur donnant le nom de grandes, hautes, élevées, sublimes' (p. 428).[16] And it is in the context, too, of this discussion of knowledge's accessibility and inaccessibility that it is fitting to turn to the two points in the *Pensées* where the term 'sublime' makes an appearance. These appearances will provide us with productive cross-currents of association, and will help us in our goal of reconsidering the current critical coupling of Longinus and Pascal.

The two fragments in question both consolidate in important ways the Pascalian insistence on the dual nature of mankind. The first defines man as drawn to a form of knowledge which comes via the material, through the senses, and which 'remplit ses hôtes d'une satisfaction bien autrement pleine et entière que la raison' (S78/L44). This form of knowledge is known as 'imagination'.

Pascal's 'imagination' is further defined as 'cette partie dominante dans l'homme', as 'cette faculté trompeuse qui semble nous être donnée exprès pour nous induire à une erreur nécessaire', as one of the powers of deception by which 'les sens abusent la raison par de fausses apparences' (S78/L44). In fact, although the 'esprit', the domain of reason, may be capable of acting independently of 'l'imagination', its constant susceptibility and the ensuing confusion make this qualification meaningless. 'L'imagination' is 'd'autant plus fourbe qu'elle ne l'est pas toujours' (S78/L44). As Antony McKenna puts it, 'Nous n'avons aucun critère de certitude qui permette de distinguer les "preuves" de la raison et les "opinions" de l'imagination: le rôle des facteurs subjectifs qui naissent de l'union de l'esprit au corps est alors incontrôlable.'[17] Imagination, in other words, is a confusing conglomeration of different levels of certainty: 'Elle fait croire, douter, nier la raison. Elle suspend les sens, elle les fait sentir' (S78/L44). Thus, 'Le plus grand philosophe du monde sur une planche plus large qu'il ne faut, s'il y a au-dessous un précipice, quoique sa raison le convainque de sa sûreté, son imagination prévaudra' (S78/L44).

Nobody, indeed, is immune from the corrupting force of imagination: 'L'imagination dispose de tout; elle fait la beauté, la justice et le bonheur qui est le tout du monde.' Creating its own, artificial, notion of beauty and justice, imagination deceives us into thinking that 'la beauté, la justice et le bonheur' can exist at all in a fallen world. This is the context of the following passage:

> Qui dispense la réputation, qui donne le respect et la vénération aux personnes, aux ouvrages, aux lois, aux grands, sinon cette faculté imaginante? Combien toutes les richesses de la terre insuffisantes sans son consentement. Ne diriez-vous pas que ce magistrat dont la vieillesse vénérable impose le respect à tout un peuple se gouverne par une raison pure et sublime, et qu'il juge des choses par leur nature sans s'arrêter à ces vaines circonstances qui ne blessent que l'imagination des faibles. Voyez-le entrer dans un sermon [...] Que le prédicateur vienne à paraître, si la nature lui a donné une voix enrouée et un

> tour de visage bizarre, que son barbier l'ait mal rasé, si le hasard l'a encore
> barbouillé de surcroît, quelque grandes vérités qu'il annonce je parie la perte
> de gravité de notre sénateur. (S78/L44)

The term 'sublime', here, in apposition to 'raison', is not used as a rhetorical term.
Combined with the 'pure', it attains a sense of absoluteness. And commingled with
the pure and the sublime, 'raison' is distinguished radically from the vain and the
circumstantial. But the passage undercuts itself with the initial negativity of 'ne
diriez-vous pas'; this 'raison pure et sublime' remains inaccessible and impossible.
Closed off from mankind in the human dimension is this faculty for understanding
which, offering absolute knowledge, might be uncorrupted by external appearances
that strike the senses before they are understood in any other manner. Finishing
with its famous 'perte de gravité', this passage situates itself at the exacting crossroads
of knowledge and ignorance.

Fragment S240/L208 takes as its subject matter the way in which human beings
contain within themselves the irreducible traces of their former state, their first
nature. Traces of perfection, though hidden, are nonetheless so powerfully present
that they never entirely fade away into the vastness of sin. Rather, they continually
draw attention to themselves by making their imperfect hosts long for something
more, something meaningful. True Christianity, in Pascal, recognizes this longing
for what it is, and uses it to counter two very human errors, the first being
located in a proud belief in the exclusivity of man's excellence, the second in an
idle, inert despair:

> La seule religion chrétienne a pu guérir ces deux vices, non pas en chassant
> l'un par l'autre par la sagesse de la terre, mais en chassant l'un et l'autre par
> la simplicité de l'Évangile. Car elle apprend aux justes qu'elle élève jusqu'à la
> participation de la divinité même, qu'en ce sublime état ils portent encore la
> source de toute la corruption qui les rend durant toute la vie sujets à l'erreur, à
> la misère, à la mort, au péché, et elle crie aux plus impies qu'ils sont capables de
> la grâce de leur rédempteur. (S240/L208)

Sublimity is a state of being, here aligned with 'la participation de la divinité
même'. Again, then, the term 'sublime' is used in a sense which surpasses a powerful
rhetorical simplicity, the 'simplicité de l'Évangile'. It is not this rhetorical simplicity,
but an 'état' granted by grace, which is defined as sublime. And Pascal further
blurs the equation of sublimity and simplicity by stating that, even in the state of
participation, men 'portent encore la source de toute la corruption qui les rend
durant toute la vie sujets à l'erreur, à la misère, à la mort, au péché'. 'La participation
de la divinité même', then, is a heightened awareness of the human condition, and
of the necessity of participation in the 'corporately sinful social tradition'.[18] And so
once again the term 'sublime' in the *Pensées*, as in 'De l'art de persuader', combines
itself with investigations into the kinds of knowledge open to human beings.

'La participation de la divinité même'

We have seen in fragment S240/L208 that if a 'participation de la divinité même' is
granted by grace, a heightened awareness of the human condition is also granted by

grace. It is true that, on one level, Pascal's *Pensées* are precise about the annihilation of heterogeneity that comes with 'la conversion véritable', in which independence is transformed into a relationship of pure dependency: 'La conversion véritable consiste à s'anéantir devant cet être universel qu'on a irrité tant de fois et qui peut vous perdre légitimement à toute heure, à reconnaître qu'on ne peut rien sans lui et qu'on n'a rien mérité de lui que sa disgrâce' (S410/L378). An investigation into the original draft of this fragment reveals that, before committing the verb 's'anéantir' to paper, Pascal crossed out 's'hum', suggesting that the transition from the humiliation to the annihilation of the self was one he wished to consummate in his text. But on a second level, the relationship of dependency which is set up and acknowledged in 'la conversion véritable' is nuanced by self-knowledge.

Fragment S410/L378 continues as follows: 'Elle [la conversion véritable] consiste à connaître qu'il y a une opposition invincible entre Dieu et nous.' It reconfigures us in our humanity. This is the kind of knowing that we saw in fragment S240/L208, the awareness granted to humanity that 'ils portent encore la source de toute la corruption qui les rend durant toute la vie sujets à l'erreur'. It is also the kind of knowing which makes an appearance in 'Sur la conversion du pécheur': 'La première chose que Dieu inspire à l'âme qu'il daigne toucher véritablement, est une connaissance et une vue tout extraordinaire par laquelle l'âme considère les choses et elle-même d'une façon toute nouvelle.'[19] Conversion reconfigures the relationship of the self to material bodies, 'les choses', and subsequently reconfigures the relationship of the 'âme' to itself. In the terms of the three orders of the *Pensées*, conversion assimilates the lower orders of existence, the 'corps' ('les choses') and the 'esprit' ('l'âme'), into the divine order of charity.[20]

Conversion brings into play, therefore, a kind of self-regard that is very different from the 'amour-propre' which means that man 'a voulu se rendre centre de lui-même' (S182/L149), which makes the self 'injuste en soi en ce qu'il se fait centre de tout', and which makes it 'injuste aux autres en ce qu'il les veut asservir, car chaque moi est l'ennemi et voudrait être le tyran de tous les autres' (S494/L597). The identity that Pascal proposes arises, rather, through an identification 'qui remplit l'âme et le cœur de ceux qu'il possède; [...] qui leur fait sentir intérieurement leur misère, et sa miséricorde infinie; qui s'unit au fond de leur âme; qui la remplit d'humilité, de joie, de confiance, d'amour; qui les rend incapables d'autre fin que de lui-même' (S690/L449). So this is a self-awareness which simultaneously takes on interiority (as God 'leur fait sentir intérieurement leur misère') and precludes 'la pente vers soi' (S680/L421). Any notion of religious experience which is not conceived of in this way is in fact dismissed, as in the case of those who claim that '"si j'avais vu un miracle [...] je me convertirais"' (S410/L378). Such people 's'imaginent que cette conversion consiste en une adoration qui se fait de Dieu comme un commerce et une conversation telle qu'ils se la figurent'. As Henri Gouhier puts it,

> Les interlocuteurs de Pascal 'se figurent' le 'commerce' avec Dieu comme une 'conversation' où chacun prend la parole; ainsi, étonné par un miracle, je me tourne de moi-même vers Dieu et lui dis mon 'adoration'; dans cette hypothèse, il est clair que rien ne m'empêche de prévoir avec assurance ma 'conversion'.[21]

An individual impulse alone cannot bring about either the conversation or the conversion: 'Si Dieu ne vient à eux, ils sont incapables d'aucune communication avec lui' (S413/L381). Gouhier's comments can be extended to the dismissal in the *Pensées* of deists: 'Ils s'imaginent qu'elle consiste simplement en l'adoration d'un Dieu considéré comme grand et puissant et éternel; ce qui est proprement le déisme, presque aussi éloigné de la religion chrétienne que l'athéisme, qui y est tout à fait contraire' (S690/L449).[22]

Perhaps the clearest embodiments of this self-centred, territorialized conception of the divine are the Jesuits of the *Lettres provinciales*, a work described by Boileau as 'le plus parfait ouvrage de prose qui soit en notre langue'.[23] Throughout the *Provinciales*, the theology of the Jesuits is shown to be entirely self-regulating, whether in its endorsement of a human, 'proximate' because earthbound, *pouvoir prochain*, or in its related denigration of *grâce efficace* (granted by God to the chosen) in favour of a generalized *grâce suffisante*:

> Les Jésuites prétendent qu'il y a une grâce donnée généralement à tous, soumise de telle sorte au libre arbitre, qu'il la rend efficace ou inefficace à son choix, sans aucun nouveau secours de Dieu, et sans qu'il manque rien de sa part pour agir effectivement; ce qui fait qu'ils l'appellent *suffisante*, parce qu'elle seule suffit pour agir. (2, 22)[24]

But the *Lettres provinciales* go beyond an external critique of such self-willed regulation. They portray self-justification in action, as the Jesuits are forced to respond with increasing urgency to the interrogation of their practices. Indeed the *Lettres provinciales* could be summed up as an examination of the different dynamics of Jesuit justification, the diffuse irony of Pascal's interlocutor bitingly focused in a single outburst: 'Béni soyez-vous, mon Père, qui justifiez ainsi les gens!' (4, 59)

The Jesuits' self-attribution of the power to condemn or to exculpate represents a scandalous qualification of the doctrine that Christians are 'astreints à prendre leurs règles hors d'eux-mêmes, et à s'informer de celles que Jésus-Christ a laissées aux anciens pour nous et retransmises aux fidèles' (S634/L769).[25] 'Ils couvrent leur prudence humaine et politique', we are told, 'du prétexte d'une prudence divine et chrétienne; comme si la foi, et la tradition qui la maintient, n'était pas toujours une et invariable dans tous les temps et dans tous les lieux' (5, 78). The censure of Arnauld is just one event in a whole list of Jesuit political ploys, with justification conjured up in whatever way is required to maintain the prevailing prominence of their company: 'Ils vivent au jour la journée' (3, 47).[26] Temporality reigns, as the Jesuits defer to the transience of circumstance: 'Vous l'entendez bien peu,' announces the Jesuit figure to his interlocutor: 'Les Pères étaient bons pour la morale de leur temps; mais ils sont trop éloignés pour celle du nôtre. Ce ne sont plus eux qui la règlent, ce sont les nouveaux casuistes' (5, 90).

Similarly, concerns of locality lead the Jesuits to suppress different truths which in fact require superimposition:

> Ainsi ils en ont pour toutes sortes de personnes et répondent si bien selon ce qu'on leur demande, que, quand ils se trouvent en des pays où un Dieu crucifié passe pour folie, ils suppriment le scandale de la Croix, et ne prêchent que Jésus-Christ glorieux, et non pas Jésus-Christ souffrant: comme ils ont fait dans les Indes et dans la Chine. (5, 76).

They privilege the particular, formulating general laws from this:

> Oui, dit le bon Père, d'un ton résolu [...] et plutôt que de dire qu'on pèche sans
> avoir la vue que l'on fait mal, et le désir de la vertu contraire, nous soutiendrons
> que tout le monde, et les impies et les infidèles, ont ces inspirations et ces désirs
> à chaque tentation. (4, 62–63)

And yet the general can, should the occasion demand it, be dismantled into the particular: 'Cette proposition [...] serait catholique dans une autre bouche; ce n'est que dans M. Arnauld que la Sorbonne l'a condamnée' (3, 51). So Jesuit doctrine, reduced by Pascal to a multivalent self-justification, is displayed in what he sees as its crassness, and shown to crumble: 'Vous reculez, lui dis-je en l'interrompant, vous reculez, mon Père' (4, 64). The Jesuits, although they might, in Pascal's vision, seek to liberate themselves and their consciences from the rigours of true Christianity, end up binding themselves to the shackles of self-justification, in all the different forms this takes. This is a purely self-imposing kind of self-regard. It is different from the heightened self-awareness which, as we saw in fragment S240/ L208, comes with 'la participation de la divinité même'. Because wider Jansenist views about 'connaissance' come into play here too, I shall discuss texts relevant to these views, in order to show, as I move into my next chapters, that Pascal's *Pensées* modify and expand upon them.

'La connaissance de soi-même'

'La conversion véritable' (S410/L378) is, in Pascal, coextensive with self-knowledge. But the question which is inextricably bound up with this statement is the following: can self-knowledge bring conversion? In 'De la connaissance de soi-même', Pierre Nicole engages with precisely this question:

> Dieu ne veut que nous nous connaissions qu'autant qu'il nous est nécessaire
> pour nous humilier, et pour nous conduire. Ainsi toute application à percer
> dans le fond de notre cœur, qui n'est pas renfermée dans ces bornes, n'est point
> agréable à Dieu, et ne nous saurait être utile.[27]

Demanded by God here is a form of self-knowledge which confines itself to engaging with the limits of human capacities. Self-knowledge equates, then, to a form of uncertainty: a knowledge of what one cannot know. We understand that this self-humiliation can, if not guarantee conversion, at least catalyse the form of existential enquiry that is desired by the divine. Uncertainty is flipped over to bring with it the possibility of knowledge.

The basic, and basically Augustinian, denigration of human reason which comes with an acknowledgement of humankind's ignorance and pitiable state is of course profoundly and broadly important in the seventeenth century, and inflects the whole lineage of critical thinking which came to be known as Jansenism.[28] Jansenism rejects all knowledge other than that which has been handed down by the church fathers, following Cornelius Jansen's objection to the scholastic notion that philosophy can be placed in the service of theology. For Jansen, the admixture of philosophical thought and theology can culminate only in the defilement of the latter, and is therefore deemed, in his correspondence with Saint-Cyran, to be quasi-heretical: 'Car, pour vous parler naivement, je tiens ferme que, après les hereticques, il n'y a gens au monde, qui ayent plus corrompu la Theologie que ces clabaudeurs de l'Escole que vous cognoissez.'[29] Jansen's impulse is not, in scholastic fashion, to rewrite or to re-explain faith, but rather to draw attention to its perpetuity, through a return to the sources of the discourses that have belonged to Christianity through the ages.

To this end, Jansen immerses himself in the thought of Saint Augustine: '[Je] m'estonne touts les jours davantage de la hauteur et profondeur de cest esprit, et que sa doctrine est si peu cognue parmy les sçavants, non de ce siècle seulement, mais de plusieurs siecles passez' (p. 69).[30] Truth is located only in Augustine's doctrinal stability:

> Tant est ce que j'ose dire avoir assé descouvert par des principes immobiles, que, quand toutes les deux escoles tant des Jesuites et des Jacobins disputeroyent jusques au jour du jugement poursuivant les traces qu'ils ont commencées, ils ne feront autre chose que s'esgarer beaucoup avantage, l'une et l'autre estant cent lieues loing de la vérité. (p. 69)

Indeed, Jansen's correspondence with Saint-Cyran reveals the sheer breadth of the usefulness and relevance he perceives in Augustine's work: the transition in the *Confessions* from uncertainty to the plenitude of knowledge available to the believer; the assault on the notion of the human capacity for perfectibility in the controversy with Pelagius; the incoherences of human history in the *De civitate Dei*. Jansen has, he writes, 'leu les livres d'importance deux, ou trois fois' (p. 69). Aiming to 'lire et relire toute ma vie', he simultaneously shows his awareness of the inflammatory nature of his thoughts:

> Je n'ose dire à personne du monde ce que je sens (selon les principes de S. Augustin), d'une grande partie des opinions de ce temps et particulierement de celles de la grace et praedestination, de peur qu'on ne me fasse le tour à Rome qu'on a fait à tant d'autres, devant que toute chose soit meur et à son temps. (p. 69)

Jansen's passionate reading of Augustine is encountered at one remove in his correspondent, the Abbé de Saint-Cyran.[31] The focus of Saint-Cyran's arguments, in defending Pierre Charron against the Jesuit François Garasse, is the incommensurability of God's judgements, the way our own judgements cannot even be placed in a relationship of proportionality to those, but exist on an entirely different plane:

> Aussi l'éminence des pensées de Dieu & de ses jugemens estant infiniment relevée par dessus les pensées charnelles & humaines, il est fort mal-aisé que voulant s'élever jusques à ce point on ne donne du nez en terre, & qu'on ne blasme les jugemens de Dieu, comme ayans de l'absurdité, de la dissonance, & de l'injustice, si on les veut assujettir à des regles di basses & disproportionnées comme sont celles de nostre raison. (p. 331)

Garasse, on the other hand, sees the human and the divine as contiguous, the former a 'raccourcy' of the latter, as in the following extract cited by Saint-Cyran:

'*La justice humaine n'est autre chose qu'un raccourcy de la justice divine, & [...] quand elle s'égare des reigles & des maximes de la justice divine, elle n'est plus justice*' (p. 335). But for Saint-Cyran, the human and the divine always exist in a relationship of incommensurability, and to state otherwise is blasphemy.

If Saint-Cyran defends Charron against Garasse, it is because Charron's propositions, 'estans conformes à la doctrine de l'Escriture, & particulierement de sainct Augustin, ont rencontré en vous une passion démesurée, qui vous porte à déchirer ce personnage, & à le décrier comme un des premiers atheïstes de ce temps' (pp. 340–41).[32] Saint-Cyran grants Charron's arguments the status of 'une doctrine si vraye, si saine et si Catholique, que je ne fais point de scrupule de l'appeller la doctrine de l'Eglise catholique, & la contraire une heresie' (p. 350). Charron is quoted as arguing specifically that '[l'intention de la religion] *est de faire bien sentir à l'homme son mal, sa foiblesse, son rien, & par là le faire courir à Dieu son bien, sa force, son tout*'. Here, Saint-Cyran asks, 'se peut-il dire au monde chose plus vraye, plus saincte, & plus solide de la Religion?' (p. 403). The preteritive stance, the statement of the inadequacy of discourse, the refusal to philosophize, is seen as praiseworthy in Charron precisely because it displays structural similarities to Augustine's own work. The texts examined here promote a form of Christian scepticism which dislocates human certainty, and forces an acknowledgement of human uncertainty, to provoke a turn towards God.[33]

These particular examples of Jansenist discourse, with their insistence upon the potential instructiveness of man's inadequacies, are perhaps most clearly paralleled in the *Pensées* in the passage known as 'le mystère de Jésus'. This attributes to Christ the following statement: 'Console-toi, tu ne me chercherais pas si tu ne m'avais trouvé' (S751/L919). The act of knowing that one has to question is itself (in this concentrated formula) to find. This emphasis on active searching is the important thing here. It takes the Pascalian endeavour away from that realm of negative theology, sometimes known as mysticism, which holds that nothing can be known in a direct or positive fashion about God, that no language can refer transitively to God, and that the approach adopted when speaking about God must be a *via negativa* — a description which works preteritively, through a statement of what God is not, and which embodies a certain passivity in its abandonment of any positive attempt to find and identify.[34] Pascal's distancing from mysticism does not alter the fact that his *Pensées*, like the other Augustinian texts under discussion, can be seen to situate themselves within a less extreme form of Christian scepticism which can make positive use of uncertainty.[35] Thus, while 'nous avons une idée de vérité invincible à tout le pyrrhonisme' (S25/L406), it is nonetheless possible that 'le pyrrhonisme sert à la religion' (S542/L658), that 'le pyrrhonisme est le vrai' (S570/L691).[36]

This dialectic between certainty and uncertainty has been profoundly appealing to Pascalian critics of a deconstructive stripe. For Paul de Man, in Pascal's 'fundamentally dialectical' pattern of reasoning, 'oppositions are, if not reconciled, at least pursued toward a totalization that remains operative as the sole principle of intelligibility'.[37] Deconstruction, preoccupied with the limitations of the artifice that is language, can easily situate Pascal's God as the Other which inevitably lies beyond human discourse. It works on the basis that a preteritive understanding of the fact that there must always be a 'beyond', even if what is 'beyond' cannot be grasped, is itself a form of knowledge.

Sara Melzer, heavily influenced by such conceptual structures, also builds a compelling argument around the notion that, in Pascal, knowledge must be acquired indirectly, through the emphasis on a fallen language's failure to represent, in other words through language's inevitable figurativeness, its incapacity to state what it means:

> Although this otherness of figural language marks our fallen state, it can also hold the key to Redemption. Language not only points to the debasement of its representative capacity; it also suggests something other than its codes and structures, something that they exclude.[38]

Melzer confirms in her conclusion that Pascal does go some way towards borrowing from mysticism, in that he 'communicates the impossibility of communicating; he makes the readers read the impossibility of reading his text' (p. 144), but that the active role played by the reader in trying (and failing) to construct meaning differs from the *a priori* renunciation of the mystics: 'Unlike negative theology, however, the *Pensées* leave it to the reader to decide if it [the otherness of all discourse] constitutes a metaphor for divine otherness, an unreadable resemblance to the otherness of God' (p. 145).

Going beyond Melzer, Nicholas Hammond makes space for a rhetorically detailed study of how, in textual terms, the instability of the human manifests itself in the *Pensées*. His study focuses in particular on the multiple shifts in meaning played out by certain key terms in Pascal's vocabulary, among which are 'ordre', 'inconstance', 'ennui', 'inquiétude', 'repos', 'bonheur', and 'justice'.[39] It is only the closeness of this reading which permits the conclusion that

> the persuasive process of the *Pensées* is energized by the reader's active participation in sorting through both the fragmentary ordering and the shifting meanings of the text. [...] Once the notion of the Fall is fully comprehended, the instability of those terms depicting the human condition becomes integral to the reader's search beyond the inadequacies of language and order.[40]

The *Pensées* do not just state human uncertainty didactically; they make the reader work through it as part of the reading process itself.[41] Pascal seeks to transfigure indifference into that which it forecloses: self-awareness. A degree of self-awareness brings with it a destabilizing doubt as to the limits of human knowledge, and marks up the relevance of faith as a means to resolve such uncertainties.

My own point in apportioning investigative space to knowledge in the *Pensées* is not just that the term 'sublime' in the fragments with which I began this chapter demands it, and submits knowledge to systemic pressure. I also hold that there are various vital questions which critics have not yet asked in this connection. These questions correspond to the various forms that knowledge can take. Does self-knowledge come exclusively with a preteritive denigration of the human capacity for understanding? Is the reader led to pursue certainty in the realm of the divine only out of a sense of human futility? If not, what other forms can an enquiring self-knowledge embody? 'Il faut se connaître soi-même', we read in S106/L72, because 'quand cela ne servirait pas à trouver le vrai, cela au moins sert à régler la vie. Et il n'y a rien de plus juste.' Pascal investigates knowledge, I suggest, by investing his text with 'la vie', with the dynamics of human experience and encounter.

We read, indeed, that 'deux choses instruisent l'homme de toute sa nature: l'instinct et l'expérience' (S161/L128). 'Instinct', in the *Pensées*, can be that 'instinct secret qui nous reste de la grandeur de notre première nature' (S168/136), or a related 'instinct impuissant du bonheur' (S182/L149).[42] In all cases, it is a privileged kind of knowledge which points up the particular limitations of a human reason 'qui voudrait juger de tout' (S142/L110). In this latter fragment, the 'connaissances des premiers principes: espace, temps, mouvement, nombres' are called 'connaissances du cœur et de l'instinct', and the term 'instinct' brings a critique of reason into explicit play: 'C'est sur ces connaissances du cœur et de l'instinct qu'il faut que la raison s'appuie et qu'elle y fonde tout son discours.'[43] But instinct can never render the act of reasoning unnecessary:

> Plût à Dieu que nous n'en eussions au contraire jamais besoin et que nous connussions toutes choses par instinct et par sentiment! Mais la nature nous a refusé ce bien, elle ne nous a au contraire donné que très peu de connaissances de cette sorte. Toutes les autres ne peuvent être acquises que par raisonnement. (S142/L110)

There is a seemingly unqualified bipolarity of 'instinct' and 'raison' here. Fragment S161/L128, though, as we have seen, has given credence to another substantival pairing and suggested a further kind of knowledge: the kind of knowledge which comes through 'expérience'.

I have been concerned with Venn-diagrammatic terms — 'sublime' and 'connaissance' — which have touched upon the hypothesis that 'expérience' can be used instructively. That this hypothesis is made thinkable in Pascal takes us beyond the preterition characteristic of wider Jansenist or *moraliste* discourse. It suggests that Pascal seeks to make accessible the divine truth of religious experience by supplying his text with the dynamics of human experience, the life we can, 'au moins [...] régler' (S106/L72). This has not, as I shall argue further in the next chapter, been sufficiently recognized. And the conclusion that we are starting to approach here is that in Pascal — as in Longinus — different levels of knowledge, experience, and encounter may define each other mutually.

Notes to Chapter 5

1. The numberings referred to are those of Sellier (in Pascal, *Pensées*, ed. by Gérard Ferreyrolles (Paris: Livre de Poche, 2000)) and Lafuma (in Pascal, *Œuvres complètes*, ed. by Louis Lafuma (Paris: Éditions du Seuil, 1963)). As I shall signal subsequently, references to the *Lettres provinciales* will also be to the Lafuma edition of the *Œuvres complètes*; references to all other works, however, will be taken from the edition by Jean Mesnard, 7 vols (Paris: Desclée de Brouwer, 1964–).

2. This fragment, which transcribes the 'nuit de feu' experienced by Pascal as his second conversion and dated by him as 23 November 1654, was written out twice, once on parchment and once on a piece of paper folded up in this, and sewn into the hem of his clothing. It is known as the 'mémorial' following the Père Guerrier's account of its discovery. See the 'Commentaire du Père Guerrier', in *Œuvres complètes*, ed. by Mesnard, III (1991), 55–56.

3. Pascal, 'De l'art de persuader', in *De l'esprit géométrique*, *Œuvres complètes*, ed. by Mesnard, III, 360–428 (p. 413).

4. 'Thus it was necessary that the mediator between God and man should have a transient mortality, and a permanent blessedness, so that through that which is transient he might be conformed to the condition of those who are doomed to die, and might bring them back from the dead to that which is permanent'. Augustine, *Concerning the City of God against the Pagans*, trans. by Henry Bettenson (Harmondsworth: Penguin, 1972), Book IX, Chapter 15.

5. 'De l'art de persuader', p. 416.

6. The 'mémorial' is cited in the parchment version. See Ferreyrolles's note 13 to fragment 742 in his edition of the *Pensées* (p. 562).

7. Richard Lockwood, *The Reader's Figure: Epideictic Rhetoric in Plato, Aristotle, Bossuet, Racine and Pascal* (Geneva: Droz, 1996), p. 267.

8. Louis Marin, 'On the Sublime, Infinity, Je Ne Sais Quoi', in *A New History of French Literature*, ed. by Denis Hollier (Cambridge, MA: Harvard University Press, 1989), pp. 340–45 (p. 343).

9. Marc Fumaroli, 'Pascal et la tradition rhétorique gallicane', in *Méthodes chez Pascal: actes du colloque tenu à Clermont-Ferrand, 10–13 juin 1976* (Paris: Presses universitaires de France, 1979), pp. 359–72 (p. 363).

10. Gilles Magniont does the same: Longinus's 'idée d'une persuasion brutale, comme imposée, rejoint notre analyse de la deixis et de son rôle dans l'argumentation pascalienne'. *Traces de la voix pascalienne: examen des marques de l'énonciation dans les 'Pensées'* (Lyons: Presses universitaires de Lyon, 2003), p. 69.

11. Sophie Hache, *La Langue du ciel: le sublime en France au XVIIe siècle* (Paris: Champion, 2000), pp. 21, 404.

12. *Œuvres complètes*, ed. by Lafuma, pp. 358–59 (Mesnard, III, 427–28), quoted in Hache, *La Langue du ciel*, p. 102.

13. Henry Chadwick, *Augustine* (Oxford: Oxford University Press, 1986), p. 107.

14. For Montaigne, 'C'est "Barroco" et "Baralipton" qui rendent leurs supposts [the subordinates to truly wise philosophers] ainsi crotez et enfumés.' 'De l'institution des enfans', in *Essais*, ed. by P. Villey, 2nd edn (Paris: Presses universitaires de France, 1965), I, 26, p. 161.

15. This is true even if, as Pierre Force points out, 'l'idéal vers lequel tend le raisonnement géométrique est l'intuition simultanée de toutes les étapes d'un raisonnement'. 'Géométrie, finesse et premiers principes de Pascal', *Romance Quarterly*, 50.2 (2003), 121–30 (p. 124).

16. Force, 'Géométrie, finesse et premiers principes de Pascal', is particularly good on how 'chez Pascal tout se tient: l'art de persuader n'est pas séparable de la réflexion sur les sciences; il est aussi intimement lié à la réflexion sur la croyance religieuse' (p. 121).

17. Antony McKenna, *Entre Descartes et Gassendi: la première édition des 'Pensées' de Pascal* (Oxford: Voltaire Foundation, 1993), p. 22. On 'imagination' see also Michael Moriarty, *Early Modern French Thought: The Age of Suspicion* (Oxford: Oxford University Press, 2003), pp. 100–50.

18. The phrase is Henry Chadwick's, in *Augustine*, p. 109.

19. 'Ecrit sur la conversion du pécheur', in *Œuvres complètes*, ed. by Mesnard, IV (1992), 35–44 (p. 40).

20. Nicholas Hammond usefully refers to the different orders as different 'planes of understanding of living' in *Playing with Truth: Language and the Human Condition in Pascal's 'Pensées'* (Oxford: Oxford University Press, 1994), p. 51.

21. Henri Gouhier, *Blaise Pascal: conversion et apologétique* (Paris: Vrin, 1986), p. 29.

22. Note also the partiality of other visions of God — those of the pagans, the Epicureans, and the Jews — described in the same fragment: 'Le Dieu des chrétiens ne consiste pas en un Dieu simplement auteur des vérités géométriques et de l'ordre des éléments; c'est la part des païens et des épicuriens [...] Il ne consiste pas seulement en un Dieu qui exerce sa providence sur la vie et sur les biens des hommes, pour donner une heureuse suite d'années à ceux qui l'adorent; c'est la portion des juifs.'

23. Samy Ben Messaoud, 'Lettre de Boileau à Antoine Arnauld: étude critique d'une copie inédite', *XVIIe siècle*, no. 201 (October–December 1998), 709–14 (p. 712).

24. References to the *Lettres provinciales* are taken from *Les Provinciales ou les lettres écrites par Louis de*

Montalte à un provincial de ses amis et aux RR. PP. Jésuites, ed. by L. Cognet (Paris: Garnier, 1965). The number of the letter is followed by the page.

25. See also the first 'Ecrit des Curés de Paris': 'Ces nouveaux théologiens, au lieu d'accommoder la vie des hommes aux préceptes de Jésus-Christ, ont entrepris d'accommoder les préceptes et les règles de Jésus-Christ aux intérêts, aux passions et aux plaisirs des hommes.' *Œuvres complètes*, ed. by Lafuma, p. 472.

26. 'C'est de cette sorte', we read, 'qu'ils se sont maintenus jusqu'à présent, tantôt par un catéchisme où un enfant condamne leurs adversaires, tantôt par une procession où la grâce suffisante mène l'efficace en triomphe, tantôt par une comédie où les diables emportent Jansénius; une autre fois par un almanach; maintenant par cette censure' (3, 381).

27. Pierre Nicole, 'De la connaissance de soi-même', in *Essais de morale*, ed. by Laurent Thirouin (Paris: Presses universitaires de France, 1999), pp. 309–79 (p. 334). The central dilemma for Nicole is the following: 'L'homme veut se voir, parce qu'il est vain. Il évite de se voir, parce qu'étant vain il ne peut souffrir la vue de ses défauts et de ses misères' (p. 312).

28. It also inflects, of course, a much more generalized *moraliste* discourse, and indeed discourses which are entirely separate from Jansenism, as the fact of the Maurist Dom Mabillon's edition of Augustine indicates.

29. 5 March 1621, in *Les Origines du jansénisme*, 1: *Correspondance de Jansénius*, ed. by Jean Orcibal (Paris: Vrin, 1947), p. 69.

30. As Orcibal notes of Jansen, 'Son originalité a consisté à traiter les œuvres du docteur d'Hippone comme des livres canoniques.' Ibid., p. 70.

31. See Jean Duvergier de Hauranne, Abbé de Saint-Cyran, 'Fautes commises par le P. François Garasse sur Charron', in *Somme des fautes et faussetez capitales contenues en la Somme Theologique du Pere François Garasse de la compagnie de Jesus, qui contient un nombre innombrable de fautes et de faussetez qu'il a commises alleguant les saincts Peres & autre autheurs seculiers* (Paris: Joseph Bouïllerot, 1626). This is a response to Garasse's *Somme théologique des veritez capitales de la religion chrestienne* (Paris: S. Chappelet, 1625).

32. Indeed, Augustine is said by Saint-Cyran to have written 'comme s'il eust voulu fournir à dessein des parolles formelles qui peussent douze cens ans apres servir de defense à Charron, & tirer une conclusion à son avantage pour abattre la vanité de vostre caquet' (p. 339).

33. The launch of the debate between Saint-Cyran and Garasse is the main point at which, writes Antony McKenna, 'est déclarée l'alliance capitale entre le pyrrhonisme chrétien et l'augustinisme dans la constitution d'une philosophie chrétienne opposée au rationalisme scolastique'. *Pascal entre Descartes et Gassendi*, p. 5. This Christian scepticism never goes as far, as we have seen with fragment S240, as an inert despair about the possibility of all knowledge: it condemns those who 'reconnaissent l'infirmité de la nature' while they 'en ignorent la dignité'. I shall discuss Christian scepticism further in Chapter 7, in the context of the seventeenth-century reception of Montaigne.

34. A coherent doctrine of 'mysticism' was first elaborated by pseudo-Dionysius the Areopagite, who writes that 'the most divine knowledge of God' is 'that which comes through unknowing', and who preaches the purges of asceticism as a means of obtaining knowledge: 'By an undivided and absolute abandonment of yourself and everything, shedding all and freed from all, you will be uplifted to the ray of the divine shadow which is above everything that is.' See *The Divine Names*, Chapter 7, section 3, p. 109, and *The Mystic Theology*, Chapter 1, section 13, p. 135, in *Pseudo-Dionysius: The Complete Works*, trans. by Colm Luibheid (New York: Paulist Press, 1987). It should be noted that critics do not always concur with the idea that Pascal moves away from mysticism. Evelyn Underhill embraces Pascal's 'mémorial' in her work on mysticism, which she defines very broadly as an expression of the human tendency to strive towards complete harmony with a transcendental order. See *Mysticism: A Study in the Nature and Development of Man's Spiritual Consciousness*, 12th edn, rev. (London: Methuen, 1930), pp. xiv, 188–90. Alan Boase writes of Pascal's 'essentially passive conception of faith', defined by Boase as 'it is not I who act but God who acts in me'. Here, 'the general character of [Pascal's] doctrine is mystical in tone, and despite their differences with regard to original sin, it is Mme Guyon and the Quietist mystics who are in many respects his true successors'. *The Fortunes of Montaigne: A History of the Essays in France* (London: Methuen, 1935), p. 374. See also Jean Mesnard: 'Il nous semble alors

impossible de ne pas découvirir dans l'œuvre de Pascal une pensée mystique. Le christianisme de Pascal s'épanouit naturellement en mystique' (*Les 'Pensées' de Pascal* (Paris: SEDES, 1993), p. 333), although this statement is nuanced in a much more detailed discussion in *Œuvres complètes*, ed. by Mesnard, III, 19–49.

35. When Richard H. Popkin terms Pascal a fideist in *The History of Scepticism from Erasmus to Spinoza* (Berkeley: University of California Press, 1979), his definition of the term is broad, and blurs into the standpoint that 'reason may play some relative or probable role in the search for, or explanation of the truth' (p. xx). Popkin's interest, in turning scepticism into fideism, is to make the story of fideism the story of modernity; according to him, the modern episteme is defined by that moment of the Reformation crisis which introduced doubt into theology. For a questioning of Popkin's definition of scepticism as fideism, see the special edition of the *Revue de synthèse* (42.2–3 (April–September 1998)) entitled *Histoire du scepticisme de Sextus Empiricus à Richard H. Popkin*, ed. by Pierre-François Moreau and Eric Brian; in particular the articles of Sylvia Giocanti, 'Histoire du fidéisme, histoire du scepticisme' (pp. 193–210), and Frédéric Brahami, 'L'Articulation du scepticisme religieux et du scepticisme profane dans l'*Histoire du scepticisme d'Erasme à Spinoza* de Richard H. Popkin' (pp. 293–305).

36. For a sophisticated analysis of Pascal's alignment with Christian scepticism, see McKenna, *Pascal entre Descartes et Gassendi*. McKenna's interest is to track the repercussions of debates about scepticism in the context of the publication history of the *Pensées*.

37. Paul de Man, 'Pascal's Allegory of Persuasion', in *Allegory and Representation*, ed. by Stephen Greenblatt (Baltimore: Johns Hopkins University Press, 1981), pp. 1–25 (p. 20).

38. Sara E. Melzer, *Discourses of the Fall: A Study of Pascal's 'Pensées'* (Berkeley: University of California Press, 1986), p. 4. Pascal, according to Melzer, is explicitly deconstructionist: 'Pascal believes, as does Derrida, that such dreams are impossible with the limits of human life because any attempt to decode a truth or an origin will be a product of the particular code one chooses. Pascal thus seeks a solution outside language; he wagers to go beyond textuality through the heart, the atextual origin of certainty' (p. 8).

39. On the instability, not just of terminology, but more specifically of the voice of the speaker in the *Pensées*, see Richard Parish, ' "Mais qui parle?" Voice and Persona in the *Pensées*', *Seventeenth-Century French Studies*, 8 (1986), pp. 23–40.

40. *Playing with Truth*, pp. 226–27.

41. See also Richard Lockwood in *The Reader's Figure*: '[Pascal] in the figuring of his reader as defective, as an uncertain receptor of the word, will locate the most important effects of his discourse, whether in theory or in practice' (p. 286).

42. For analysis of the term 'instinct' in Pascal, see in particular McKenna, *Pascal entre Descartes et Gassendi*, pp. 23–25; Buford Norman, *Portraits of Thought, Knowledge, Methods and Styles in Pascal* (Columbus: Ohio State University Press, 1988), pp. 26–34, 40–42; Gouhier, *Conversion et apologétique*, pp. 60–70.

43. We are in the territory of the 'vérités de notre portée' of 'De l'art de persuader'. Antony McKenna notes that 'ainsi, tout en reprenant le cadre de la psychologie cartésienne, Pascal retourne contre Descartes sa définition des "idées primitives" ', since the latter's definition relies upon an 'esprit' which, purely intellectual, can detach itself from all material circumstances. *Pascal entre Descartes et Gassendi*, p. 25. I shall turn to this in the next chapter.

CHAPTER 6

❖

Knowledge, Experience, and the Uses of 'Expérience' for Pascal

We see with Pascal that religious experience may bring with it a revelatory, redemptive, and ineffable 'certitude, certitude'. The next stage of my argument will engage more closely with the question of how Pascal seeks to communicate this knowledge, this experience. Continuing my re-statement of the forceful sublimity sometimes imputed to Pascal, I shall develop the notion that Longinian structures and strictures hold a more complex interest for us as we look at Pascal's work. How does Pascal persuade his readers that religious experience is open to them also? How does he bring about the enquiring self-awareness which, as we saw in Chapter 5, is a prerequisite for that experience ('tu ne me chercherais pas si tu ne m'avais trouvé', S751/L919)? I shall question the supposition that religious experience can be precipitated only through a denigration of 'raison' which, dictating human uncertainty, is presumed to open the reader up to the 'sentiment du cœur' without which faith is 'inutile pour le salut' (S142/L110). To this end, I shall focus on the second epistemological tool offered to us in fragment S161/L128: 'Deux choses instruisent l'homme de toute sa nature: l'instinct et l'expérience.' This fragment suggests that the instruction required to make the reader susceptible to the God-given experience of 'participation' can be conveyed through inserting into text a different level of 'expérience'. Pascal displays not just a fall from (certain) religious experience into (uncertain) discourse, but an assiduous attachment to, and belief in, the transformative potential of, texts which delve into human 'expérience'.

Analysing experience and art in his work on redemption, Leo Bersani writes that 'in the work of art, a certain type of representation of experience will operate both as an escape from the objects of representation and as a justification (retroactive, even posthumous) for having had any experiences at all. [...] Literary repetition is an annihilating salvation'.[1] Bersani's comments, psychoanalytically oriented, serve to delineate the myriad ways in which experience, irreducible to representation, can be redemptively formed and manipulated in its passage into textuality. 'In Proust', writes Bersani, 'art simultaneously erases, repeats and redeems life' (p. 11). Art is enslaved to life, but Bersani puts across an infinitely creative flexibility available to the writer in deciding to translate expérience into discourse. Pascal, writing with a feverishness he shares with Proust, knows and exploits this flexibility.

What I wish to suggest here, in other words, is that art for Pascal is not only a realm which is inferior, inadequate, to experience or to knowledge, doomed to transmitting experience and knowledge preteritively, through the conveying of its own incapacity to convey. Critics of Pascal have written of a fall 'from truth into language', have stated that 'stories, signs and narrative must replace truth and epistemology in the Pascalian fallen world', that in the *Pensées*, 'inevitably, we are forced out of pure epistemology and into a practical problem of persuasion'.[2] These comments suggest a shift from one mode (ineffable knowledge) to another inferior mode (discourse, persuasion), a fall 'from', a move 'out of'. Religious experience and the human representation of it are incommensurate. But what I seek to propose in my reading of the *Pensées* is a tactical and Longinian manipulation of this position.

'Expérience' and Instruction

In the *Lettres provinciales*, it is the Jesuits' blind eye to 'expérience' which renders their doctrine of *pouvoir prochain* (making redemption purely dependent upon the sinner's statement of regret) so erroneous: 'Je doute que l'expérience ait fait connaître à vos Pères que tous ceux qui font ces promesses les tiennent, et je suis trompé s'ils n'éprouvent souvent le contraire' (Letter 10, p. 177). It is the experience that 'libertins qui ne cherchent qu'à douter de la religion', on the other hand, *do* acknowledge which enables them to turn away from this and all doctrine: 'N'est-il pas visible qu'étant convaincus par leur propre expérience de la fausseté de votre doctrine en ce point [qu'ils sentent, à chaque péché qu'ils commettent, un avertissement et un désir intérieur de s'en abstenir], que vous dites être de foi, ils en étendront la conséquence à tous les autres?' (4, 61). And it is the experience of the injured man, in the parable of the second letter, which enables him to ask for God's grace and strike out on his own (just as the Jansenists, so the parable implies, separate themselves off from the domination of the Church by the Jesuits): 'Après avoir fait essai de ses forces, et reconnu par expérience la vérité de sa faiblesse [...] il demanda à Dieu les forces qu'il confessait n'avoir pas; il en reçut miséricorde, et par son secours, arriva heureusement dans sa maison' (2, 30–31).[3]

To possess 'expérience', here, is to have made an 'essai'. This is experience gained through experiment, indicative of that semantic chiasmus which has Furetière define the noun 'experience' as an 'espreuve qu'on fait de quelque chose', which makes the verb 'experimenter' synonymous with 'faire experience de' and which, today, means that the French 'expérience' is still the most obvious translation of the English 'scientific experiment'.[4] Individual 'expériences', 'essais', or 'espreuves' can be cumulative and, when integrated, approach a kind of 'expérience' which is an asymptote of 'connaissance': 'Expérience signifie aussi, Connoissance des choses acquises par un long usage.'[5] Experience implies a rather different kind of knowledge of self from that promoted in the broad discourse of 'la connaissance de soi-même' discussed in the last chapter. It implies a knowledge which comes from a participation in the external world.

This participation is, in fact, etymologically inherent to the term 'experience'. Stripped down to its historical bases, the verb 'to experience' reveals the Indo-

European root '-per' (going through, engaging with). 'Experience' is, at this fundamental level, bound up with 'peril' (exposure to danger) and 'piracy' (exposure to the high seas).[6] The gaining of experience, the approaching of 'connaissance', require exposure; not necessarily to danger or to adventure, although certainly to these also, but to all that which can be seen, heard, felt. In English, this slippage between experience and the experiential is embodied in the way in which 'experience' is also a transitive verb: experience (a generalized knowledge in the form of the substantive) is gained as a result of what one experiences (transitively, at individual points of time, in response to individual stimuli). La Bruyère intertwines 'expérience' and the experiential with a use of 'avoir l'expérience de': 'Celui qui a eu l'expérience d'un grand amour néglige l'amitié.'[7] The individual experience of 'un grand amour' is a microcosm, a thumbnail sketch, of the general experience gained. La Bruyère's subject (and any reader who is captured within the net cast by the maxim) is, in this regard, 'expérimenté'.

The opposite of experience in all these senses would seem to be indifference. As apathy, lack of interest, or detachment, indifference extinguishes experiential engagement and neutralizes any sense of peril. In the *Dictionnaire de l'Académie française*, the indifferent is that 'qui touche peu, dont on ne se soucie point'; an indifferent person 'n'a pas plus de penchant pour une chose que pour une autre, pour un parti que pour un autre'. This is how indifference appears in the *Pensées*, where it exists in the form of the 'négligence' which Pascal's dialectician makes his own 'monstre': 'Qu'il se trouve des hommes indifférents à la perte de leur être et au péril d'une éternité de misères, cela n'est point naturel' (S681/L427).[8] 'Naturel' is used in a non-theological sense here; indifference is, for Pascal, quite simply inhuman. This fragment turns around the apologetic movement (from the human to the divine) to bring religion into the lived, experiential present: 'L'immortalité de l'âme est une chose qui importe si fort, qui nous touche si profondément, qu'il faut avoir perdu tout sentiment pour être dans l'indifférence de savoir ce qui en est' (S681/L427).

But merely describing this movement, whereby 'l'immortalité de l'âme' becomes something which 'nous importe' and 'nous touche', is not enough to counter indifference. Doing so would not in itself differentiate Pascal's argumentation from that of the *Meditationes de prima philosophia, in qua dei existentia et animae immortalitas demonstrantur*. Pascal's attempt to force the readers of the *Pensées* to engage with this question of 'l'immortalité de l'âme [...] qui importe si fort', though, has to embody a difference in priorities, establish a distance, between his work and that of Descartes. This same distance is, in fragment S196/L164, also gouged out between Pascal's speaker and the thought of Copernicus: 'Je trouve bon qu'on n'approfondisse pas l'opinion de Copernic, mais ceci: Il importe à toute la vie de savoir si l'âme est mortelle ou immortelle.' 'Toute la vie' is at stake, and a recognition of this is crucial; and it is apposite, then, that one of the key ways in which Pascal elaborates upon the distance between his own and Cartesian patterns of thinking is via the vital, dynamic pressure of the term 'expérience'. A discussion of this will feed back into our wider analysis of how Pascal sets about intimating a kind of knowledge which, for him, makes absolute sense of 'toute la vie'.

Descartes

What Descartes fails to take into account in Pascal is 'les deux infinis' of fragment S230/L199, far beyond the stretch of human vision:

> Les philosophes ont bien plutôt prétendu d'y arriver, et c'est là où tous ont achoppé. C'est ce qui a donné lieu à ces titres si ordinaires: *Des principes des choses, Des principes de la philosophie*, et aux semblables, aussi fastueux en effet quoique moins en apparence que cet autre qui crève les yeux: *De omni scibili.* (S230/L199)

In response to Descartes's conception, in *Les principes de la philosophie*, of the universe as *res extensa*, as made up of 'une matière étendue en longueur, largeur et profondeur, dont les parties ont des figures et des mouvements divers', Pascal draws up fragment S118/L84, headed 'Descartes':

> Il faut dire en gros: 'Cela se fait par figure et mouvement', car cela est vrai. Mais de dire quelles et composer la machine, cela est ridicule, car cela est inutile et incertain et pénible. Et quand cela serait vrai, nous n'estimons pas que toute la philosophie vaille une heure de peine.[9]

Descartes's desire to 'composer la machine', to see the universe as an immense mechanism whose every movement is explicable as the functioning of a component, demonstrates an urge to totalization which, for Pascal, is excessively presumptuous and doomed to error.[10]

In accordance with such fragments, critics have based their conclusions regarding the intertextual relationship between Pascal and Descartes primarily on the reason–instinct dichotomy to be found in the *Pensées*. Philippe Sellier, making Pascal's denigration of reason chime with Augustine's elevation of the 'cœur', writes that 'cette volonté de tout régenter, qui constitue le rationalisme, est mise en échec à tout moment. [...] On va retrouver ici l'une des pentes de la pensée augustinienne: l'insistance sur la faiblesse d'une raison qui voudrait cependant tout prouver et tend à rejeter comme faux ce qui échappe à ses prises.'[11] Stephen C. Bold, seeking to be more succinct, comes up with the following formulation: 'To borrow a familiar distinction from Pascal's epistemology, I might paraphrase and say that "la raison cartésienne ne connaît pas les raisons augustiniennes du cœur".'[12] Nicholas Hammond concludes an article on Pascal's reference to 'Descartes inutile et incertain' (S445/L887) with the following assertion: 'Without the "sentiment de cœur", Pascal deems all human faith to be useless. This would explain why Descartes is "inutile et incertain", for the "sentiment de cœur" plays no part in his philosophy.'[13] There are, however, further characteristics which define Pascal's engagement with Descartes. We need to consider, for example, Pascal's *Préface sur le Traité du vide*.

The *Préface sur le Traité du vide* targets those who 'rapportent la seule autorité pour preuve dans les matières physiques, au lieu du raisonnement ou des expériences'.[14] If, in matters of theology, 'c'est l'autorité seule', an unchanging authority passed down through the centuries, 'qui nous en peut éclaircir' (p. 778), other subjects, such as 'la géométrie, l'arithmétique, la musique, la physique, la médecine, l'architecture, et toutes les sciences qui sont soumises à l'expérience et au raisonnement, doivent être augmentées pour devenir parfaites' (p. 779). These are subjects in which 'la preuve consiste en expériences, et non en démonstrations' (p. 784): proof lies, in other words, in (cumulative) experiment.[15] Mesnard aligns the *Préface* and 'De l'art de persuader': 'Le progrès s'accomplit sur deux plans: enchaînement sans cesse prolongé des conséquences à partir des principes, constitué en physique par les expériences, qui sont en ce domaine l'ultime point d'appui d'un raisonnement; mais aussi, par l'accroissement du nombre des expériences, multiplication des principes mêmes.'[16] General principles and axioms stem from — knowledge is dependent upon — experiment: 'Quand les anciens ont assuré que la nature ne souffrait point de vide, ils ont entendu qu'elle n'en souffrait point dans toutes les expériences qu'ils avaient vues' (p. 784). 'L'expérience des siècles' (p. 783) is dependent upon what can be seen, heard, felt in an experimental environment, and thereafter integrated into a generalized knowledge and experience.[17] Experiment and experience are, once again, copiously intertwined.

The 1651 *Préface* cited here is the culminating point of the debate about scientific experiment, and about the nature of the vacuum, which had produced the *Expériences nouvelles touchant le vide* (1647), the correspondence with the Jesuit Père Noël and with Le Pailleur, the head of the Mersenne academy from 1648 (1647–48), the *Récit de la grande expérience de l'équilibre des liqueurs* (1648) and the posthumously published *Traités de l'équilibre des liqueurs et de la pesanteur de la masse de l'air* (1663). Throughout, the experimental character of this research was naturally at the heart of debate. The key experiment on which Pascal's research focuses is that anticipated in the *Expériences nouvelles* and finally narrated in the *Récit de la grande expérience*, after Florin Périer (standing in for Pascal) had peformed it on the Puy de Dôme. This experiment showed that the fluctuations in mercury in a configuration of test tubes (effectively a Torricelli tube, or a barometer) were due to atmospheric pressure, and produced a vacuum.[18]

Written in the midst of the debate about the vacuum, Noël's initial letter to Pascal commences as follows: 'J'ai lu vos *Expériences touchant le vide*, que je trouve fort belles et ingénieuses, mais je n'entends pas ce vide apparent qui paraît dans le tube après la descente, soit de l'eau, soit du vif-argent. Je dis que c'est un corps.'[19] As Pascal notes in his letter to Le Pailleur, 'Cette matière, qu'il [Noël] appelle air subtil, est la même que celle que M. Descartes nomme matière subtile.'[20] Pascal asserts his own position against that of Descartes throughout this debate. The Cartesian concept of *res extensa*, of the universe as made up of all-pervasive matter, excludes the possibility of the existence of a vacuum or 'vide'.[21] Pascal's response to the notion of *res extensa* revolves around the term 'expérience'.

Pascal progresses from experiment to subsequent demonstration, relaying 'quantité d'expériences nouvelles que j'ai faites touchant le vide, et les conséquences que j'en ai tirées'.[22] Noël starts with (as it turns out, says Pascal, faulty) principles, and tries to make these fit experimental results: 'il s'est imaginé une définition du corps qu'il a conçue exprès, en sorte qu'elle convînt à notre espace, afin qu'il pût en tirer sa conséquence avec facilité' (p. 568). Pascal and Noël disagree on where to draw the line between the description and the explanation of experiments, and it is certainly possible to argue, as does Desmond M. Clarke, that Pascal inconsistently 'fudged the distinction between observation and theory to his own advantage'.[23] Throughout, though, Noël's supposed indifference to experiment is what is targeted by Pascal: 'Il est évident qu'il n'a vu aucune des expériences dont il parle' (p. 573); 'Il ne connaît les expériences que par récit' (p. 574). Pascal's most hyperbolic criticism, therefore, opposes the Jesuit's conceptual tyranny over 'la nature', 'les éléments', and 'l'univers':

> Mais je voudrais bien savoir de ce Père d'où lui vient cet ascendant qu'il a sur la nature, et cet empire qu'il exerce si absolument sur les éléments, qui lui servent avec tant de dépendance qu'ils changent de propriétés à mesure qu'il change de pensées, et que l'univers accommode ses effets à l'inconstance de ses intentions. (p. 571)

If, as Pascal concludes his letter by arguing, the Père Noël's 'façon d'agir est bien différente de la mienne', it is because the latter does not 'agir' at all: rather, he 'produit ses opinions à mesure qu'il les conçoit' (p. 575). There are similarities between this statement and Pascal's reported accusation that Descartes's science, lacking experimental rigour — making experiment guaranteed only by deduction — constitutes a 'roman de la nature': 'Feu M. Pascal appelait la philosophie cartésienne le roman de la nature, semblable à peu près à l'histoire de Don Quichotte.'[24] In 'De l'esprit géométrique', geometry offers 'vérités de notre portée', basic truths which are comparable to the kind of knowledge that comes through the 'cœur' or the 'instinct' (S142/L110); in his writings about the vacuum, Pascal grants 'expériences' a similarly foundational status. We have here the two terms of the pairing in fragment (S161/L128): 'Deux choses instruisent l'homme de toute sa nature: l'instinct et l'expérience.'

So a persistent belief in a subtle form of matter is a form of closure to the knowledge gained through experiment and experience. Pascal's accusation that Cartesianism demonstrates inadequacy in the philosophical domain is, then, just as important as the accusation that Descartes confuses the relative importance of the philosophical and the theological. We have witnessed two levels in Pascal on which Cartesianism is criticized. One pertains to 'le cœur', which Cartesianism neglects; the other to 'l'expérience', which it also neglects. Both 'le cœur' and 'l'expérience' can, for Pascal, open up knowledge. Pascal thus makes 'l'expérience', as well as 'l'instinct', a necessary complement to 'la raison'. Cartesian science falls down because it ignores the epistemological import of both 'expérience' and 'instinct'.

If Pascal 'se moquait fort' regarding Descartes's 'matière subtile', we are however told that 'il était de son sentiment sur l'automate'; and Pascal's writings on this 'automate' are also revelatory when it comes to the use he makes of 'expérience'.[25] The 'automate' is the body which is opposed to the 'âme immortelle' in Cartesian dualism. But the 'automate' is also that part of the 'âme' which is susceptible to mechanistic behaviour: 'Car il ne faut pas se méconnaître: nous sommes automate autant qu'esprit' (S661/L821). Pascal's term for the conviction which ensues from our status as 'automates' is 'la coutume': 'la coutume fait nos preuves les plus fortes et les plus crues: elle incline l'automate, qui entraîne l'esprit sans qu'il y pense. Qui a démontré qu'il sera demain jour, et que nous mourrons? Et qu'y a-t-il de plus cru?' (S661/L821)

One of the advantages of 'la machine' for Pascal is that it means his readers can choose to be convinced by incorporating certain practices into their daily lives. Faith can be tested, tried out, tried on by the 'automate':

> Vous voulez aller à la foi, et vous n'en savez pas le chemin? [...] Apprenez de ceux qui ont été liés comme vous et qui parient maintenant tout leur bien: ce sont gens qui savent ce chemin que vous voulez suivre et guéris d'un mal dont vous voulez guérir. Suivez la manière par où ils ont commencé: c'est en faisant tout comme s'ils croyaient, en prenant de l'eau bénite, en faisant dire des messes etc. (S680/L418)

S39/L5, which also needs to be examined here, is 'une lettre d'exhortation à un ami pour le porter à chercher':

> Et il répondrait qu'il serait heureux de trouver quelque lumière, mais que selon cette religion même, quand il croirait ainsi, cela ne lui servirait de rien et qu'ainsi il aime autant ne point chercher. Et à cela lui répondre: 'la machine'.

What 'la machine' achieves is the removal of obstacles to faith: 'Après la lettre qu'on doit chercher Dieu, faire la lettre d'ôter les obstacles, qui est le discours de la machine' (S45/L11).

Clearly, though, the 'machine' also has limitations. It is limited first because those who employ it are not necessarily 'ceux à qui Dieu a donné la religion par sentiment du cœur [...] sans quoi la foi n'est qu'humaine et inutile pour le salut' (S142/L110). 'Il faut que l'extérieur soit joint à l'intérieur pour obtenir de Dieu' (S767/L944). Mechanical efforts towards faith may resemble the efforts of those who imitate the external manifestations of the faith of Teresa of Ávila, for example, without embodying her 'profonde humilité': 'On se tue d'imiter ses discours, pensant imiter son état' (S756/L928). If this initial level of action 'vous fera croire' (S680/L418), it also 'vous abêtira', which, as Ferreyrolles notes in his edition of the *Pensées*, 'ne signifie pas se rendre stupide, mais utiliser ce qui est commun à l'homme et à l'animal' (p. 465, n. 1). For another example of mechanistic behaviour, we may turn to fragment S139/L107: 'Le bec du perroquet qu'il essuie, quoi qu'il soit net'. And here, the reader is forced into contact with a more precise analysis of a further problem with the 'machine'.

This further problem, equally important, is that mechanistic action precludes 'expérience'. It closes off our senses to 'expérience' first in the sense of the experimental. This is clearly stated in scientific mode in fragment S617/L736:

> Lorsqu'on est accoutumé à se servir de mauvaises raisons pour prouver des effets de la nature, on ne veut plus recevoir les bonnes, lorsqu'elles sont découvertes. L'exemple qu'on en donna fut sur la circulation du sang, pour rendre raison pourquoi la veine enfle au-dessous de la ligature.

And it also precludes what the *Préface sur le Traité du vide* termed the 'augmentation' of knowledge. The workings of 'la machine' exclude the capacity to integrate the data received through experiment into experience: into the kind of dynamic, lifeful 'expérience' with which Pascal endows 'De l'art de persuader': 'Voilà ce que je sais par une longue expérience de toutes sortes de livres et de personnes.'[26] So again, Pascal criticizes the machine's (and therefore Descartes's) inadequacy with regard to the 'cœur', but, moving further, its inadequacy with regard to 'l'expérience'. Engaging with the 'machine' does not constitute experiment, nor can it be integrated into experience. What I want to suggest now, however, is that we do find the mechanics of an 'integrable' experiment in the *Pensées*, and that the *Pensées* are packed with the experiments, exposures, and encounters which can prefigure knowledge and experience. If Descartes neglects the epistemological import of 'expérience', Pascal makes sure that the readers of the *Pensées* do not. To this end, he returns constantly to the etymological roots of the term 'expérience': to the stratum of meaning identified with 'moving through', 'engaging with', 'encountering'.

'Le mouvement' and 'le péril'

'Le mouvement', in the *Pensées*, lies first within the ambit of 'instinct'; along with 'espace', 'temps', and 'nombres' it is, in fragment S142/L110, one of the forms of knowledge which are 'aussi ferme qu'aucune de celles que nos raisonnements nous donnent'. It is one of those 'connaissances du cœur qu'il faut que la raison s'appuie et qu'elle y fonde tout son discours'. This is reiterated in S680/L419: 'Qui doute donc que notre âme, étant accoutumée à voir nombre, espace, mouvement, croie cela et rien que cela?' (Those who do espouse this kind of doubt might be subjected to the corrosive sarcasm of S164/L131: 'Que fera donc l'homme en cet état? Doutera-t-il de tout? Doutera-t-il s'il veille, si on le pince, si on le brûle? Doutera-t-il qu'il doute? Doutera-t-il s'il est?') The readers of the *Pensées* are, inasmuch as they are human beings, obliged to move. And in this, the self-evidence of 'le mouvement' belongs both to the domain of 'instinct' and to the domain of 'expérience'. Movement in the world, the fact of being embarked upon life, equates to an initial level of compulsory, non-negotiable 'expérience': 'vous êtes embarqué' (S681/L427).

A comparably fundamental level of 'expérience' comes with that further etymological relation, 'le péril'. This, too, is mandatory in the *Pensées*. 'Craindre la mort hors du péril, et non dans le péril,' reads fragment S594/L716, 'car il faut être homme.' Rather than publicizing the quality of manliness, this fragment establishes a schema according to which 'il faut être dans le péril'. Peril should be accepted rather than feared in Pascal's optic, since the very state of humanity is perilous; on the other hand, a refusal to accept this fact is dangerous. This is an important rewriting of Don Gomès's 'à vaincre sans péril, on triomphe sans gloire', a slogan which is rendered irrelevant if it is impossible to live 'sans péril'.[27] We might take tangential note here of the Theban statesman in fragment S560/L681. Epaminondas turns in the middle of a battlefield (as Montaigne explains) 'au rencontre de son hoste et de son amy'.[28] Pascal inserts the encounter into his text as follows:

> Je n'admire point l'excès d'une vertu, comme de la valeur, si je ne vois en même temps l'excès de la vertu opposée, comme en Epaminondas, qui avait l'extrême valeur et l'extrême bénignité. Car autrement ce n'est pas monter, c'est tomber. On ne montre pas sa grandeur pour être à une extrémité, mais bien en touchant les deux à la fois et remplissant tout l'entre-deux. Mais peut-être que ce n'est qu'un soudain mouvement de l'âme de l'un à l'autre de ces extrêmes et qu'elle n'est jamais en effet qu'un point, comme le tison de feu. Soit, mais au moins cela marque l'agilité de l'âme, si cela n'en marque l'étendue.

Pascal allows judgements to overlap and be overridden in the writing out of the fragment, as the value allocated to 'grandeur' and to 'étendue' is redistributed in favour of 'agilité'. What should constitute Epaminondas's renown for the speaker here is not his valour but a basic 'agilité de l'âme'. Standard notions of glory and danger are adjusted; and their adjustment does important work in the *Pensées* as a whole.

The everyday peril with which Pascal is concerned resonates slightly differently from the 'péril d'une éternité de misères' (S681/L427) which describes damnation. It subsists even when the threat of damnation might seem to subside: 'la peur des saints qui avaient toujours suivi le plus sûr' (S598/L721). Indeed, 'la vie ordinaire des hommes est semblable à celle des saints' (S306/L275). Pascal brackets off any future state to place stress on the fearful exigencies of human existence: 'on expose certainement à l'infini qui est incertain' (S680/L427).

The body is engaged in all this, but not in an unthinking, mechanistic way. Movement is also relationality: 'L'homme [...] a rapport à tout ce qu'il connaît: il a besoin de lieu pour le contenir, de temps pour durer, de mouvement pour vivre' (S230/L199). So, by forcing his readers to engage with their own movement, Pascal forces them into this sustained 'rapport'. Fragment S41/L248 is interesting in this regard:

> La foi est différente de la preuve. L'une est humaine, l'autre est un don de Dieu. *Justus ex fide vivit.* C'est de cette foi que Dieu lui-même met dans le cœur dont la preuve est souvent l'instrument. *Fides ex auditu.* Mais cette foi est dans le cœur et fait dire non *Scio* mais *Credo.*

The provenance of both quotations in this fragment is Paul's letter to the Romans, the first translated by Sacy as 'le juste vit de la foi' and the second as 'la foi vient de ce qu'on a entendu'. As Tetsuya Shiokawa notes, we can assume that the noun 'la foi' here does not change its meaning from one instance of usage to the next:

> Qu'il soit question de la cause occasionnelle de la foi dans la première ['le juste vit de la foi'], ou du rôle que joue la foi formée dans la dernière ['la foi vient de ce qu'on a entendu'], toutes les deux visent le même objet qu'elles regardent chacun sous un angle différent.[29]

What the juxtaposition of the two proposals tells us, effectively, is that the just live on the basis of what they have heard. Pascal's point of reference, alongside prophecy heard and made real in the proof-giving form of Christ the redeemer (S221/L189), is the accumulated human experience of hearing others. Listening, with the 'rapport' it generates, has to be a sustained mode of existence.

Of paramount importance to Pascal is the fact that humankind's encounters in and 'rapports' with the world entail, inevitably, the question 'par où?':

> L'homme a besoin d'éléments pour le composer, de chaleur et d'aliments pour se nourrir, d'air pour respirer. Il voit la lumière, il sent les corps, enfin tout tombe sous son alliance. Il faut donc, pour connaître l'homme, savoir d'où vient qu'il a besoin d'air pour subsister, et pour connaître l'air, savoir par où il a ce rapport à la vie de l'homme, etc. (S230/L199)

What is important, then, about Pascal's textual deployment of 'le péril' and 'le mouvement', and the rapports they generate, is that it grants such force to the trivial fact of existence itself. There is a kind of self-awareness which comes with relationality, through the vital dynamics of the 'par où', as readers are forced to enquire about their own limitations, their own 'besoins', their own 'rapport à la vie'. And what this seems to suggest is that the very fact of human relationality (no matter how false subsequent social relationships might turn out to be) can prefigure searching enquiry of the kind found in fragment S751/L919: 'Tu ne me chercherais pas si tu ne m'avais trouvé'.[30]

It is in this connection, I argue, that we should read fragment S161/L128: 'Deux choses instruisent l'homme de toute sa nature: l'instinct et l'expérience.' Human experiences, the movements of human interrelationships, are 'vérités de notre portée'. These are basic, but have an instructive capacity. Given this, they have the potential to open the reader up to the reviewing of self-perception which is a necessary precursor to faith. Human experiences are the basis for further, potential, levels of experience. The possibility of faith, and of faithful experience — the overarching concern of the *Pensées* — can follow from a trivial level of identification with one's fellow human beings: it depends upon the 'd'où' and the 'par où' which come with the 'rapport'. This is, as I shall now discuss further, a provocative and powerful proposition.

'Expérience' as Figure

What I am suggesting here is that certain kinds of experience can, in the *Pensées* — as indeed in the other works under consideration in this book — be thought through in terms of, aided and abetted by, others. Beyond my discussion thus far, local support is also lent to this suggestion by the letter written by Blaise and Jacqueline Pascal on 1 April 1648.[31] This letter is often quoted by critics in the interest of revealing Pascal's support for the notion that God is outwardly manifest in, figured in, the visible universe: 'car, comme nous avons souvent dit entre nous, les choses corporelles ne sont qu'une image des spirituelles, et Dieu a représenté les choses invisibles dans les visibles' (p. 582). In fact, the catalyst for this observation is not 'les choses' at all, but rather the sibling bond: 'l'alliance que la nature a faite entre nous' (p. 581). This relationship ('l'alliance que la nature a faite') figures that formed as a result of the siblings' common Christianity ('celle que la grâce y a faite'). Further, the formation of the former 'alliance' (at birth) is made the figure of the formation of the latter (at the moment of revelation, or rebirth):

> car il faut avouer que c'est proprement depuis ce temps (que M. de Saint-Cyran veut qu'on appelle le commencement de la vie) que nous devons nous considérer comme véritablement parents, et qu'il a plu à Dieu de nous joindre aussi bien dans son nouveau monde par l'esprit, comme il avait fait dans le terrestre par la chair. (p. 581)

This, then, is why 'nous devons admirer que Dieu nous ait donné et la figure et la réalité de cette alliance' (p. 582). The term 'figure' explicitly includes the movements of human interrelationships, the fact of being 'unis', of having an 'alliance', as well as 'les choses visibles'. Hence the 'double obligation' placed upon Christians:

> Ceux que Dieu, par la régénération, a retiré gratuitement du péché [...] ont une double obligation de le servir et de l'honorer, puisque en tant que créatures ils doivent se tenir dans l'ordre des créatures et ne pas profaner le lieu qu'ils remplissent, et qu'en tant que chrétiens, ils doivent sans cesse aspirer à se rendre dignes de faire partie du Corps de Jésus-Christ. (p. 583)

The Christian bond is figured not simply as the sibling relationship, but as the bond shared by humanity, in nothing other than its common human status. 'Nous sommes membres du tout', reads fragment S401/L368, and this identification with the 'tout' requires an initial, trivial, identification with a purely human 'nous'. Relationality, one's place in 'l'ordre des créatures', can force a thinking through of spirituality. And readers of the *Pensées*, brought to an understanding of the human 'rapport', can be opened up to the possibility that life itself can have figurative force: 'La vie ordinaire des hommes', we know, 'est semblable à celle des saints' (S306/L275).

Only with this understanding of the *Pensées*, which grants 'expérience' a role comparable in importance to 'instinct', can we appreciate the apposition of S580/L702: 'les mouvements de la grâce, la dureté de cœur, les circonstances extérieures'. And only from the ensuing perspective can the reader capture the full import of the analogy made in S756/L927: 'Le moindre mouvement importe à toute la nature: la mer entière change pour une pierre. Ainsi dans la grâce la moindre action importe pour ses suites à tout, donc tout est important.' The movements in the external world which equate to experiment, along with the accumulation of the knowledge thus sought which equates to experience, are necessary for exposure to grace. Pascal weaves into the fabric of the *Pensées* both the 'moindre[s]' movements and the reflexive knowledge in question.

An allegorical structure based on movement, then, permeates the *Pensées*. Says the fragment headed 'Descartes', 'Il faut dire en gros: "Cela se fait par figure et mouvement", car cela est vrai' (this before it gets to its key qualification: 'Mais de dire quelles et composer la machine, cela est ridicule', L84/S118). Fragment S306/L275 reads 'et même la grâce n'est qu'une figure de la gloire'. As Pierre Force has noted, the 'n'est que' of this formulation in no sense impinges upon the significance of grace for Pascal: 'Il [Pascal] ne refuse à la grâce ni existence ni signification autonomes.'[32] But what it does mean is that there is a progression from the former to the latter. We read in a further letter from Blaise and Jacqueline Pascal to Gilberte that 'dans les bienheureux Dieu renouvelle continuellement leur béatitude, qui est un effet et une suite de la grâce'.[33] And this letter reinforces our understanding of the nature of the 'figure' Pascal is describing in S306/L275, for it shows that 'gloire' is a continual movement, a renewing and reworking, just as grace too is a movement:

> Ainsi la continuation de la justice des fidèles n'est autre chose que la continuation de l'infusion de la grâce, et non pas une seule grâce qui subsiste toujours; et c'est ce qui nous apprend parfaitement la dépendance perpétuelle où nous sommes de la miséricorde de Dieu [...] On ne peut conserver la grâce ancienne que par l'acquisition d'une nouvelle grâce. (p. 697)

It is not simply the case that grace figures glory; more accurately, the movements of grace figure the movements of glory. We can read also in this regard the letter of

1 April 1648, with its emphasis on verbs of movement, on the need for Christians to 'passer' and 'monter':

> C'est une erreur bien préjudiciable et bien ordinaire parmi les chrétiens et parmi ceux-là mêmes qui font profession de piété de se persuader qu'il y ait un certain degré de perfection dans lequel on soit en assurance et qu'il ne soit pas nécessaire de passer, puisqu'il n'y en a point qui ne soit mauvais si on s'y arrête, et dont on puisse éviter de tomber qu'en montant plus haut. (p. 583)

The allegorical chain identified in the two letters I have mentioned starts with 'l'ordre de créatures' (p. 583). It depends upon participation in, and movement within, this order: 'Il faut que *nous nous servions* du lieu même où nous sommes tombés pour nous relever de notre chute' (p. 582, my emphases). The incarnation brought Christ to this 'lieu même', a fact witnessed to in Scripture: certified and proven by tradition and by authority. Movements within this 'lieu', and the 'rapport' they bring with them — adding to tradition and authority, then — are a necessary precursor to the movements of grace. Until readers move in the world and engage with it experientially, they will be closed off, in their stationary, indifferent position, to the admission of faith, to the movements of God's grace, and thus to the movements of beatitude. The possibility of 'participation avec la divinité même' (S240/L208), the love of universal being, can be stimulated in this way by the experience of movement in, of a participatory 'rapport' with, the world around one.

The novelty of Pascal's persuasive strategy is signalled in fragment S789/L953:

> Il me prend envie de vous le montrer par une étrange supposition. Je dirai donc: 'Quand Dieu ne nous soutiendrait pas par une Providence particulière, pour le bien de l'Eglise, je veux vous montrer qu'en parlant même humainement nous ne pouvons périr'. Accordez-moi ce principe, et je vous prouverai tout.

This is proof through experiment, proof on a human level, through speaking 'humainement'. We cannot perish 'même parlant humainement' because the movements of human interrelationships (the stuff of life itself) can have a figurative import. The starting point for Pascal's strategy of persuasion, I have suggested, is that which is experienced on a human level: 'Accordez-moi ce principe, et je vous prouverai tout.'

One use of the term 'figure' in the *Pensées* relates to the notion, which we have touched upon briefly already, that the visible can 'figure' the invisible. This is the straightforwardly Pauline belief that God is present in the world, that 'les perfections invisibles de Dieu, sa puissance éternelle et sa divinité sont devenues visibles depuis la création du monde, par la connoissance que ses créatures nous en donnent'.[34] Fragment S306/L275 paraphrases such a belief: 'Dieu, voulant faire paraître qu'il pouvait former un peuple saint d'une sainteté invisible et le remplir d'une gloire éternelle, a fait des choses visibles.' But to acknowledge this is, as Pascal points out in his correspondence, to run the risk of idolatry.[35] Further limitations of the material 'figure' are clearly visible in the dialogic form of fragment S38/L3:

> 'Et quoi ne dites-vous pas vous-même que le ciel et les oiseaux prouvent Dieu?' Non. 'Et votre religion ne le dit-elle pas?' Non. Car encore que cela est vrai en un sens pour quelques âmes à qui Dieu donna cette lumière, néanmoins cela est faux à l'égard du plupart.

The belief that the visible can figure the invisible is useful only to shore up the faith of those who already believe: 'il est certain [que ceux] qui ont la foi voient incontinent que tout ce qui est n'est autre chose que l'ouvrage du Dieu qu'ils adorent' (S644/L781). Pascal posits this use of the figure in the *Pensées* only to reject it as a persuasive tool. When stigmatizing those contemporary apologists who limit their use of the 'figure' to making the externally visible universe an allegory of divine order, Pascal's dialectician calls on his own instructive experience: 'et je vois par raison et par expérience que rien n'est plus propre à [...] en faire naître le mépris' (S644/L781).

In a further manifestation of the 'figure' in the *Pensées*, the Old Testament or Law is the figure of the spiritual content of the New: 'Le Vieux Testament est un chiffre' (S307/L276); 'Saint Paul dit que les juifs ont peint les choses célestes' (S279/L247). The Jewish religion stands for the purely figurative: 'La religion des juifs a donc été formé sur la ressemblance de la vérité du Messie' (S667/L826).[36] The Old Testament prophets are the architects of the figurative: 'Leurs discours expriment très clairement la promesse des biens temporels et [...] ils disent néanmoins que leurs discours sont obscurs, et que leur sens ne sera pas entendu. D'où il paraît que ce sens secret n'était pas celui qu'ils exprimaient à découvert' (S737/L501). Further, the population of the Old Testament is aligned with that of the New: 'J.-C. figuré par Joseph' (S474/L570).

The way of interpreting Scripture whereby the events of the Old Testament are seen as having foreshadowed, according to God's plan of salvation, future realities, is known as typology, from the Greek 'tupoi', 'examples', 'figures'. It goes back to patristic exegesis, as Philippe Sellier notes in his work on Pascal and Augustine: 'Tous deux ont longuement développé leur réflexion sur les deux grands ordres de réalités qui peu à peu se transfigurent pour ceux qui croient: l'univers, d'une part, c'est-à-dire la nature physique, le cours des événements, les hommes; et d'autre part l'Ecriture sainte'.[37] The importance of typology for Augustine is signalled in Book v, Chapter 14 of the *Confessions*, when he listens to Ambrose explaining the Old Testament by virtue of the New:

> Après lui avoir vu expliquer selon le sens spirituel et allégorique plusieurs endroits de la vieille Loi, je commençai à condamner cette fausse créance que j'avais eue qu'il fût impossible de répondre à ceux qui font mille railleries, et vomissent mille blasphèmes contre la Loi et les Prophètes.[38]

Augustine turns in *De Trinitate* from a semiological understanding of allegory ('Qu'est-ce donc qu'une allégorie, sinon une trope où l'on donne à entendre une chose par une autre?') towards a typological distinction between *allegoria in verbis* and *allegoria in factis*:

> Lorsque l'Apôtre parle d'allégorie ce n'est pas à propos de mots, mais à propos d'un fait: dans les passages où il montre que les deux fils d'Abraham, celui de la servante et celui de la femme libre (ce ne sont pas là des paroles mais des faits) signifient les deux Testaments.[39]

Pierre Force is one critic who, arguing against the predominance of typology in Pascal's persuasive strategy, has successfully re-examined Pascal's use of the 'figure'. Force argues that Augustinian typology is disregarded by Pascal in favour of that lexical symbolism which takes as the raw material for allegory not facts but individual words:

> Pascal fait parfois appel au symbolisme des choses. Quand il dit que Noé et Joseph ont été la figure du Messie, il fait de l'exégèse typologique. Cependant, lorsque Pascal mentionne l'histoire et la loi, c'est le plus souvent à travers ce qu'en disent les prophètes'.[40]

By working 'à travers ce qu'en disent les prophètes', what Pascal effectively does — and this is the starting point for Force's study — is to 'propose des règles de lecture applicables à tout texte littéraire' (p. 22). These 'règles de lecture' are available to anyone, and so the unbelieving reader will be encouraged to get to grips with religious texts, and thus inevitably become susceptible to grace. This textual strategy is shown to have been influenced by Pascal's knowledge of Raymond Martini's *Pugio fidei* and of Origen.[41]

Force states that the necessity of the interpretative act within Pascal's persuasive strategy takes Pascal away from Augustinian exegesis. 'Le monde est silencieux,' he argues; 'seuls les textes parlent' (p. 112). It is only by placing the reader in a situation where Scripture is seen as textual material to be understood like any other that Pascal can cross the initial threshold of indifference and make the question of faith impose itself. Here, I suggest that Pascal does indeed expand upon Augustine's *allegoria in factis*, but he does so in order to subordinate this figuring of punctual facts or events to a kind of typology which takes trivial experiences and movements as its starting point. If the external is made the foundation for allegory in the *Pensées*, it is in the form of exposure to experience. This exposure can make the question of faith pertinent. Pascal assimilates to Augustinian typology a form of allegory which takes as its raw material the experience that his reader is necessarily embarked upon.

This all lends a new emphasis to Pascal's comment on 'repos': 'le repos entier est la mort' (S529bis/L641). A lack of movement, or in other words a lack of 'expérience', precludes progression into further levels of experience. This kind of figuring takes as its foundation an 'expérience' which, in Pascal's text, and thanks to an imposing applicability to the reader, does not disintegrate into discursivity. 'La figure a été faite sur la vérité. Et la vérité a été reconnue sur la figure' (L826/S667). Pascal starts with movement, with the experiential, knowing that he is giving a pragmatic slant to his own work, as it addresses the unbeliever, making it diverge from proofs which rely on 'l'autorité seule'; and so he meshes text and extra-discursive experience, making belief itself, in the end, overlap with domains in which 'la preuve consiste en expériences et non en démonstrations'.[42]

The cluster of terms — 'sublime', 'connaissance', 'expérience', 'rapport', 'mouvement' — which has provided the raw material for this study gives us an understanding of the *Pensées* which makes individual 'expérience', as a trivial, present, and immediate level of movement and engagement, epistemologically beneficial. Thus it is that Pascal's speaker can state to his reader that 'c'est à vous de commencer' (S659/L816). Pascal goes some way towards mitigating, in the *Pensées*, the notion that the knowledge obtainable by humankind is entirely ambiguous and unreliable. Indeed, we read in fragment S579/L701, largely neglected in critical studies of

Pascal, that 'les appréhensions des sens sont toujours vraies'. This fragment does not so much attribute absolute fidelity to the senses as state simply that the fact of sensory apprehension is beyond doubt. A passage from the eighteenth *Lettre provinciale* needs to be understood similarly:

> Et, comme Dieu a voulu se servir de l'entremise des sens pour donner entrée à la foi, *fides ex auditu*, tant s'en faut que la foi détruise la certitude des sens, que ce serait au contraire détruire la foi que de vouloir révoquer en doute le rapport fidèle des sens.[43]

We unfailingly have a 'rapport' to the world around us; inasmuch as this is the case, the 'rapport' is 'fidèle'. The 'rapport fidèle des sens' is engaged in a 'rapport à tout ce qu'il connaît', in a 'd'où vient qu'il a besoin d'air', in a 'par où [l'air] a ce rapport à la vie de l'homme, etc.' (S230/L199). Seen thus, Pascal's argument cannot be reduced to the statement that all knowledge which comes through the senses is faulty. Pascal inveigles the external into a persuasive policy of interpretation in which exposure to experience can be instructive. Exposure, figuring its own enquiring integration into experience, can also figure the enquiry which will interpose the question of faith into 'la vie ordinaire': 'La vie ordinaire des hommes est semblable à celle des saints' (S306/L275). Pascal places the 'certitude, certitude' of the 'mémorial' within the reach of all: 'La seule religion chrétienne est proportionnée à tous, étant mêlée d'extérieur et d'intérieur' (S252/L219).

We have seen, then, that Pascal seeks to convey an unsayable knowledge and love of the divine and, in the course of his attempt, weaves a fascinating web around the terms of human interaction. The *Pensées*, like *Peri hypsous*, interrogate certainty by investigating how 'expérience' and encounter, inserted into text, might provide a means of lighting upon it. Writing that 'deux choses instruisent l'homme de toute sa nature: l'instinct et l'expérience' (S161/L128), Pascal plays on the different experimental/experiential strata of the latter term. The variegations of 'expérience', and experiential knowledge, can be used persuasively.

'Je ne demande pas de vous une créance aveugle', is the voice of God in the prosopopeia of fragment S182/L149. Pascal redefines the standardly Augustinian parameters of Christian scepticism discussed in the last chapter — the dislocation of 'raison' in order to open the reader up to a kind of knowledge that will come through the 'cœur' — and modifies these parameters with available 'expérience'. In this, it is not just his relationship to Descartes which can be scrutinized to instructive effect, but further his relationship to Montaigne. This will be the starting point for my next chapter.

Notes to Chapter 6

1. Leo Bersani, *The Culture of Redemption* (Cambridge, MA: Harvard University Press, 1990), p. 11.
2. Sara E. Melzer, *Discourses of the Fall: A Study of Pascal's 'Pensées'* (Berkeley: University of California Press, 1986), Chapter 2 ('The Fall from Truth into Language') and p. 149, n. 11; Richard Lockwood, *The Reader's Figure: Epideictic Rhetoric in Plato, Aristotle, Bossuet, Racine and Pascal* (Geneva: Droz, 1996), p. 278.
3. For a reading of this parable, see J. Deprun, 'La Parabole de la seconde *Provinciale*', in *Méthodes chez Pascal: actes du colloque tenu à Clermont-Ferrand, 10–13 juin 1976* (Paris: Presses universitaires de France, 1979), pp. 241–52.

4. *Le Dictionnaire universel d'Antoine Furetière* (The Hague: Arnout & Reinier Leers, 1690). See also Richelet's definitions: 'Experience, s.f. [usus, experientia]: Action de la personne qui experimente, qui eprouve & essaie' and 'Experimenter, v.a. [experiri, tintare, facere periculum]: Eprouver: essaier: faire experience (Il faut experimenter cela)'. *Le Nouveau Dictionnaire françois de Pierre Richelet* (Lyons: Jean-Baptiste Girin, 1719).

5. *Dictionnaire de l'Académie française* (Paris: Jean-Baptiste Coignard, 1694). Much will be made of this by Montaigne, who will be discussed in the next chapter; for Montaigne drawing upon the meaning of *essai*, see in particular Richard Scholar, *The Je-Ne-Sais-Quoi in Early Modern Europe: Encounters with a Certain Something* (Oxford: Oxford University Press, 2005), pp. 256–57.

6. 'EXPÉRIENCE n. f. est un emprunt (v. 1265) au latin *experientia* "épreuve, essai, tentative" et "expérience acquise, pratique", dérivé de *experiri* "faire l'essai de" (→ expert). Le verbe est formé de *ex-* et de *peritus* "qui a l'expérience de, habile à", participe passé d'un verbe *periri* non attesté. *Periri* est sans doute en rapport avec le grec *peira* "expérience" (→ empirique) et se rattache à l'importante racine indoeuropéenne *per-* "aller de l'avant, pénétrer dans" (→ péril, pirate, pore, port).' *Dictionnaire historique de la langue française,* ed. by Alain Rey (Paris: Le Robert, 1993).

7. 'Du Cœur', 8, in Jean de La Bruyère, *Les Caractères ou les mœurs de ce siècle,* ed. by Robert Pignarre (Paris: Garnier-Flammarion, 1965).

8. See Nicholas Hammond, *Playing with Truth: Language and the Human Condition in Pascal's 'Pensées'* (Oxford: Oxford University Press, 1994), pp. 8–10, on the appellation 'dialectician' and its appropriateness for Pascal's speaker.

9. *Principes de la philosophie,* Part II, Article 1, in René Descartes, *Œuvres philosophiques,* ed. by F. Alquié, 3 vols (Paris: Garnier, 1988–89), III, 147. Fragment S445/L887 also pairs the adjectives 'inutile et incertain' in relation to Descartes.

10. Descartes, as the title of the *Meditationes* itself indicates clearly enough, does not neglect God altogether. As Michel Le Guern notes, Descartes 'cherche lui aussi à délimiter les domaines de la théologie et de la philosophie' (*Pascal et Descartes* (Paris: Nizet, 1971), p. 160). But the use that Descartes makes of the divine, his relegation of God to the status of a principle which undergoes subsequent subordination to a philosophical argument, incurs Pascal's disdain, as in the account given by Marguerite Périer: 'Il ne pouvait souffrir un de ses principes sur la formation de toutes choses et il disait très souvent: "Je ne puis pardonner à Descartes; il voudrait bien, dans toute sa philosophie, se pouvoir passer de Dieu, mais il n'a pas pu s'empêcher de lui faire donner une chiquenaude pour mettre le monde en mouvement; après cela il n'a plus que faire de Dieu."' 'Mémoire sur Pascal et sa famille', in *Œuvres complètes,* ed. by Jean Mesnard, 7 vols (Paris: Desclée de Brouwer, 1964–), I, 1090–1105 (p. 1105). It should be noted that a seventeenth-century 'philosophie' encompasses the sphere of the sciences as well as what we would call philosophy today.

11. Philippe Sellier, *Pascal et saint Augustin* (Paris: Albin Michel, 1995), p. 46. For an article on the Augustinian distinction between 'la foi' and 'l'intelligence', see M. R. Gagnebet, 'La Théologie augustinienne type de théologie affective', *Revue Thomiste,* 44.1 (1938), 3–39.

12. Stephen C. Bold, *Pascal Geometer: Discovery and Invention in Seventeenth-Century France* (Geneva: Droz, 1996), p. 113.

13. Nicholas Hammond, 'Pascal and "Descartes inutile et incertain"', *Seventeenth-Century French Studies,* 16 (1994), 59–63 (p. 63).

14. *Préface sur le Traité du vide,* in *Œuvres complètes,* ed. by Mesnard, II (1970), 777–85 (p. 779).

15. When Peter Dear writes that Pascal's 'expériences' (which he translates as 'experiences') are 'universal statements about how things happen in the world, suitable for Pascal's subsequent use of them in deriving other universal statements about nature', it is important to nuance this with Pascal's statement that 'dans toutes les matières dont la preuve consiste en expériences et non en démonstrations, on ne peut faire aucune assertion universelle que par la générale énumération de toutes les parties ou de tous les cas différents. C'est ainsi que, quand nous disons que le diamant est le plus dur de tous les corps, nous entendons de tous les corps que nous connaissons' (p. 784). Universal statements stemming from 'expérience' are always subject to alteration. Peter Dear, *Discipline and Experience: The Mathematical Way in the Scientific Revolution* (Chicago: University of Chicago Press, 1995), p. 181. The distinction Dear makes between 'maxim' and 'experience' on p. 187 is important here.

16. *Œuvres complètes,* ed. by Mesnard, III (1991), 360–428 (p. 380).

17. See also Mesnard's note comparing Pascal to Bacon and Auzoult: 'Plus particulière à Pascal l'affirmation que le progrès de l'humanité dans l'acquisition du savoir tient à la multiplication des expériences, mais, si cette affirmation est étrangère à Descartes, plus soucieux de métaphysique, elle rejoint la position de Bacon et s'accorde avec des vues exprimées à la même époque par Auzoult' (*Œuvres complètes*, ed. by Mesnard, II, 774–75).

18. For a detailed account of this and other experiments, see Dominique Descotes, *L'Argumentation chez Pascal* (Paris: Presses universitaires de France, 1993), pp. 267–88. In fact, there is a certain amount of debate about whether Pascal or Descartes first construed the experiment which took place on the Puy de Dôme. On three occasions, surviving letters written by Descartes claim that he was the source of the idea which was only then acted upon by Pascal. See two letters to M. de Carcavy (*Œuvres complètes*, ed. by Mesnard, II, 717, 719) and one to Mersenne (ibid., II, 548–56). The doubt that ensues from this correspondence does not detract from Pascal's emphasis on the importance of experiment, which I shall focus on here. Mesnard writes: 'On ne saurait déposséder Pascal d'un mérite qui ne saurait être sousestimé, celui d'être passé de l'idée à l'acte' (ibid., II, 658). And as Christian Licoppe notes, 'Pascal revendique bien la singularité et la propriété de ces expériences qu'il estime "avoir fait [...] avec beaucoup de frais, de peine et de temps".' *La Formation de la pratique scientifique: le discours de l'expérience en France et en Angleterre (1630–1820)* (Paris: Éditions de la découverte, 1996), p. 22.

19. *Lettre à Monsieur Pascal, à Paris*, in *Œuvres complètes*, ed. by Mesnard, II, 513–18 (p. 513).

20. *Lettre de Pascal à Le Pailleur*, ibid., 556–76 (p. 572).

21. See Article 19 of the *Principes*: 'la nature de la substance matérielle ou du corps ne consiste qu'en ce qu'il est quelque chose d'étendu'. This 'extension' is also proper, states Descartes, to an 'espace vide'. An 'espace vide', in other words, also has the property of taking up space. Thus 'pour ce qui est du vide, au sens que les philosophes prennent ce mot, à savoir, pour un espace où il n'y a point de substance, il est évident qu'il n'y a point d'espace en l'univers qui soit tel, parce que l'extension de l'espace ou du lieu intérieur n'est point différente de l'extension du corps' (Article 16). *Principes de la philosophie*, in Descartes, *Œuvres philosophiques*, III, 165, 161. It is often assumed that this stance shares a common ground with the dictum that 'nature abhors a vacuum', but this is disputable. See Desmond M. Clarke: 'Whilst he [Descartes] agreed with Pascal and Noël that it is the weight of the air, rather than the fear of a vacuum, that supports the column of mercury in a Torricelli tube, he still wished to claim that the apparently empty space at the top of the tube was filled with subtle matter.' 'Pascal's Philosophy of Science', in *The Cambridge Companion to Pascal*, ed. by Nicholas Hammond (Cambridge: Cambridge University Press, 2003), pp. 102–21 (p. 102).

22. *Expériences nouvelles touchant le vide*, in *Œuvres complètes*, ed. by Mesnard, II, 498–508 (p. 498).

23. 'Pascal's Philosophy of Science', p. 115. On the *Traité de la pesanteur de la masse de l'air*, Clarke writes: '[Pascal] claims that, if the experiment works (i.e., if a balloon filled with air inflates as it is moved up a mountain), that confirms his theory. But if it fails to inflate, that must be due to some defect in the experiment!' (p. 115). Nowhere in Pascal, as Clarke notes (pp. 109, 115), do we find the notion that scientific theories are only ever merely probable; nor, as Peter Dear states, do we find the notion that Pascal's accounts of his own experiments might be less than convincing (*Discipline and Experience*, p. 185).

24. 'Extrait des *Opuscules posthumes* de Menjot', in *Œuvres complètes*, ed. by Mesnard, I, 831.

25. Périer, 'Mémoire sur Pascal et sa famille', p. 1105.

26. 'De l'art de persuader', p. 426. This is the kind of experience which 'nous fait voir une différence énorme entre la dévotion et la bonté' (S397/L365), and which is attributed to Solomon and to Job in fragment S22/L403: 'Salomon et Job ont le mieux connu et le mieux porté de la misère de l'homme, l'un le plus heureux et l'autre le plus malheureux. L'un connaissant la vanité des plaisirs par expérience, l'autre la réalité des maux.'

27. Corneille, *Le Cid*, Act II, scene 2, line 434, in *Œuvres complètes*, ed. by André Stegmann (Paris: Éditions du Seuil, 1963).

28. Montaigne, *De l'utile et de l'honnête*, in *Essais*, ed. by P. Villey, 2nd edn (Paris: Presses universitaires de France, 1965), III. 1, p. 801.

29. '*Justus ex fide vivit* et *fides ex auditu*: deux aspects de la foi dans l'apologétique pascalienne', in *Pascal: l'exercice de l'esprit*, ed. by Christian Meurillon (= *Revue des sciences humaines*, no. 244 (December 1996)), pp. 159–78 (p. 165).

30. See, for the most recent discussion of these false, friable social relationships, Michael Moriarty, *Early Modern French Thought: The Age of Suspicion* (Oxford: Oxford University Press, 2003). As Moriarty makes clear, our 'true' immaterial substance or soul or 'metaphysical' being is never the being we display in our relationships with others; but to say this does not diminish the trivial fact of the relationship, or its potential usefulness in betraying (through the questioning the relationship engenders: 'd'où vient'?) the limitations and neediness of our material beings.

31. *Lettre de Blaise et Jacqueline Pascal à leur sœur Gilberte.* Mesnard notes that 'écrite de la main de Jacqueline Pascal, selon le P. Guerrier qui en vit l'original, cette lettre est rédigée au nom du frère et de la sœur. Pourtant, lorsqu'est employée la première personne du singulier, l'accord du participe montre que c'est le frère qui parle.' *Œuvres complètes*, ed. by Mesnard, II, 580.

32. Pierre Force, *Le Problème herméneutique chez Pascal* (Paris: Vrin, 1989), p. 90. Force's comments follow on from those of Jeanne Russier, in her commentary upon fragment L501 'l'Ancien Testament n'est que figuratif': 'des expressions renfermant le fameux *que* pour traduire des textes latins ne contenant aucune formule d'exclusion'. *La Foi selon Pascal* (Paris: Presses universitaires de France, 1949), p. 391, quoted in Force, p. 90.

33. 5 November 1648, *Œuvres complètes*, ed. by Mesnard, II, 696.

34. Romans 1. 20, in the translation of Sacy: *La Sainte Bible, traduite en français par Lemaistre de Sacy*, ed. by l'Abbé Jacquet (Paris: Garnier, [n.d.]).

35. See the First Epistle of St John: 'N'aimez ni le monde, ni rien de ce qui est dans le monde. Si quelqu'un aime le monde, l'amour du Père n'est point en lui | Car tout ce qui est dans le monde est ou concupiscence de la chair, ou concupiscence des yeux, ou orgueil de la vie; ce qui ne vient pas du Père, mais du monde. | Or le monde passe, et la concupiscence du monde passe avec lui; mais celui qui fait la volonté de Dieu, demeure éternellement' (1 John 2. 15–17, in the translation of Sacy). See also Pascal's letter of 1 April 1648: 'Quelque ressemblance que la nature créée ait avec son Créateur, et encore que les moindres choses et les plus petites et les plus viles parties du monde représentent au moins par leur unité la parfaite unité qui ne se trouve qu'en Dieu, on ne peut pas légitimement leur porter le souverain respect, parce qu'il n'y a rien de si abominable aux yeux de Dieu et des hommes que l'idolâtrie, à cause qu'on y rend à la créature l'honneur qui n'est dû qu'au Créateur', in *Œuvres complètes*, ed. by Mesnard, II, 580–83 (pp. 582–83).

36. In his letter of 1 April 1648, Pascal refers to 'cet aveuglement charnel et judaïque qui fait prendre la figure pour la réalité' (*Œuvres complètes*, ed. by Mesnard, II, 538).

37. *Pascal et saint Augustin*, p. 361.

38. *Confessions*, trans. by Arnauld d'Andilly, ed. by Philippe Sellier (Paris: Gallimard, 1993), Book V, Chapter 14, p. 178. The hostile critics in question are the Manichees.

39. *De Trinitate*, trans. by Paul Agaësse, in *Œuvres de saint Augustin*, XV–XVI (Paris: Études augustiniennes, 1991), XV. 9. 15. The biblical passage in question is Galatians 4. 22. See also the case put forward for the typological interpretation of Scripture in *De Doctrina christiana*. For an example of Jansenist typological exegesis, see Sacy, *La Genèse traduite en françois, avec l'explication du sens litteral & du sens spirituel, tirée des saint Peres et des Auteurs ecclesiastiques*, new edn (Paris: Guillaume Desprez and Jean Desessatz, 1725).

40. Force, *Le Problème herméneutique*, p. 103.

41. The *Pugio fidei*, a thirteenth-century text by Raymond Martini, reveals rabbinical exegesis to consist in reconciling the contradictions of Scripture. Origen's 'geste fondateur' for Christian exegesis is that he, comparably, 'tire de l'Ecriture même le principe de son interprétation' (*Le Problème herméneutique*, p. 284); Pascal, writing of the 'preuve par l'Ecriture même', of the 'preuve des deux Testaments à la fois' (S305/L274), of the need to read 'tous ces passages ensemble' (S290/L259), 'répète à sa façon le geste fondateur d'Origène' (p. 284); he also thereby offers a Christian reinterpretation of Jewish hermeneutics as set out in the *Pugio fidei*. Pascal distances himself from Augustine in this regard; he is 'paradoxalement plus proche d'Origène et de certains exégètes de la Renaissance que de saint Augustin' (p. 62).

42. *Préface sur le Traité du vide*, p. 784. As we saw earlier, in matters of theology, 'C'est l'autorité seule qui nous en peut éclaircir [...] Elle y est inséparable de la vérité [...] Nous la connaissons que par elle' (p. 778).

43. *Œuvres complètes*, ed. by Lafuma, p. 467.

CHAPTER 7

❖

Embodiments of Experience:
Montaigne and Augustine

Beyond critical analyses of the discursive fragmentation in the *Pensées*,[1] I have suggested that, by splintering his authorial utterances as he does, splaying them into the voices of different personae, Pascal also comprehends — in a move I have described as Longinian — differing levels or modes of experience. The text of the *Pensées* enacts the conceptual slide between varying stages of knowledge which is inherent to the concept of 'expérience'. This reading has offered a new understanding of the way in which the certainties of a 'participation avec la divinité même' (S240/L208) can be conveyed by Pascal. I have, therefore, sought to re-examine the persuasive structures of Pascal's text, attempting in so doing to move away from a simplistic opposition of faith and reason. What I want to develop in this chapter, since it is important to this understanding of Pascal, is the idea that Pascal's emphasis on 'expérience' troubles accepted accounts of influence. Montaigne in the *Essais* and Augustine in the *Confessions* can each offer new insights for Pascal studies if they are seen to embody the kind of engagement with experience which the *Pensées* demand.

The *Entretien de Pascal et Sacy* and the Use of Montaigne

If Montaigne is seen as useful to Pascal, it is generally because the *Apologie de Raymond Sebond* delineates doubt. This doubt, aiming to 'froisser et fouler aux pieds l'orgueil et l'humaine fierté', can, as I mentioned in Chapter 5 when discussing the role of uncertainty in broadly Augustinian thought, be seen to militate against a human arrogance.[2] It can be deemed to be 'une étape provisoire mais nécessaire pour convertir le libertin'.[3] It is the *Entretien* between Pascal and Isaac Le Maistre de Sacy, his 'directeur de conscience', which is seen as most revelatory in this regard:

> It is in the *Entretien avec M. de Sacy* that we see most clearly the influence of Montaigne on the notion of interpretation in the *Pensées*. Although the excessive doubt and uncertainty, which 'roule sur elle-même dans un cercle perpetuel et sans repos', are perceived ultimately to be self-defeating, the way in which Montaigne 'se moque de toutes les assurances' helps to avoid complacency about the powers of the human mind.[4]

In Pascal's presentation, Montaigne 'combat avec une fermeté invincible les hérétiques de son temps, sur ce qu'ils s'assuraient de connaître seuls le véritable sens de l'Ecriture, et c'est de là encore qu'il foudroie plus vigoureusement l'impiété horrible de ceux qui osent assurer que Dieu n'est point' (p. 602). The currency of uncertainty can be exchanged specifically for a Christian humility, for an awareness of one's own inadequacies and a concomitant sense of piety. Pascal's contemporaries are, however, less ready to see in Montaigne a figure who embodies this utility.

Sacy, faced in the *Entretien* with a Montaigne who 'détruit insensiblement tout ce qui passe pour le plus certain parmi les hommes', who 'se moque de toutes les assurances', responds by demanding 'à quoi sert un bien, quand on en use si mal?' (p. 602). Montaigne is dismissed by Sacy because, even if the end product of his doubt is a humiliation of self, his overall goal is not purposefully Christian. Sacy's theological training has encouraged him to apply in his teaching a paradigm which Montaigne ignores:

> Vous pouvez juger qu'ayant passé ma vie comme j'ai fait, on m'a peu conseillé de lire cet auteur, dont tous les ouvrages n'ont rien de ce que nous devons principalement rechercher dans nos lectures, selon la règle de saint Augustin, parce que ses paroles ne paraissent pas sortir d'un grand fonds d'humilité et de piété. (p. 606)

Sacy administers Augustine's dictum concerning those who lead their lives without recourse to faith: 'Il met dans tout ce qu'il dit la foi à part; ainsi nous, qui avons la foi, devons de même mettre à part tout ce qu'il dit' (p. 606).

Sacy's dismissive discourse finds an echo in Arnauld and Nicole's 1662 *La Logique ou l'art de penser*. From their *Premier discours*, Arnauld and Nicole denounce the doubt of a scepticism not specifically oriented towards Christianity as no more morally valuable than its counterpart, dogmatism. If dogmatism is the tyrannical discourse of those who believe themselves capable of decision-making and dictatorship without submission to the divine, then scepticism is no less brazenly self-sufficient. Thus 'le pyrrhonisme' is 'une extravagance de l'esprit humain, qui, paraissant contraire à la témérité de ceux qui croient et qui décident tout, vient néanmoins de la même source, qui est le défaut d'attention'.[5]

This lack of attention (the opposite of a conscious self-humiliation before God) is precisely what engendered Sacy's criticism of Montaigne in the *Entretien*. In the *Logique*, it is carried over into the extended discussion which follows: 'Car, comme les uns [dogmatists] ne veulent pas se donner la peine de discerner les erreurs, les autres [sceptics] ne veulent pas prendre celle d'envisager la vérité avec le soin nécessaire pour en apercevoir l'évidence' (p. 12). Throughout *La Logique*, indeed, the vocabulary that Arnauld and Nicole employ in relation to scepticism is one of intellectual idleness, an unwillingness to 'se donner la peine de discerner', a 'défaut d'application': 'La moindre lueur suffit aux uns pour les persuader de choses très-fausses, et elle suffit aux autres pour les faire douter des choses les plus certaines: mais, dans les uns et dans les autres, c'est le même défaut d'application qui produit des effets si différents' (p. 12). For Arnauld and Nicole too, the sceptics (and especially Montaigne) fail to apply their own theory in a useful and productive way: 'Ces personnes [those like Montaigne] qui mettent leur plaisir à douter de tout, empêchent leur esprit de s'appliquer à ce qui pourrait les persuader, ou ne s'y appliquent qu'imparfaitement, et ils tombent par là dans une incertitude volontaire à l'égard des choses de la Religion' (p. 13). In order to justify themselves, the interrogatory structures of scepticism need to draw a deliberate contrast between their own human uncertainties and the resolution of doubt with the divine. As it is, the self-sufficiency discerned on the part of the sceptics in general, and of Montaigne in particular, is a lack of application and an ignorance of or indifference to 'les choses de la Religion'. Montaigne's *Essais* are fabricated out of 'paroles horribles, et qui marquent une extinction entière de tout sentiment de la religion' (p. 252).[6]

Like that of Sacy in the *Entretien*, Arnauld and Nicole's discourse on scepticism is Augustinian in origin. They understand scepticism only as they understand Augustine to have done so: as a threshold to be crossed on the path to belief. As we know from the *Confessions*, Augustine escaped the doctrine of Manichaeism, a religion which derided the inconsistencies and crudities of the Bible, only after coming into contact with the overarching doubt of academic scepticism.[7] The role played by the Academics in the mechanics of Augustine's conversion is defined at the end of Book v of the *Confessions*:

> Aussi selon la coutume des Académiciens (au moins comme on explique d'ordinaire leurs sentiments), doutant de tout sans pouvoir me déterminer à rien, je résolus d'abandonner les Manichéens. Car dans l'incertitude où j'étais, je ne croyais pas devoir demeurer dans une secte dont la doctrine me paraissait moins probable que celle de beaucoup de Philosophes, auxquels néanmoins j'étais très éloigné d'avoir recours pour trouver la guérison de mon âme, ne rencontrant parmi eux aucune trace du nom et de la connaissance salutaire de Jésus-Christ. Je résolus donc enfin de demeurer Catéchumène dans l'Eglise Catholique que mon père et ma mère m'avaient tant recommandée, jusqu'à ce qu'il me parût quelque chose de plus certain que je puisse suivre, et qui pût me régler dans la conduite de ma vie. (v. 14, 179)

Scepticism is a hesitation, a pause, a heightened awareness of doubt which can be superficially useful in catalysing a turn away from false dogma, but which can be truly useful only when applied or transposed into the religious domain to indicate that only God provides the certainty that is lacking.[8] What the *Confessions* make clear is the temporal progression of Augustine's scepticism: doubt is succeeded by certainty. Nevertheless, the hesitation or pause itself is railed against in the *Confessions* ('je différais de jour en jour, ô mon Seigneur et mon Dieu, de me convertir et de vivre en vous, et ne différais un seul jour de mourir en moi', vi. 11, 208), and is thought sacrilegious enough in its own right to provoke the *Contra Academicos*: 'Avant même mon baptême, j'ai commencé par écrire un ouvrage contre les Académiciens ou sur les Académiciens, afin d'écarter de mon esprit par toutes les raisons possibles, car ils m'impressionnaient aussi, leurs arguments, qui insinuent dans de nombreux esprits le désespoir de trouver le vrai.'[9]

Foreign to Augustine here is a distinction between different schools of scepticism and different structures of doubt. All scepticism is seen as 'le désespoir de trouver le vrai'. Sextus Empiricus, however, whose *Outlines of Pyrrhonism* provides us with the only primary sources of the philosophy of Pyrrho, makes a tripartite distinction between those philosophers who make positive assertions (the dogmatists, stating 'I know'), those who make negative assertions (the Academics, stating 'I do not know'), and those who refuse to make any assertions at all, on the grounds that, while still enquiring, they do not have the capacity to do so. These philosophers, who do not despair of truth but merely suspend it, are the Pyrrhonists.[10] Jean-Paul Dumont notes that 'si saint Augustin n'avait pas eu pour le grec l'horreur qu'il avoue si souvent, il aurait pu, avec Sextus Empiricus, maintenir une distinction entre l'académie pour qui tout échappe à la compréhension et les Sceptiques qui poursuivent la recherche'.[11]

The Port-Royal thinkers cited follow Augustine in this regard. They, as we have seen, assume that scepticism excludes truth utterly, in its 'négligence à se rendre attentif autant qu'il faut pour discerner la vérité'.[12] Doubt, for them, is straightforward, unqualified. What is overlooked in their assimilation of Pyrrhonism to Academic scepticism is the fact that Montaigne does not himself espouse an unqualified doubt. Rather, and as I shall explain, he qualifies doubt with the certainties of experience. Pascal will be seen both to show and to use his awareness of this. The usefulness Pascal perceives in Montaigne does not just stem, therefore, from structures of doubt, but rather from structures of experience.

Montaigne's 'Fantasies'

Montaigne is careful to make the same tripartite distinction between different schools of philosophy as Sextus Empiricus, going so far as to paraphrase, in the *Apologie de Raimond Sebond*, the passage from Sextus cited earlier:

> Quiconque cherche quelque chose, il en vient à ce point: ou qu'il dit qu'il l'a trouvée, ou qu'elle ne se peut trouver, ou qu'il en est encore en queste. Toute la philosophie est departie en ces trois genres. Aristoteles, Epicurus, les Stoiciens et autres ont pensé l'avoir trouvé [...]. Clitomachus, Carneades et les Academiciens ont desesperé de leur queste, et jugé que la verité ne se pouvoit concevoir par nos moyens [...]. Pyrrho et autres Skeptiques ou Epechistes disent qu'ils sont encore en cherche de la vérité. Ceux-cy jugent que ceux qui pensent l'avoir trouvée, se trompent infiniment; et qu'il y a encore de la vanité trop hardie en second degré qui asseure que les forces humaines ne sont pas capables d'y atteindre. (II. 12, 502)

He reformulates his position in 'Des boyteux': 'La fierté de ceux qui attribuoyent à l'esprit humain la capacité de toutes choses causa en d'autres, par despit et par emulation, cette opinion qu'il n'est capable d'aucune chose. Les uns tiennent en ignorance cette mesme extremité que les autres tiennent en science' (III. 11, 1035). It is the movement, the asking, which is important for Montaigne, not just the static confrontation of dogmatism and doubt. Montaigne's identification is thus with the Pyrrhonists rather than the Academics. But there is an expansion to be perceived also: 'Je voy les philosophes Pyrrhoniens qui ne peuvent exprimer leur generale conception en aucune maniere de parler: car il leur faudrait un nouveau langage' (II. 12, 527). Montaigne identifies with Pyrrhonism, in fact, only when he redefines its structures, which he states to be 'plus seurement conceuë par interrogation: Que sçay-je? Comme je la porte à la devise d'une balance'.[13]

Montaigne thus applies himself to his doubt, and persistently asks himself to examine his own level of and desire for knowledge. While his appraisal of his own, human, capacity for truth is condemnatory — 'Moy qui m'espie de plus prez

[...] à peine oseray-je dire la vanité et la foiblesse que je trouve chez moy' (II. 12, 565) — it starts and finishes with his own enquiring act of enunciation, positive in its dynamism.[14] In 'Des livres', Montaigne writes: 'Ce sont icy mes fantasies, par lesquelles je ne tasche point à donner à connaistre les choses, mais moy [...]. Aussi je ne pleuvy aucune certitude, si ce n'est de faire connoistre jusques à quel poinct monte, pour cette heure, la connoissance que j'en ay' (II. 10, 407–08). The 'nouveau langage' of Montaigne's Pyrrhonism is a language of the present tense — a language 'pour cette heure' — a language of affective immediacy, of simultaneities and coexistences. If Pyrrho, seeking to display a commitment to immediacy, 'a voulu se faire homme vivant, discourant et raisonnant, jouissant de tous plaisirs et commoditez naturelles' (II. 12, 505), Montaigne makes both pleasure and certainty a function of his own, individual, 'fantasie'.

This rewriting of Pyrrhonism to take account of 'fantasie' is of vital importance both to our understanding of Montaigne and, I want to argue here, to our understanding of Pascal's later appropriation of his work. What it implies is the impossibility of that balanced weighing up of different options upon which the Pyrrhonism of Sextus Empiricus's *Outlines* depends. Sextus's definition of 'What Scepticism Is' reads as follows:

> Scepticism is an ability, or mental attitude, which opposes appearances to judgements in any way whatsoever, with the result that, owing to the equipollence of the objects and the reasons thus opposed, we are brought firstly to a state of mental suspense [epochē] and next to a state of 'unperturbedness' or quietude [ataraxia]. (*Outlines of Pyrrhonism*, I.8, p. 7)

But in Montaigne, balance gives way to flux. The self-identity of ataraxia is never attained, as Montaigne cannot sidestep the force of his individual 'fantasie', cannot even contemplate a 'state of mental suspense':

> Maintes fois (comme il m'advient de faire volontiers) ayant pris pour exercice et pour esbat à maintenir une contraire opinion à la mienne, mon esprit, s'appliquant et tournant de ce costé là, m'y attache si bien que je ne trouve plus raison de mon premier advis et m'en despars. Je m'entraine quasi où je penche, comment que ce soit, et m'emporte de mon pois. (II. 12, 566)

What Sextus precludes when he writes of 'epochē' is this fierce embodiment of a point of view ('je m'entraine quasi où je penche'). What makes his 'equipollence' (from 'pollere', to be strong) impossible for Montaigne is the sheer weight of the latter's 'fantasie' as it swings from one stance to another: 'Je [...] m'emporte de mon pois.'

It is, then, Montaigne's 'fantasie' which differentiates him radically from the Greek sceptics. It necessitates the following critique:

> Ils [les Pyrrhoniens] debattent d'une bien molle façon. Ils ne craignent point la revenche à leur dispute. Quand ils disent que le poisant va contre bas, ils seroient bien marris qu'on les en creut; et cherchent qu'on les contredie, pour engendrer la dubitation et surceance de jugement, qui est leur fin. Ils ne mettent pas en avant leurs propositions que pour combattre celles que nous ayons en nostre creance. Si vous prenez la leur, ils prendront *aussi volontiers* la contraire à soustenir: tout leur est un; ils *n'y ont aucun choix*. (II. 12, 503, my emphases)

Individual 'fantasie' has, according to Montaigne here, absolutely no role to play in the elaboration of Pyrrhonism. It is this that necessitates Montaigne's condemnatory and distancing formulation, his refusal to assimilate his own voice to theirs, his insistence that 'il leur faudrait un nouveau langage' (II. 12, 527), which is prepared in the 'Apologie' with the obsessive repetition of the pronoun 'leur': 'Or cette assiette de leur jugement, droicte et inflexible, recevant tous objects sans application et consentement, les achemine à leur Ataraxie' (II. 12, 503). What we find in Montaigne is precisely an all-embracing 'application', an unruly and unpredictable 'consentement':

> Ce que je tiens aujourd'huy et ce que je croy, je le tiens et le croy de toute ma croyance; tous mes utils et tous mes ressorts empoignent cette opinion et m'en respondent sur tout ce qu'ils peuvent. Je ne sçaurois embrasser aucune verité ni conserver avec plus de force que je ne fay cette-ci. J'y suis tout entier, j'y suis voyrement. (II. 12, 563)

Montaigne embodies, in the most vigorous terms, a form of 'croyance'. In this passage, Montaigne's 'croyance' is secular: its object is 'ce que je tiens aujourd'huy'. But what is of interest is the degree of engagement it divulges. Montaigne puts forward in his *Essais* a form of scepticism which could not possibly be accused of indifference, of having 'pas plus de penchant pour une chose que pour une autre, pour un parti que pour une autre', of refusing to be moved.[15] Montaigne is moved by whatever he encounters: his 'fantasies humaines et miennes' are 'non comme arrestées et matiere d'opinion'; they are, fundamentally, 'instruisables non instruisants' (I. 56, 323).

It follows from this analysis that when Pascal writes of 'les braves pyrrhoniens et leur ataraxie, doute et suspension perpetuelle' (S111/L76), he is following Montaigne's repetition of the pronoun 'leur' in relation to the Pyrrhonists. He is not, in other words, targeting Montaigne, but citing him. Correspondingly, we cannot assume that those fragments written against the Pyrrhonists, and written in a highly derogatory language, have the effect of disparaging the author of the *Essais*. S141/L109, headed 'Contre le pyrrhonisme', is one example of such a fragment, censuring 'la cabale pyrrhonienne' and their 'ambiguïté ambiguë'. And fragment S164/L131 contains the following famous onslaught: 'Doutera-t-il de tout? Doutera-t-il s'il veille, si on le pince, si on le brûle? Doutera-t-il qu'il doute? Doutera-t-il s'il est?'. This fragment builds its criticism on the basis of the 'neutralité' which is the 'essence de la cabale'. 'Ils ne sont pas pour eux-mêmes,' continues Pascal, 'ils sont neutres, indifférents, suspendus à tout sans s'excepter.' They are, in other words, all the things that Montaigne, with his 'fantasies humaines et miennes', is not.

For Montaigne, of course, 'nous sommes tous du vulgaire' (II. 12, 570). We cannot and must not abstract ourselves from the analysis of the movement and flux of our everyday lives. Knowledge can be experiential rather than theoretical: 'Je ne suis pas un philosophe' (III. 9, 950). Vulgarity in Montaigne, in the sense of a complicity with the everyday, is a criterion for wisdom. It is in these very human, immediate terms that Montaigne's 'nouveau langage' for scepticism is taken on by Pascal, as the *Pensées* too seek a complicity with the ordinary: 'Il faut se connaître soi-même. Quand cela ne servirait pas à trouver le vrai, cela au moins sert à régler la vie. Et il n'y a rien de plus juste' (S106/L72). And in this context, it is no surprise to learn from Bernard Croquette's research that the essay which yields the highest number of recollections in the *Pensées* is 'De l'expérience'.[16]

One fragment which bears a particularly close relationship to 'De l'expérience' is S181/L148. This takes as its starting point the assertion that 'tous les hommes recherchent d'etre heureux'. The fragment continues as follows:

> Une épreuve si longue, si continuelle et si uniforme devrait bien nous convaincre de notre impuissance d'arriver au bien par nos efforts. Mais l'exemple nous instruit peu. Il n'est jamais si parfaitement semblable qu'il n'y ait quelque délicate différence et c'est de là que nous attendons que notre attente ne sera pas déçue, en cette occasion comme en l'autre, et ainsi le présent ne nous satisfaisant jamais, l'expérience nous pipe, et de malheur en malheur nous mène jusqu'à la mort qui en est un comble éternel.

When set against the generalization of example, experience 'nous pipe': it catches us out and trips us up, sets reality against the banality of 'notre impuissance d'arriver au bien par nos efforts'. Individual experience is intractable; it jars against the smoothing out of the 'continuel' and the 'uniforme'. In Montaigne's terms, taken from 'De l'expérience', it 'cloche':

> Toutes choses se tiennent par quelque similitude, tout exemple cloche, et la relation qui se tire de l'experience est tousjours defaillante et imparfaicte; on joinct toutefois les comparaisons par quelque coin. Ainsi servent des lois, et s'assortissent ainsi à chacun de nos affaires, par quelque interpretation destournée, contrainte et biaise. (III. 13, 1070)

Montaigne, like Pascal in his adaptation of this passage, states that, when we are faced with experience itself, all abstraction into law is 'defaillante et imparfaicte'. And as Pascal brings the *Pensées* back to the fact of experience, fractures his thoughts into a level of experience to which a reader of the *Pensées* might be able to relate, Montaigne, with his focus on his 'fantasies humaines et miennes', becomes indispensable as a particular kind of model.

There are, then, two main issues here: the specificity of Montaigne's doubt (as it is qualified by experience), and the specificity of Pascal's appreciation of this. Jean Mesnard hints that Montaigne's sceptical position is specific and original, but only in order to make the point that Pascal, like his contemporaries, misunderstands it. Mesnard writes that Pascal, 'nourri de la lecture des *Essais*, qu'il était porté, avec tout son siècle, à interpréter dans le sens d'un pur scepticisme, a envisagé avec complaisance cette mise en question de tout le savoir'.[17] Philippe Sellier suggests, in an acute observation, that Pascal appreciates the specificity of Montaigne's position on scepticism. Further, he posits a certain degree of assimilation between the two:

> La réaction purement augustinienne eût consisté à riposter à la modernisation du scepticisme en se bornant à récrire le *Contra Academicos*. Plus subtil, Pascal, selon son habitude, va reprendre un instant les arguments de ses adversaires, pour s'en faire bientôt des armes contre eux. Mais une telle position exigeait un doigté extrême.[18]

But what remains to be questioned here is Sellier's assumption that Pascal is a kind of double agent, identifying with Montaigne all the better to betray him afterwards. Pascal, in the reading I propose here, never leaves Montaigne behind him. Scepticism, in Montaigne's writing of it, is given the task of judging and narrating the endless mobilities of his actions and experiences, of following his forceful 'fantasies', and, in this regard, Pascal aligns and allies himself with the author of the *Essais*.

It should be noted, moreover, that this intertextual identification between Pascal and Montaigne is played out on one very basic level in the *Entretien*. It comes with the crumbling of boundaries between the two authors in response to the active pleasures of the reading encounter.[19] The 'memoir-writer' Fontaine refers repeatedly to Pascal's own desire, his own pleasures, and the role these have played in his reading of Montaigne. Montaigne is an author whom, states Pascal, 'je ne puis voir sans joie' (p. 608), whose work offers 'un plaisir extrême' (p. 609). Thus Pascal's identification with Montaigne, in the discourse he addresses to Sacy, is a metaphorically corporal enthusiasm: 'Il lui avoua être extrêmement édifié de la solidité de tout ce qu'il venait de lui représenter. Cependant, étant encore tout plein de son auteur, il ne put se retenir' (p. 608). Pascal sets against the 'solidité', the resoluteness, of Sacy's Augustinianism, for it is this which has just been demonstrated to him, the pleasurable movement of his own reading. Montaigne's discourse, in Pascal's formulation, is 'naïve, familière, plaisante, enjouée, et pour ainsi dire folâtre. Elle suit ce qui la charme, et badine négligemment des accidents bons et mauvais' (p. 609). But just as Montaigne's writing 'suit ce qui la charme', so does Pascal, in the *Entretien*, by citing him at such length, and by stating that he reads Montaigne because he gets an active pleasure in doing so.

Montaigne's goal, in summary, is to 's'entendre bien en soy' (III. 13, 1073); we have seen that it was the Pyrrhonists' incapacity to 's'entendre bien en soy', to follow their own 'fantasie', which catalysed his criticism of them in the 'Apologie'. The achievement of this goal offers absolute fulfilment: 'C'est une absolue perfection, et comme divine, de scavoyr jouyr loiallement de son estre' (III. 13, 1115). And Montaigne explicitly signals what we may perceive as his usefulness to Pascal when he writes that his 'absolue perfection' is 'comme divine'. Montaigne, closed off to and uninterested in non-experiential or abstract knowledge, takes the human and points it away from indifference. Montaigne can find satisfaction only as long as he self-consciously follows the present trajectory of his desire. This engagement is a step which has to be undertaken by the readers of the *Pensées*, as they move away from indifference in the course of Pascal's process of persuasion. A promotion of human experience, rather than a denigration of human reason (the dynamic of Christian scepticism), is thus the chief point of intertextual contact between Pascal and Montaigne.

The fact remains, of course, that Montaigne's 'absolue perfection' is *only* 'comme divine'. Montaigne, in various different ways, 'a tort' (S454/L525); Pascal targets his 'mœurs' (S534/L649), his 'mots lascifs' (S559/L680). But above all, Montaigne is wrong in the readiness with which he assigns the absolute, attributing perfection to the knowledge of how to 'jouyr loiallement de son estre' (III. 13, 1115), attributing 'certitude' to the fact of being able to follow his own thought as it moves ('Je ne pleuvy aucune certitude, si ce n'est de faire connoistre jusques à quel poinct monte, pour cette heure, la connoissance que j'en ay', II. 10, 408). There are, writes Pascal, 'deux cent quatre-vingts sortes de souverain bien chez Montaigne' (S27/L408). Montaigne's task is finding a satisfaction which might be adequate to his desire for knowledge; Pascal's is building a desire for knowledge which might be adequate to the satisfaction he proposes. Montaigne's experience is a necessary stage that Pascal's reader has to pass through. Montaigne's porous, copious, supple essays, if they make a deliberate attempt to 'capture the multiple accidents of the world',[20] do not put these in the service of the more powerful understanding that Pascal, in the end, wants to communicate. 'Expérience' and encounter are of interest to Pascal only because they can prefigure (and so, in text, figure) a Pascalian 'certitude, certitude'. The leap of faith is to be broken down into a progression of 'expériences'. This figuring, as we saw in Chapter 6, is the sublime action of the *Pensées*.

The *Confessions*

In the *Entretien avec Monsieur de Sacy* as in the *Pensées*, the 'nouveau langage' that Montaigne applies to scepticism is an object of fascination for Pascal. It permits of a kind of identification which has not yet been examined closely, and which forges a rift between the Pascalian standpoint and the more rigid thought patterns of Sacy. This is not to imply a lack of Augustinian principles on Pascal's part. It suggests, rather, that Pascal's Augustinianism is broader than the readings allowed for by his Jansenist contemporaries. As such, the Augustinian leap in the *Confessions* from human uncertainty to divine plenitude, the accomplishment of which provoked the *Contra Academicos*, is not Pascal's only or overriding structural model. We also have to take into account the long distention, the experiential progression, which is the text of the *Confessions* as a whole.

One passage of the *Entretien* is of particular interest in the context of how Pascal's Augustinianism may differ from that of Sacy. In his second extended response to Sacy, Pascal breaks from his defence of Montaigne's usefulness to make the following statement: 'Tant il est vrai ce que vous venez de me dire de saint Augustin, et que je trouve d'une grande étendue: *Non enim uno modo sacrificatur transgressoribus angelis, etc.* Car en effet on leur rend hommage en bien de manières' (p. 610).[21] Sacy's citation, *non enim uno modo sacrificatur transgressoribus angelis*, is from Book 1, Chapter 17 of the *Confessions*. Here, Augustine refers to his youthful taste for reciting Homer, which gained him plaudits from his contemporaries and the respect of his teachers, and reproaches himself for such a use of his own talents:

> Ne les pouvais-je point employer, Seigneur, à réciter et à chanter vos louanges, que vous avez vous-mêmes dictées dans vos Ecritures saintes, qui eussent soutenu et affermi la mobilité légère et volage de mon cœur, comme les branches des arbres soutiennent et arrêtent les pampres de vigne qui y sont enlacés et attachés: qui l'eussent empêché de s'évaporer et de se perdre dans le vague de ces chimériques rêveries, et d'être la proie et le jouet des esprits impurs qui volent dans l'air? Car il y a plusieurs manières de sacrifier aux anges rebelles.[22]

The 'leur' of Pascal's reference signals, then, the fallen angels, or 'anges rebelles', of the paganism which permeated classical literature. What I want to focus on here, however, is the fact that Pascal earmarks Sacy's statement as being 'd'une grande étendue'. Pascal seeks, precisely, to expand upon Sacy's conclusions.

Book I of the *Confessions*, the origin of the quotation in question, is about the vain curiosities of childhood and the punishments received. It is the source of a further reference to Augustine made by Sacy, when the latter states to Pascal that Augustine 'vous a rappelé de ce plaisir dangereux, *a jucunditate pestifera* dit saint Augustin, qui rend graces à Dieu de ce qu'il lui a pardonné les péchés qu'il avait commis en goûtant trop la vanité' (p. 607). The passage cited by Sacy here (I. 14, 53) functions in two ways. It emphasizes first the power of God's redemptive grace:

> Mais votre sagesse, ô mon Dieu, renferme dans les bornes de vos lois cette curiosité qui n'est que trop libre d'elle-même, en retenant par cette crainte ses débordements et ses excès [...] C'est ainsi que par ces amertumes salutaires vous nous rappelez à vous, en nous retirant de cette douceur pernicieuse [*a jucunditate pestifere*] qui nous avait éloignés de vous.

And it also, fundamentally, makes the route to redemption a series of experiences: 'Et cet ordre admirable de votre justice s'étend, depuis les petites peines dont on punit les enfants, jusqu'aux grands supplices qui peuvent exercer la patience des Martyrs.'

Sacy's references to Augustine are, I would suggest, of limited interest to Pascal when the lesson drawn from them is that 'Dieu [...] a pardonné les péchés' (Sacy's conclusion on p. 607). They are of much wider import for Pascalian argumentation if that lesson reveals the different stages in the progression of experience towards conversion. As the most recent English translation of Augustine's 'amertumes salutaires' has it: 'Your laws have the power to temper bitter experience in a constructive way.'[23]

If Pascal's Augustinianism is broader than Sacy's, it is because of this emphasis on (bitter) experience. In his *Lettres spirituelles*, Sacy sums up Augustinian piety as follows: 'Toute la piété, selon saint Augustin, consiste à nous connoître & à connoître Dieu; à nous connoître pour nous haïr & pour nous séparer de nous-mêmes, à connoître Dieu pour l'aimer et pour nous tenir toûjours unis à lui.'[24] But this extract does not sum up the *Confessions*. Augustine's text traces out, not a linear exposition of the doctrine 'nous connoître pour nous haïr', but, as one critic terms it, a 'circulation capricieuse' between the piously self-deprecating and the individually experienced.[25] In another formulation, the *Confessions* constitute a 'record of an imitable, soterial experience'; the experience in question is, in other words, *both* soterial (pertaining to eternal salvation) *and* imitable (pertaining to ordinary life).[26] Pascal uses Augustine, as he uses Montaigne, to rewrite the epistemological dynamic of the faith–reason dichotomy, inserting the fact of human encounters, and the need for them, into his text.[27]

Such an angle of vision makes clear the full ambiguity of the 'moi haïssable' of S494/L597. It is not the case, as Vincent Carraud asserts in a chapter on Pascal entitled 'La destruction de l'égologie', that Pascal's persuasive project is defined through a will to 'outrepasser, universaliser et radicaliser la confusion et la discontinuité jusqu'à faire apparaître l'insubstantialité de l'*ego*'.[28] Pascal's fragment S534/L649, on Montaigne, reads: 'Ce qu'il a de mauvais, j'entends hors les mœurs, pût être corrigé en un moment si on l'eût averti qu'il faisait trop d'histoires et qu'il parlait trop de soi.' But this supposedly instantaneous correction would annihilate the *Essais*. It would preclude Pascal's appropriation of them: 'Ce n'est pas dans Montaigne mais dans moi que je trouve tout ce que j'y vois' (S568/L689). Terence Cave notes the juxtaposition of this latter fragment with S567/L688, in which Pascal asks 'qu'est-ce que le moi?'.[29] This latter interrogation itself proves that the 'moi' for Pascal is not just 'haïssable', to be suppressed without question.[30] Montaigne's discourse, like that indeed of the pseudonymous and anagrammed Pascal, Salomon de Tultie, is of the kind which 'est le plus d'usage, qui s'insinue le mieux, qui demeure le plus dans la mémoire, et qui fait le plus citer, parce qu'elle est toute composée de pensées nées sur les entretiens ordinaires de la vie' (S618/L745). The 'moi' is 'injuste en soi, en ce qu'il se fait centre de tout' and 'incommode aux autres, en ce qu'il les veut asservir' (S494/L597). But if Montaigne 'parlait trop de soi' (S534/L597), he also embodies that shifting engagement with encounter, experience, and 'les entretiens ordinaires de la vie' (S618/L745) which, as I have suggested throughout, Pascal seeks to instil in his readers.

As Pascal's dialectician states about Montaigne in S559/L680, 'Son livre n'étant point fait pour porter à la piété il n'y était pas obligé, mais on est toujours obligé de n'en point détourner.' But Pascal does turn away from piety: in the *Entretien* because of his attachments as reader to the texts he encounters, and in the *Pensées* because of the projection of his voice into a level of experience which has not yet encountered that piety. There are different routes to certainty:

> Ce fut ainsi que ces deux personnes d'un si bel esprit s'accordèrent enfin au sujet de la lecture de ces philosophes, où ils arrivèrent néanmoins d'une manière un peu différente: M. de Sacy y étant arrivé tout d'un coup par la claire vue du christianisme, et M. Pascal n'y étant arrivé qu'après beaucoup de détours en s'attachant aux principes de ces philosophes. (p. 612)

If Sacy has a direct, unmediated, 'claire vue du christianisme', Pascal's enquiry into absolute knowledge privileges the 'détours' made *en route*.

It is incontrovertible that, as Michael Moriarty puts it in a chapter entitled 'Pascal's Critique of Experience', 'one of the effects of the Fall has been to distort our very relationship with ourselves and with the world, subjecting us to an all-pervasive illusion'.[31] But Pascal persists, provocatively, in giving weight to experience. His detours into human experience and encounter represent 'la digression sur chaque point qui a rapport à la fin' (S329/L298), but this 'fin' makes the digression no less real. As he states in the *Entretien*:

> Je vous demande pardon, Monsieur, de m'emporter devant vous dans la théologie, au lieu de demeurer dans la philosophie, qui était seule mon sujet; mais il m'y a conduit insensiblement; et il est difficile de n'y pas entrer, quelque vérité qu'on traite, parce qu'il est le centre de toutes les vérités. (p. 611)

And just as disciplines may converge upon this centre, so may ways of speaking, writing, reading, and living. Brought to a basic awareness of what it is to be an experiential being, readers may be brought out of indifference and led, seemingly 'insensiblement', to 'le centre de toutes les vérités'.

We saw at the beginning of this section that the 'mémorial' was that 'certitude, certitude' which was granted to Pascal in a 'nuit de feu' and which, bestowing unrestricted, unmitigated knowledge, could be narrated only in epiphanic terms: '*Père juste, le monde ne t'a point connu, mais je t'ai connu.* Joie, joie, joie, pleurs de joie' (S742/L913). Pascal, following the 'nuit de feu', sets himself the task of showing that religious experience can signify unqualified knowledge. This goal requires the writing down of nuances of 'connaissance' and 'expérience'. Pascal shows that experience in and of the world, like 'les parties du monde', can be the foundation of such allegorically formed chains of signification as are to be found in S230/L199: 'Les parties du monde ont toutes un tel rapport et un tel enchaînement l'une avec l'autre que je crois impossible de connaître l'une sans l'autre et sans le tout.' I have sought to relay some of the 'rapports' and 'enchaînements' of Pascal's writing here — by observing the permeable boundaries of terms like 'sublime', 'connaissance', and 'expérience'; by bearing witness in this context to Pascal's own intertextual relationships; and by showing that Pascal does not just communicate, in all this, some sublimely impressive force. Rather, he gets across the extraordinary truth in which he is interested through his own powerful, Longinian, alertness to the common ground it shares with ordinary life.

Notes to Chapter 7

1. See the earlier references to Paul de Man, 'Pascal's Allegory of Persuasion', in *Allegory and Representation*, ed. by Stephen Greenblatt (Baltimore: Johns Hopkins University Press, 1981), pp. 1–25; Sara E. Melzer, *Discourses of the Fall: A Study of Pascal's 'Pensées'* (Berkeley: University of California Press, 1986); Richard Parish, '"Mais qui parle?" Voice and Persona in the *Pensées*', *Seventeenth-Century French Studies*, 8 (1986), 23–40; Nicholas Hammond, *Playing with Truth: Language and the Human Condition in Pascal's 'Pensées'* (Oxford: Oxford University Press, 1994); Richard Lockwood, *The Reader's Figure: Epideictic Rhetoric in Plato, Aristotle, Bossuet, Racine and Pascal* (Geneva: Droz, 1996).
2. Montaigne, 'Apologie de Raimond Sebond', in *Essais*, ed. by P. Villey, 2nd edn (Paris: Presses universitaires de France, 1965), II. 12, p. 448.
3. Elaine Limbrick, 'Le Pyrrhonisme est le vrai', in *Mélanges sur la littérature de la Renaissance, à la mémoire de V.-L. Saulnier* (Geneva: Droz, 1984), pp. 439–55 (p. 442). Limbrick writes that 'pour Pascal, comme pour beaucoup d'apologistes de christianisme du dix-septième siècle, le pyrrhonisme était un instrument méthodique qui servait à démontrer la faiblesse de la raison humaine afin de convaincre l'incrédule que ni les sens ni la raison n'étaient capables d'atteindre la vérité qui reposait uniquement dans le sein de Dieu' (p. 442).
4. Hammond, *Playing with Truth*, p. 48. Much research has focused on the status of the *Entretien*, as it occurs in Nicolas Fontaine's *Mémoires*. Fontaine writes that, a few weeks after the 'nuit de feu' of conversion, Pascal 'enfin étant touché de Dieu soumit cet esprit si élevé au doux joug de Jésus-Christ [...] Il vint à Paris se jeter entre les bras de Monsieur Singlin, résolu de faire tout ce qu'il lui ordonnerait. M. Singlin crut en voyant ce grand génie qu'il ferait bien de l'envoyer à Port-Royal des Champs, où M. Arnauld lui prêterait le collet en ce qui regardait ses hautes sciences, et où M. de Saci lui apprendrait à les mépriser'. 'Entretien de M. de Pascal avec M. de Saci', in Nicolas Fontaine, *Mémoires ou histoire des solitaires de Port-Royal,* ed. by Pascale Thouvenin (Paris: Champion, 2001), pp. 597–612 (p. 597; page references to this edition will be cited in brackets in the main text). However, while conversations between Pascal and Sacy certainly took place, the notion that the *Entretien* derives from one or more of them is tendentious. It is assumed that Fontaine in fact built his narration around certain documents in his possession, although these documents have never been found and so their exact status is unknown. Pierre Courcelle, in his critical edition, suggests that Fontaine used 'notes personnelles' made by both Pascal

and Sacy in preparation for a series of conversations, along with two of their letters, and then conflated these into a single 'entretien'. He thus argues for a certain basis in orality (*L'Entretien de Pascal et Sacy: ses sources et ses énigmes* (Paris: Vrin, 1960), pp. 141–65). Mesnard, in his *Œuvres complètes*, 7 vols (Paris: Desclée de Brouwer, 1964–), cites 'difficultés majeures' associated with this hypothesis, among which the following: 'Comment les deux recueils seraient-ils venus à la fois aux mains de Fontaine?' (III (1991), 247). Mesnard puts forward the convincing suggestion that 'ce que Fontaine a eu en main, c'est un document d'un type extrêmement répandu, un écrit de Pascal dans les marges duquel Sacy avait porté ses observations' (p. 248). Since Fontaine was Sacy's secretary, such a document could easily have fallen into his hands upon Sacy's death. See also Mesnard's introduction to the *Entretien (original inédit)*; texte établi, présenté et annoté par Pascale Mengotti-Thouvenin et Jean Mesnard (Paris: Desclée de Brouwer, 1994), pp. 11–77: 'Pour construire le rôle de Sacy, peut-être disposait-il de notes, de références, de citations, portées par le solitaire sur le manuscrit qu'il avait reçu, ou sur des feuillets joints' (p. 57). For a recent edition of the text, see *Entretien avec Sacy sur la philosophie, extrait des Mémoires de Fontaine*; présentation et lecture de Richard Scholar (Arles: Actes Sud, 2003).

5. Antoine Arnauld and Pierre Nicole, *La Logique ou l'art de penser*, ed. by Charles Jourdain (Paris: Gallimard, 1992), p. 12.

6. More recently, critics have made much space for the debate about whether Montaigne's discourse in fact displays an 'extinction' of religious belief. See, for programmatic statements of Montaigne's Catholicism, Michael Screech's *Montaigne and Melancholy: The Wisdom of the Essays* (London: Duckworth, 1983); see also Marc Fumaroli's introduction to the French translation ('Ce que nous découvrons ici pour la première fois, et que seul Screech pouvait nous faire découvrir, c'est tout simplement la dimension religieuse des *Essais*, la spiritualité à l'*intérieur* de la sagesse de Montaigne': *Montaigne et la mélancolie* (Paris: Presses universitaires de France, 1992), p. ix). Nonetheless, the argument of Sacy, Arnauld, and Nicole that Montaigne glosses over faith and sidelines the sacred is convincing. 'Des prières' is telling here: Montaigne proffers his work 'd'une manière laïque, non clericale, mais tres-religieuse tousjours' (I. 56, 323). The practice of religion is not incompatible with a lack of interest in it. On this, see Sylvia Giocanti's comment: 'L'*Apologie de Raymond Sebond* [...] permet aussi de ne plus avoir à parler de la religion. Le chapitre des *Essais* où est reléguée la religion permet à Montaigne de justifier ce fait qu'il n'en parlera presque plus' ('Histoire du fidéisme, histoire du scepticisme', in *Histoire du scepticisme de Sextus Empiricus à Richard H. Popkin*, ed. by Pierre-François Moreau and Eric Brian (= *Revue de synthèse*, 42.2–3 (April–September 1998)), pp. 193–210 (p. 204). It should be noted, furthermore, that the usefulness Pascal perceives in Montaigne does not imply that he thinks the latter is devout; as he states in the *Entretien*, 'étant né dans un Etat chrétien, il fait profession de la religion catholique, et en cela il n'a rien de particulier' (p. 601).

7. The Manichees, writes Augustine, held that 'les Ecritures du Nouveau Testament avaient été falsifiées par quelques personnes qui voulaient mêler la loi des Juifs avec la foi de l'Eglise; quoique cependant ils ne pussent eux-mêmes produire aucun exemplaire plus correct qui servît de preuve à cette falsification prétendue'. *Confessions*, trans. by Arnauld d'Andilly, ed. by Philippe Sellier (Paris: Gallimard, 1993), Book V, Chapter 11, pp. 173–74.

8. On the intermediary stage of doubt, see Sacy's awareness in the *Entretien* that 'c'est aussi par ce même doute des académiciens que saint Augustin quitta l'hérésie des manichéens' (p. 607).

9. *Révisions*, I. 1, quoted in Philippe Sellier, *Pascal et saint Augustin* (Paris: Albin Michel, 1995), p. 41. See also the account of the delay in Monica's reaction to the news of her son's move into the church: 'Son cœur [...] ne tressaillit point d'une joie immodérée, lorsqu'elle apprit que vous aviez déjà fait en moi une si grande partie de ce qu'elle vous demandait tous les jours avec tant de larmes qu'il vous plut d'y faire [...] elle savait avec certitude que vous ne manqueriez pas d'accomplir la dernière partie qui restait de cet ouvrage' (*Confessions*, VI. 1, 182).

10. 'The natural result of my investigation is that the investigators either discover the object of search or deny that it is discoverable and confess it to be inapprehensible or persist in their search. So, too, with regard to the objects investigated by philosophy, this is probably why some have claimed that it cannot be apprehended, while others again go on enquiring. Those who believe that they have discovered it are the "Dogmatists", specially so called — Aristotle, for example, and Epicurus and the Stoics and certain others; Clitomachus and Carneades and

the other Academics treat it as inapprehensible: the Sceptics keep on searching. Hence it seems reasonable to hold that the main types of philosophy are three — the Dogmatic, the Academic and the Sceptic.' Sextus Empiricus, *Outlines of Pyrrhonism*, 1, 1–4, trans. by R. G. Bury, Loeb Classical Library, 273 (Cambridge, MA: Harvard University Press, 1990), pp. 2–3. Charles Schmitt writes with regard to the philosophy of Pyrrho that Sextus 'seems to have been an accurate compiler, but to have contributed nothing original to the movement himself'. 'The Rediscovery of Ancient Skepticism in Modern Times', in *The Skeptical Tradition*, ed. by Myles Burnyeat (Berkeley: University of California Press, 1983), pp. 225–31 (p. 226).

11. Jean-Paul Dumont, *Le Scepticisme et le phénomène* (Paris: Vrin, 1972), p. 31.

12. *La Logique*, p. 13.

13. Montaigne's difference from Charron can be seen most radically at this point. Transforming Montaigne's argument into a series of maxims and thus utterly neglecting its interrogatory structure, Charron makes his own motto a dogmatic negativity: 'Je diray icy que j'ay fait graver sur la porte de ma petite maison que j'ay fait bastir à Condom l'an 1600 ce mot, *Je ne sçay.*' *De la sagesse*, ed. by Barbara de Negroni (Paris: Fayard, 1986), p. 402. Pascal, on the other hand, fully recognizes in the *Entretien* that for Montaigne the *structure* of the 'que sais-je?' is everything: 'Sur ce principe [du 'Que sais-je?'] roulent tous ses discours et tous ses Essais et c'est la seule chose qu'il prétend y établir, quoiqu'il ne fasse pas toujours remarquer son intention' (p. 602). And thus he fully recognizes the structural differences between Montaigne and Charron: 'Les divisions de Charron attristent et ennuient' (S644/L780).

14. André Tournon notes that 'chercher, discourir, raisonner, ce programme implique que le pyrrhonisme, tel que le comprend Montaigne, n'est pas une doctrine négative et destructrice'. *Montaigne, la glose et l'essai* (Lyons: Presses universitaires de Lyon, 1983), p. 245 n. 76. In a later article, he once again stresses the force of this self-application: 'L'écrivain y engage sa parole.' 'Images du pyrrhonisme selon quelques écrivains de la Renaissance', in *Les Humanistes et l'antiquité grecque*, ed. by Mitchiko Ishigami-Iagolnitzer (Paris: CNRS, 1991), pp. 27–37 (p. 35).

15. As we saw in Chapter 6, this is the definition of 'indifferent' in the *Dictionnaire de l'Académie française*.

16. Bernard Croquette, *Pascal et Montaigne: étude des réminiscences des Essais dans l'œuvre de Pascal* (Geneva: Droz, 1974), p. 109.

17. Jean Mesnard, 'Pascal et la vérité', *Chroniques de Port-Royal*, 17–18 (1962), 21–40 (p. 22). Mesnard assimilates into his own writing a blurring of the terms scepticism and Pyrrhonism, referring indiscriminately to 'le scepticisme' and 'le pyrrhonisme'. Commencing 'sur le chemin de la vérité, le niveau le plus bas est représenté par le scepticisme', he later continues his argument as follows: 'Mais, si le pyrrhonisme ne constitue qu'une étape dans le cheminement vers la vérité, il n'en demeure pas moins une étape nécessaire.' 'Pascal et la vérité', pp. 22, 24.

18. *Pascal et saint Augustin*, p. 42.

19. One of the most striking characteristics of the text, this is often ignored. See, as an exception, Richard Scholar, who notes that 'Pascal affiche le "plaisir" que lui procurent ses lectures d'Epictète et de Montaigne'. 'La Force de l'imagination de Montaigne: Camus, Malebranche, Pascal', *Littératures classiques*, 45 (2002), 127–38 (p. 137).

20. Richard Scholar, *The Je-Ne-Sais-Quoi in Early Modern Europe: Encounters with a Certain Something* (Oxford: Oxford University Press, 2005), p. 258.

21. Pascal is referring back to Sacy's citation of Augustine on p. 606.

22. Augustine, *Confessions*, 1. 17, 58.

23. Augustine, *Confessions*, trans. by Henry Chadwick (Oxford: Oxford University Press, 1998), Book 1, Chapter 14, p. 17.

24. *Lettres chrestiennes et spirituelles de Messire Isaac Louis Le Maistre de Sacy*, 2 vols (Paris: Elie Josset, 1690), II, 169.

25. 'Ainsi s'amorce une circulation capricieuse, parce que vivante et, comme telle, imprévue, entre les faits objectifs — parfois même les plus négligeables — de la vie d'Augustin entre 354 et 388, les questions que ces expériences vécues posent rétrospectivement à la réflexion philosophique de l'Augustin de 395–97 sur les labyrinthes de l'âme humaine et des comportements humains, enfin les épanchements du sentiment religieux que provoquent cette évocation et cette réflexion,

lorsqu'elles sont confrontées à la Parole de Dieu dans l'Ecriture sainte.' Jacques Fontaine, 'Genres et styles dans les *Confessions* de saint Augustin', *L'Information littéraire*, 42.1 (1990), 13–20 (p. 17).

26. John Sturrock, *The Language of Autobiography: Studies in the First Person Singular* (Cambridge: Cambridge University Press, 1993), p. 22. Sturrock notes that centuries of readers have tried to strip Augustine of his story, citing one critic as follows: 'Such, not an autobiography, is the object of the *Confessions*; a praise and confession of God's unmerited goodness, but of himself only so much, as might illustrate out of what depth God's mercy had raised him.' E. B. Pusey, 'Preface', *The Confessions of St Augustine*, quoted in Sturrock, *The Language of Autobiography*, p. 23.

27. Jean Mesnard describes Pascal's reference to 'ce que vous venez de me dire de saint Augustin, et que je trouve d'une grande étendue' as 'rigoureusement inutile à l'exposé des idées, qu'il n'a d'autre effet que de ralentir' (*Œuvres complètes*, ed. by Mesnard, I, 247). Mesnard does not see why Pascal would have made such a reference to Augustine in the first place: 'Il fait intervenir saint Augustin dans un raisonnement dont toute la profondeur vient de ce qu'il se fonde sur l'utilisation des seuls auteurs profanes' (p. 247). But if Montaigne is of interest to Pascal not just in relation to his status as 'auteur profane' but also because he embodies the kind of anti-indifference, or engagement with experience, which Pascal tries so ardently to instil in the readers of the *Pensées*, then it is easy to see why the Augustine of the *Confessions*, as 'record of an imitable, soterial experience', might also be brought into play at this point.

28. Vincent Carraud, *Pascal et la philosophie* (Paris: Presses universitaires de France, 1992), p. 294.

29. Terence Cave, *Pré-histoires: textes troublés au seuil de la modernité* (Geneva: Droz, 1999), p. 125.

30. Of interest here is Jean Mesnard's singling out of the following, renowned, passage of *La Logique*: 'Feu M. Pascal, qui savait autant de véritable rhétorique, que personne en ait jamais su, portait cette règle jusques à prétendre, qu'un honnête homme doit éviter de se nommer, et même de se servir des mots *je*, et de *moi*.' As Mesnard notes, 'De cette analyse se dégage l'exigence d'une ascèse personnelle pour aller à la découverte de la vérité. Mais Nicole insiste surtout sur une *autre* conséquence qui, comme il le reconnaît lui-même, lui a été suggérée par Pascal. Elle est d'ordre rhétorique: celui qui veut convaincre autrui doit s'effacer dans son discours, afin de ne pas exciter chez l'auditeur cette jalousie spontanée qui entraînerait une sorte de dégoût pour les arguments présentés. Le meilleur commentaire du propos de Pascal recueilli par Nicole, dont le sens complet n'a pas toujours été compris faute de recours au contexte, n'est pas seulement fourni par la célèbre *pensée*: "le moi est haïssable" mais par celle-ci, non moins célèbre: "On se persuade mieux, pour l'ordinaire, pour les raisons qu'on a soi-même trouvées que par celles qui sont venues dans l'esprit des autres."' *Œuvres complètes*, ed. by Mesnard, I, 993.

31. Michael Moriarty, *Early Modern French Thought: The Age of Suspicion* (Oxford: Oxford University Press, 2003), p. 100.

CHAPTER 8

❖

Translations and Reflections

When, in the years preceding the publication of his *Œuvres diverses* in 1674, Boileau came to spend 'quelques-unes de mes veilles' translating Longinus into French for the first time, he found that the treatise had been properly understood only by 'un très petit nombre de savants'.[1] Boileau's preface to his translation takes care to specify, therefore, that 'il faut donc sçavoir que par Sublime, Longin n'entend pas ce que les Orateurs appellent le stile sublime: mais cet extraordinaire et ce merveilleux qui frape dans le discours, et qui fait qu'un ouvrage enleve, ravit, transporte' (p. 338). Boileau immerses himself in the Longinian sublime, its enmeshing of the listener or reader in its arousal of intense emotional experience, its rejection of sublimity as a 'style' of language, even one opposed to mediocrity. With his collected works of 1674, his preoccupation stamps itself upon the cover of the volume, entitled *Œuvres diverses du sieur D***, avec le Traité du Sublime ou du merveilleux dans le discours, traduit du grec de Longin*. I shall consider in this chapter the acquisitive emphases of his translation and commentary, before turning to an anonymous translator of Longinus whose manuscript work is all the more compelling for having eluded critical interest.[2]

In any analysis of Boileau's translation of Longinus, Jules Brody's 1958 *Boileau and Longinus*, mentioned briefly in my Introduction, is a necessary starting point. Brody understands Boileau's œuvre, including the (often seen to be drily legislative) *Art poétique*, to reject rules for rules' sake and to focus instead on the emotional effects of literature. Brody thus seeks to restore to Boileau 'unity of thought' (p. 141). In order to attain this goal, Brody offers a useful study of the differences in emphasis between Longinus's Greek and Boileau's French. In the following key passage, for example, Brody marks Boileau's interpolations as follows:

> Si [...] *nous ne sentons point* qu'il nous élève l'âme, et nous laisse dans l'esprit une idée qui soit *même* au-dessus de ce que nous venons d'entendre; mais si au contraire, en le regardant avec attention *nous trouvons* qu'il tombe et ne se soutienne pas, il n'y a point là de grand *puisqu'enfin ce n'est qu'un son de paroles qui frappe simplement l'oreille, et dont il ne demeure rien dans l'esprit*. La marque *infaillible* du sublime, c'est quand *nous sentons* qu'un discours nous laisse beaucoup à penser, *qu'il fait d'abord un effet sur nous*, auquel il est bien difficile, pour ne pas dire impossible, de résister.[3]

The reflexive emphasis is revealed to be stronger here than in the original Greek: 'With his interpolated "nous ne sentons point", "nous sentons" and "nous trouvons", Boileau gives the subjective reactions of the reader more prominence than they had in the original' (p. 95). Boileau, it seems, is 'deeply preoccupied with the emotive effects of literature' (p. 100).

Brody helps to restratify his contemporaries' thinking on the rigid and rule-bound Boileau. His statement that 'the urge to blend with Longinus' words an added touch of mystery never left Boileau' (p. 55) supports the belief, expressed in Brody's later article on Platonism and classicism, that we need to 'restituer au classicisme la base métaphysique qui, une fois, dut être la sienne'.[4] And he encourages the supposition that any seventeenth-century interest in Longinus is a result of the latter's affiliation with the Platonist tradition. Thus we read Slobodan Vitanovic's comment that:

> Boileau se distingue dans son siècle et s'écarte de la majeure partie de ses prédécesseurs et contemporains par le fait même qu'il a longuement travaillé et réfléchi le traité *Du Sublime*, ce qui lui a permis de se mettre en contact plus étroit avec la tradition platonicienne, et des écoles rhétoriques grecques de l'enthousiasme.[5]

Nicholas Cronk, too, appreciates Brody's suggestion that classicism may be 'platonist in the very essence of its conception', and builds his thesis around the notion that '[Longinus] can be read in a way which brings his thought close to Plato's'.[6] I have throughout been interested in the way that the ineffability and theory-free quality of sublime moments are, in Longinus, accompanied by an investigation into hard details about human interaction (and I have argued that only with caution can one bring Longinus's complex thought in line with Plato's own, differently complex, œuvre). A close analysis of those moments when Boileau comments explicitly upon his own engagement with Longinus can help to delineate his preoccupation with this clash of concerns.

Expansions and Exemplifications

In the 1674 preface to his translation, Boileau condemns in vituperative terms 'ces hommes accoûtumez aux débauches et aux excés des Poëtes modernes, et qui n'admirant que ce qu'ils n'entendent point, ne pensent pas qu'un Auteur se soit élevé, s'ils ne l'ont entierement perdu de veuë' (p. 337). Nothing could show more clearly the transference into Boileau's own work of the Longinian notion that elevation is not merely ascension, but is rather and only ever a movement towards other readers. The sublime is excluded by a 'perte de vue'. Boileau dismisses those who cannot cope with the Longinian redefinition of sublimity, and who, unimaginatively, 'chercheront le Sublime dans le Sublime' (p. 337). The first thing to say about Boileau's understanding of the sublime, then, is that he follows Longinus — and the other seventeenth-century authors mentioned in Chapter 4 — in making sublimity not just the lofty, but the well communicated. This places a particular burden upon Boileau as translator. A translator who has Latin as his medium of choice can 'traduire le Grec mot par mot' (p. 336), on the grounds that any clumsiness or obsoleteness of expression can be put down to the archaisms of the linguistic tools available. 'En effet, le lecteur, qui bien souvent n'y conçoit rien, s'en prend plutost à soi-mesme qu'à l'ignorance du Traducteur' (pp. 336–37). No such buffer zone surrounds Boileau: 'Tout ce que le Lecteur n'entend point s'appelle un galimatthias, dont le Traducteur tout seul est responsable' (p. 337).

Boileau's *Réflexion X*, written around 1710, is coherent in moving away from a preoccupation with 'les grands mots' (p. 550). These, 'selon les habiles connoisseurs, font en effet si peu l'essence entiere du Sublime, qu'il y a mesme dans les bons Ecrivains des endroits sublimes, dont la grandeur vient de la petitesse energique des paroles' (p. 550). Energy carries with it, is defined in terms of, transference. Boileau backs up his statement with Longinus's example from Herodotus: 'Cleoment estant devenu furieux, il prit un couteau, dont il se hacha la chair en petits morceaux; et s'estant ainsi dechiqueté luy-mesme il mourut' (p. 550). This shocking utterance, states Boileau, is irremediably 'bas'. But 'on y sent toutefois une certaine force energique, qui marquant l'horreur de la chose qui y est enoncée, a je ne sçay quoy de sublime'. Cleomenes's madness is transferred by Herodotus via a discourse which is itself direct to the point of being 'déchiqueté'; we shall see in a moment that this sublimity is also particularly preoccupying to another, anonymous translator of Longinus.

Réflexion X is written in response to a persistent misunderstanding of Longinus on the part of Pierre-Daniel Huet. Huet had presupposed that the Longinian sublime could be corralled quite happily into definitions of sublime style; and that Longinus's simply expressed example from Genesis (the *Fiat lux*) was correspondingly nonsensical.[7] Boileau, on the other hand, backs up Longinus's citation with his own analysis of the Scripture which precedes that: 'Moyse ayant ainsi expliqué dans une narration également courte, simple, et noble, les merveilles de la Creation, songe aussitost à *faire connoistre* aux hommes l'Autheur de ses merveilles' (p. 551, my emphases). Moses' rhetorical skill with the figure of apostrophe is put in the service of the knowledge he seeks, sublimely, to impart (only thus may he himself be qualified as 'grand'): '*Pour cela* donc ce grand Prophete n'ignorant pas que le meilleur moyen de faire connoistre les Personnages qu'on introduit, c'est de les faire agir; il met d'abord Dieu en action, et le fait parler' (p. 551, my emphases). Sublimity is not just height (the highest entity of all is not here notable for his height but rather for being a 'Personnage'), but the transmission of knowledge via 'action'. On the following page, Boileau modifies the clearly controversial notion that God can be manipulated as a character:

> Avec tout cela neantmoins, respondrez-vous, on ne me persuadera jamais que Moyse, en escrivant la Bible, ait songé à tous ces agréments, et à toutes ces petites finesses de l'Escole [...]. Asseurément Moyse n'y a point pensé; mais l'Esprit Divin qui l'inspiroit y a pensé pour luy, et les y a mises en œuvre, avec d'autant plus d'art, qu'on ne s'aperçoit point qu'il y ait aucun art. (p. 554)

Agency is, in this case, safely reattributed to the divine.[8] The fact remains, however, that Boileau has made divinity and the communication of it only fitfully distinguishable.

A comparison with the 1664 *Dissertation sur Joconde* may be of service in explaining how Boileau's remarks about Longinus take us beyond a 'touch of mystery', divert us from the 'divine, immortal, intelligible, uniform'.[9] Boileau is preoccupied in the *Dissertation* with 'ces sortes de beautés [...] qu'il faut sentir, et qui ne se prouvent point'.[10] These he goes on to qualify as an ineffable 'je ne sais quoi': 'C'est ce je ne sai quoi qui nous charme, et sans laquelle la beauté n'auroit ni grace ni beauté.'

But contemplating his correspondent's 'Ami', immune to such charms, Boileau continues as follows:

> Mais après tout, c'est un je ne sai quoi; et si vôtre ami est aveugle, je ne m'engage pas à lui faire voir clair; et c'est aussi pourquoi vous me dispenserés, s'il vous plait, de répondre à toutes les vaines objections qu'il vous a faites. Ce seroit combattre des Fantômes qui s'évanoüissent d'eux-mêmes. (p. 316)

The 'je ne sais quoi' appears twice in this passage. Its first manifestation is as that which 'nous charme'. Though indefinable, it is instantly recognizable, offering a direct and unmediated form of understanding ('qui ne se prouv[e] point'). Interpretation, here, is unnecessary. The 'je ne sais quoi' is coextensive with the effect it produces, which is to say the effect of absolute, intuitive, pleasurable charm. The self is redefined, reoriented through a kind of intoxication. Since that intense emotional engagement is posited as being common to all, the 'je' is subsumed within the 'nous'. The 'je ne sais quoi', here, is effectively an 'on ne sait quoi', existing purely in the maxim-like realm of universal affectivity (what 'we' can always pleasurably sense). Hence it is this quality 'sans laquelle la beauté n'auroit ni grace ni beauté'. It can be perceived by all as the defining constitutive element of beauty. Without epistemological characteristics of its own, its status is marked out within a closed circuit of reciprocal perception.

There is also, however, a supplementary definition: 'Mais après tout, c'est un je ne sais quoi; et si vôtre ami est aveugle, je ne m'engage pas à lui faire voir clair.' This is clearly more than a tautological expansion which states merely that the 'je ne sais quoi' is (after all) a 'je ne sais quoi'. The repetition troubles rather than verifies, for there is a certain modification in process. An interlocutor, 'vôtre ami', is excluded from the common belief structure of the 'nous'. Boileau thus qualifies that definition of the sublime which rests on tacit intuition and mutual understanding, bringing into question the 'nous' as inclusive force. The strongly deprecatory tone of these lines is designed to open up a moral gap between Boileau's discourse and that of his ignorant interlocutor, but the distance put between the two is logical also. The 'je' and the 'nous' cannot be as one. The dialogic form fractures and reopens the proposed summing up of individual experience inherent in the previous, all-encompassing definition of the sublime. Thus Boileau makes the conceptual shift from the 'on ne sait quoi' to the '*je* ne sais quoi'. His statement is a quite trivial '*I* don't know'. The 'je ne sais quoi', in this second definition, is the syntactic equivalent of the 'je ne m'engage pas', reinstating the 'je' as active subject rather than blurring it into a 'nous'. We find here a moment of interrogation, in other words, where the preoccupation with the communally experienced 'ineffability' of the 'je ne sais quoi' is broken down into its individual building blocks. There is a separate focus on the individual encounter with the sublime, on the reactions of the differentiated 'je'.[11]

Brody cites the *Dissertation* to support his argument about the underlying coherence of Boileau's œuvre: 'A good part of his preface of 1701 seems to have been lifted out of the *Dissertation sur Joconde* (1664).'[12] Let us consider briefly, then, the preface that Boileau writes for the 1701 edition of his *Œuvres complètes*. It contains the following series of assertions:

> Que si on me demande ce que c'est que cet agrément et ce sel, Je répondray que
> c'est un je ne sçai quoy qu'on peut beaucoup mieux sentir, que dire. A mon avis
> neanmoins, il consiste principalement à ne jamais presenter au Lecteur que des
> pensées vraies et des expressions justes. L'Esprit de l'Homme est naturellement
> pleine d'un nombre infini d'idées confuses du Vrai, que souvent il n'entrevoit
> qu'à demi; et rien ne lui est plus agréable que lorsqu'on lui offre quelqu'une
> de ces idées bien éclaircie, et mise dans un beau jour. Qu'est-ce qu'une
> pensée neuve, brillante, extraordinaire? Ce n'est point, comme se persuadent
> les Ignorans, une pensée que personne n'a jamais euë, ni dû avoir. C'est au
> contraire une pensée qui a dû venir à tout le monde, et que quelqu'un s'avise le
> premier à exprimer. (p. 1)

The 'je ne sais quoi' as maxim, as indicative of universal truth, cannot be supported without a coexistent shift into the realm of the subjective: 'a mon avis neanmoins'. Beyond the apodictic, the 'je ne sais quoi' tells an untidier story, as the 'je ne sais quoi' as eternal, infinite, all-encompassing signifier is tempered by Boileau's investigation into the mechanics of each individual instance. And Boileau's answer to the question projected, 'Qu'est-ce qu'une pensée neuve, brillante, extraordinaire?', is individual vision: the capacity to 's'aviser'.

Similarly, throughout his writings on the sublime, Boileau shows his awareness that one is never merely a recipient of sublime experience, but rather becomes an interlocutor oneself, aware of one's own critical, appraising activity. A 'désappropriation du sujet à soi-même' never quite occurs.[13] Boileau cannot move his discussion of the sublime away from the notion that 'il s'agit de sçavoir en quoy consiste ce merveilleux' (p. 538). 'Je croy qu'on ne trouvera pas mauvais', writes Boileau in his *Réflexion XII*, 'qu'au defaut de Longin, j'en hazarde icy une [definition] de ma façon, qui au moins en donne une imparfaite idée' (p. 562). This is the sublime 'de ma façon'. With the recognition of the force of affectivity comes the awareness of individual engagement with it. The blurring of coordinates which takes place in moments of overwhelming experience coexists with a self-consciousness regarding the blurring taking place; and this self-consciousness itself comes to define the moments in question. Boileau's intersection of absolute affective understanding and a reflexive move to grasp this conceptually is common to his analyses of both the 'je ne sais quoi' and the sublime. But the sublime contrives to offer us more for discussion as, and specifically as, a meeting of minds via a discourse of encounter.

Boileau chooses one particular passage from his translation of Longinus to stand at the head of his 'douzième réflexion' on the sublime. It reads as follows:

> Car tout ce qui est veritablement sublime a cela de propre, quand on l'escoute,
> qu'il esleve l'ame, et luy fait concevoir une plus haute opinion d'elle-mesme, la
> remplissant de joye, et de je ne sçay quel noble orgueil, comme si c'estoit elle
> qui eust produit les choses qu'elle vient simplement d'entendre. (p. 562)

And it provokes the following observation: 'Voila une tres-belle description du Sublime, et d'autant plus belle, qu'elle est elle-mesme tres-sublime.' Not only can Longinus scrutinize the sublime, but he can also epitomize it in his own work. When Louis Marin writes that 'part of Boileau's argument is that the special value of the *Traité du sublime* lies in its author's capacity not simply to analyse but also to exemplify the sublime', his point is that Boileau interprets 'the sublime *work* as inextricably fused with a sublime *life*'.[14] But this does not explain adequately why this passage should be picked out as sublime.

This passage from Longinus, as we saw in Chapter 1, is a rejection of the idea that the sublimity of a sublime author is something intrinsic to that author. The sublime here is in the tenuous position of having to be confirmed by a reader who is specified as a reader capable of a certain self-reflexivity ('luy fait concevoir une plus haute opinion d'elle-mesme'). It is worth noting that Boileau is anyway designating as 'tres-sublime' a passage which, as Brody tells us, he has himself modified to an important degree.[15] The sublime might 'persuade avec empire', but this forceful sublime discourse is also fragile and shifting, as each sublime encounter is different, defined by the particular effect it has on the recipient, and as each individual is in turn defined by the sublime encounter. It seems from this relativism that this passage can be singled out by Boileau as 'tres-sublime' only if he wishes to propose that the sublime is a discourse which does not talk in absolutes.

Correspondingly, when Huet suggests that 'les grandes choses sont grandes en elles-mesmes', Boileau categorizes this in *Réflexion X* as 'la proposition du monde la moins soustenable et la plus grossiere' (p. 553). A quantitatively defined sublimity, as we have seen throughout, does not exist. It is not that, as Marc Fumaroli suggests following Longinus's Jesuit readers, 'le verbe y est animé d'une énergie qui participe du divin'.[16] Boileau makes us grapple with a theory in which sublimity is entirely dependent, not upon a quality, but upon other hermeneutic standpoints. And Boileau's anecdote about Longinus and Zenobia, which has been enlisted to show Boileau's appreciation of nobility as an essential component of sublimity,[17] can also be seen to put forward suggestively the message that an absolute 'greatness' is not the primary referent of discussion.

Longinus, so Boileau tells us, was one of the statesmen in the party accompanying Zenobia, Queen of Palmyra, when both she and her city were under siege to the emperor Aurelian in the third century AD (Boileau's factual error as to the authorship of *Peri hypsous* does not, of course, invalidate any interest in the way in which his anecdote about Longinus is given anchorage in his preface). Aurelian had tried to take Palmyra by force, but had resorted to siege after being surprised by vicious resistance. Eventually, he dispatched a letter proposing to spare Zenobia's life should she surrender within a certain time. Zenobia, writes Boileau, asked Longinus to compose a response.

Boileau's citation of Longinus's rejoinder to Aurelian is lengthy. It culminates as follows:

> Nous attendons le secours des Perses. Les Sarazins arment pour nous. Les Armeniens se sont déclarez en notre faveur. Une troupe de voleurs dans la Syrie a défait ton armée. Juge ce que tu dois attendre, quand toutes ces forces seront jointes. Tu rabattras de cet orgueil avec lequel, comme maistre absolu de toutes choses, tu m'ordonnes de me rendre.[18]

The letter is shot through with an emphatic insistence on 'vertu': 'C'est la vertu, Aurelien, qui doit tout faire dans la guerre' (p. 335). Longinus, esteemed by Zenobia, reveals the justification for her esteem in the content of his composition. This ties in logically with Boileau's own framing of the letter: he has introduced his diegesis with the assertions that 'Longin ne fut pas simplement un Critique habile: ce fut un Ministre d'Etat considerable' (p. 334), that 'il suffit, pour faire son éloge, de dire qu'il fut consideré de Zenobie cette fameuse Reine des Palmyriens' (p. 334). But Boileau's 'il suffit' denies itself, illogically, its own sufficiency. Having supposedly defined and circumscribed his interest in this way, Boileau devotes paragraph upon paragraph to further anecdote.

What emerges from the letter Boileau cites in such superabundant detail, above and beyond Longinus's already apparent virtue, is a defining contempt for the egregious folly of declaring oneself 'maistre absolu de toutes choses'. The letter pits itself against the attribution of exclusive rectitude. Its weapon in so doing is the energy and potency of heterogeneous 'Perses', 'Sarazins', 'Armeniens': 'Juge ce que tu dois attendre, quand toutes ces forces seront jointes.' Fabrications of forces are set against 'orgueil', and they seek to assail its sense of security. Longinus's virtue becomes tied to his writing down of this endeavour in his letter.

Aurelian attacked and Longinus died — denounced, apparently, as the writer of Zenobia's letter when Palmyra was eventually taken. And the proliferating 'apparently's of this anecdote echo on the level of form the heterogeneity which is pitted against absoluteness in the letter in question. We move in the space of Boileau's retelling of things from Porphyrus to Flavius Vopiscus to Zosimus as sources of information. The prolonged insertion of the anecdote shows Boileau's preference for 'la petite histoire', complexities of incidental detail, over a linear account, which would have been perfectly reducible to Longinus's heroic death in the service of Zenobia. 'Le Philosophe Porphyre, qui avoit esté son disciple, parle de lui comme d'un prodige. *Si on l'en croit*, son jugement estoit la regle du bon sens' (p. 334, my emphases). Boileau does not in fact describe here fixed notions of mastery, greatness, impressiveness, or virtue.

Certain concrete textual additions to Longinus's treatise are also instructive. It is important that, in his Chapter 7, we find the discourse of Alexander signalled, but lacking, in Longinus's Greek:

> C'est particulierement aux grands Hommes qu'il échappe de dire des choses extraordinaires. Voyez, par exemple, ce que répondit Alexandre quand Darius luy offrit la moitié de l'Asie avec sa fille en mariage. *Pour moy*, luy disoit Parmenion, *si j'estois Alexandre j'accepterois ces offres.* — *Et moy aussi*, répliqua ce Prince, *si j'estois Parmenion.* N'est-il pas vrai qu'il falloit estre Alexandre pour faire cette réponse? (p. 351)

This addition, along with others to which I shall turn in the context of the *Querelle des Anciens et des Modernes*, was first filled out in a note by Longinus's editor Petra in 1612.[19] Its presence in Boileau's text — his decision to follow Petra here — makes clearer Longinus's transformation of grandeur into a logic of successful everyday communication.

Boileau was not the only seventeenth-century translator of Longinus to follow Petra's edition in adducing this anecdote. The anonymous translator whose work I mentioned in the Introduction does the same. And it is worth noting, in the context of additions and modifications to Longinus's text, that this version of the treatise, while written in the copperplate of a professional 'copiste', also provides us with scribbled variations and mutations, marginal notes (some in Greek), and even the distracted doodles of the translator at work. I shall turn now to these arresting moments. When are individual terms translated, signalled, repeated, and reused in emphatic ways? Where are the particularly heavily worked passages of marginal notes?[20]

Additions and Modifications

Illuminating in this regard is the locus of resolute rewriting to be found on folio 143. At this point in *Peri hypsous*, Longinus has just cited one particular example of sublimity, namely the fear, in Book XV of the *Iliad*, of sailors in the face of a storm.[21] This fear, suggests Longinus, and as we saw in Chapter 1, is perfectly conveyed by Homer's contorted discourse. It is conveyed by his extraordinary conflation of prepositions, for instance (Homer forces 'into an abnormal union prepositions not normally compounded', 10.6). Attempting to do justice to Longinus's analysis of Homer, the translator writes that 'le nombre et les parolles de cette expression semblent le mouvement que cette passion donne aux esprits de ceux qui en sont agités'.

   This turn of phrase, it can be seen, replaces the more prolonged 'il tourmente pour ainsy dire son vers de la même maniere que la passion de la peur qui'il descrit, tourmente l'esprit de ceux qui sont dans ce danger, et par la Compression de ces paroles, descrit ce qu'il y a d'extreme'. Concentrated agitation is acquired by and assimilated into the translation as its author works. Jotted into the margin, then crossed out, we see the words ὑπ 'ἐκ θανάτοιο, 'hypo' ('under') and 'ek' ('from') being two prepositions juxtaposed by Homer to create a new sense of movement, sublimely shared in Longinus by the reader of the *Iliad*.[22] Syntagms and synapses spark off each other in Longinus's analysis of Homer's text, and the translator sutures layers of scribbling into the main body of the translation at precisely this point.

   The author of this translation is, indeed, particularly sensitive to and interested in the identification through discourse which is key to the Longinian sublime (and the translation of the title, 'De la sublimité du discours', is in itself enough to stamp upon the reader the importance of language as opposed to genius in general within the sublime encounter). He is particularly vociferous in condemning the two opposing poles of behaviour, tumidity and puerility, which preclude sublimity. We read of tumidity that 'il n'y a rien de si difficile que de se défendre de cette vicieuse extrémité' and of puerility that it is 'une autre extrémité vitieuse et autant éloigné de la véritable grandeur que celluy dont nous venons de parler' (fol. 130ᵛ). The hyperbole here is striking: Boileau, by way of comparison, has, in the first instance, 'il n'y a rien de plus difficile à éviter que l'Enflure', and in the second, 'Il y a encore un troisième défaut opposé au Grand, qui regarde le Pathetique' (p. 344), and the Loeb edition has 'tumidity seems to be one of the hardest faults to guard against' and 'puerility is the exact opposite of grandeur' (3.3–4). Moving on to the following passage, which decries authorial use of inappropriate emotion, we find that editorial emphasis shifts towards precise differentiation: we come to a criticism of those who 'employent en public des passions qu'ils se sont fait dans leur cabinet, qui leur sont fort propres mais qui d'ailleurs n'ont aucun rapport avec la matiére qu'ils traittent, et cela *avec aussi peu de jugement* que si l'yvresse leur avoit dicté leurs discours' (fol. 131, my emphases). Boileau finishes with 'comme s'ils estoient yvres' (p. 344); the Loeb edition also has 'as if they were drunk' (3.5). The translation in question here stresses, periphrastically, a cognitive dimension which is revealed as necessary to the sublime. Minds whose ingenuity has been attenuated by intoxication cannot produce or attain sublimity; sublimity itself, therefore, is more than intoxication.

We have seen that the reader theorized in Longinus works with the cognitive element to his version of the sublime: in the sublime moment, it is 'as if we had ourselves produced what we had heard' (7.2). This agile movement between sublimity and cognition in Longinus justifies the latter's claim that his own treatise can be useful, can provide 'that assistance which should be every author's chief aim' (1.1): to encourage particular ways of thinking about the sublime is to render graspable sublime experience. Longinus's initial assessment of the use value of the sublime is another instance of this translator's revealing emphases and re-emphases:

> Mais puisque vous [Terentianus] mavez commandé d'écrire aussi de la meme manière pour vostre usage particulier, voyons si entre les réflexions que j'ai faites sur son sujet il y en a quelqu'une qui puisse estre utile à une personne qui est dans l'emploi et dans le maniement des affaires du monde. (fol. 127^{v})

This latter phrase, 'une personne qui est dans l'emploi et dans le maniement des affaires du monde', is a very real anchoring of Longinus's 'andrāsi politikois' to the transactional world of social engagement.[23] The initial translation, underlined, written over, and finally crossed out altogether, is as follows: 'Mais ce sera à vous de juger de touttes les parties de cet ouvrage, et d'en disposer comme il vous plaira.' But this statement is devoid of any specification regarding the domain in which Terentianus's 'disposition' is to take place; indeed it is devoid of any translation of 'andrāsi politikois' at all. Clearly, it requires modification of the kind we find in the margin. The translator brings Terentianus's position as 'user' of a theory of the sublime close to the mechanisms of everyday life. Longinus's address of Terentianus serves in any account to point up the pragmatism of the Longinian sublime, but this reworked translation grants pragmatism a particular force.

The suggestion that sublimity should not be divorced from 'le maniement des affaires du monde' is echoed in another point of interest: that section of *Peri hypsous* which suggests that Homer has less propensity to produce the sublime in his old age than in his youth (we looked in Chapter 1 at the way that grandeur *tout court* does not equate to the sublime: 'In the *Odyssey* one may liken Homer to the setting sun; the grandeur remains without the intensity', 9.13). In the translation with which we are concerned, 'le monde' goes on to exert a particular pressure upon the translator: 'On n'y trouve plus ce genre de discours si adroittement tourné, qui a tant l'air *du monde* et *tout plein d'images veritables*, que l'on voit dans l'Iliade' (fol. 140, my emphases). Boileau's version — 'il n'a plus cette même force, et, s'il faut ainsi parler, cette même volubilité de discours si propre pour l'action, et mêlée de tant d'images naïves des choses' — seeks to get Longinus's sense across by anchoring sublimity to 'naïveté'.[24] But this translator, returning specifically to 'le monde' which generalized Terentianus's field of experience in the first section of the treatise, makes in a particularly imposing way the point that the populous and variegated social world of the *Iliad* is the source of its sublimity.

In Longinus, something in an agile, swift-moving text anchored in the actions and events of 'le monde' can correspond to something in the active, inquisitive reader to create 'hypsos'. Encountering Longinus's comparison of Hyperides and Demosthenes later in the treatise, the translator pauses at the point where the former, an embodiment of solid, dependable virtues, is nonetheless shown to miss completely the mark of the sublime. The virtues in question are initially summed up as 'paresseuses' (fol. 151), a term which successfully deprives Hyperides of sublime action in a similar way to Boileau's depiction of his 'langueur d'esprit qui n'échauffe' (p. 388), or the statement in English that his qualities as a writer 'do not trouble the peace of the audience' (34.4). But it is accompanied by a further, brief, marginal annotation. Hyperides' virtues, in this supplementary suggestion, 'n'ont point d'action' (fol. 151). We find in this supplement a striking and dramatic portraiture of the necessary catalyst for 'hypsos'.

Peri hypsous sets up an initial difference — which the rest of the treatise will, as we know, nuance and develop — between rhetorical skill and sublimity:

> Invariably what inspires wonder, with its power of amazing us, always prevails over what is merely convincing and pleasing. For our persuasions are usually under our own control, while these things exercise an irresistible power and mastery, and get the better of every listener. (1.4)

The vocabulary employed by Longinus here is scrupulously clear: 'ekplēsso', to amaze, astound; 'kratēo', to hold sway; 'dunasteia', power, lordship, domination; these all precisely opposed to 'pithanon', the persuasive, plausible, the domain of rhetoric. Such oppositions run unhindered through Boileau's version of the text in question, which moors them firmly to the term 'Sublime' itself. This 'Sublime', then,

> ravit, il transporte, et produit en nous une certaine admiration mêlée d'étonnement et de surprise, qui est toute autre chose que de plaire seulement, ou de persuader. Nous pouvons dire à l'égard de la persuasion, que pour l'ordinaire elle n'a sur nous qu'autant de puissance que nous voulons. Il n'en est pas ainsi du Sublime. Il donne au Discours une certaine vigueur noble, une force invincible qui enleve l'ame de quiconque nous écoute. (pp. 341–42)

Boileau's 'puissance', 'vigueur', and 'force', faithful to Longinus, make 'la persuasion' seem a vapid and cumbersome means of communication.

The translator with whom we are concerned, however, reorchestrates this theme. What comes across here is less the friable quality of persuasion than the limitations of 'la probabilité':

> Le merveilleux l'emporte sur tout et éblouit pour ainsi dire le probable et les lieux dont on se sert pour gaigner l'esprit de l'auditeur. Il est en nostre pouvoir de ne nous pas rendre aux discours par lesquels on tache d'établir la probabilité d'une chose. Mais les choses qui sont dites avec cette autorité et force que la

sublimité donne au discours gouvernent souverainement l'esprit de l'auditeur.
(fol. 128; this whole passage appears in marginal annotation)

The capacity of the Longinian sublime to 'gouverne[r] souverainement' is conveyed precisely here, but its superiority, and superior durability, have changed. They take as the object of their sovereignty not the plausible or persuasive, but 'le probable', 'la probabilité'.

Clearly — and preceding discussions of 'vraisemblance' have already touched upon these matters — the probable (associated with regularity, consistency) is the rhetorical foundation for the persuasive (what people can be prepared or expected to believe). But there are also clear nuances here, and the translator's shift from one nuance to another stands out on the surface of the text. It stands out particularly, of course, precisely because, as we have seen, probability and persuasion were fought over around the time it was written in vicious debates about dramatic sequence and structure, about whether plots should be conceived on the basis of the opinions that an audience can be supposed to hold. The precise catalyst for these debates is Aristotle's distinction between 'pithanon', the plausible (the term Longinus uses), and 'eikos', the probable.[25] And this translator, turning one key term of debate, 'pithanon', into another, 'le probable', seems suggestively close to these arguments about the key criteria brought into play in portraying human lives.

Let us return in this context to the way that Longinus's readers are said to be able to identify sublimely with the images, drawn from real life, of Homer's *Iliad*. 'Les narrations de l'Odyssée', we are told, 'ne sont pas sans fautes et sont pour la plus part peu vraye semblables' (fol. 140^v); this statement is followed on the same page by a further commentary on the *Odyssey*: 'Et encore après tout en tous ces beaux endroits on voit bien plus de fables que de descriptions d'incidents vray-semblables.' Compare Boileau's rendering: 'A tout propos il s'égare dans des imaginations et des fables incroyables [...] joint qu'en tous ces endroits-là il y a bien plus de fable et de narration que d'action' (p. 355), and the English 'henceforth we see the ebbing tide of Homer's greatness, as he wanders in the realm of the fabulous and the incredible [...] in every one of these passages the mythical element predominates over the real' (9.13–14). Given the straightforward availability of a language of myth to translate the Greek 'mythikon', the translator's use of 'le vraisemblable' seems supererogatory. The way Longinus calls upon action and events to exert pressure upon mere narrative is couched in terms of one of the most controversial of all seventeenth-century theoretical terms. One might respond that, since Longinus's argument here takes up the question of structure in relation to believability, there is some overlap between any version of the treatise and dramatic theory. But this translation seems revealingly precise in its choice of terminology. The 'vraisemblable' inserts itself recalcitrantly and repetitively into the text, just as 'le probable' and 'la probabilité' did earlier.

It is interesting, finally, that this translator's 'vraisemblable', made to be the opposite of the fabulous narrative distention of the *Odyssey*, is applied to an *Iliad* 'tout plein d'images véritables'. In seventeenth-century debate, as we saw in Chapter 3, one of the main concerns behind the regulation of dramatic theory is that the 'vraisemblable' and the 'véritable' should be brought out of alignment:

'La vérité ne fait les choses que comme elles sont; & la vray-semblance les fait comme elles doivent être.'[26] Dramatic discourse, according to Rapin and his regulatory critical avatars, should, moreover, be pared down, streamlined into the 'unités' of time, place, and action. The 'vraisemblable', then, should not be 'tout plein' of anything, and certainly not of heterogeneous 'images véritables'. But the treatise on the sublime cannot be corralled into streamlined systems of checks and controls, and this translation invokes terminology and rewrites passages in such a way as to create emphases which are appropriately unruly. It is to checks and controls, though, that I now return, in the context of the most vicious seventeenth-century quarrel precipitated by the Longinian sublime.

Notes to Chapter 8

1. *Traité du sublime ou du merveilleux dans le discours, traduit du grec de Longin*, in Boileau, *Œuvres complètes*, ed. by Antoine Adam and Françoise Escal (Paris: Gallimard, 1966), p. 336. Page references to this edition will be cited in brackets.

2. This is the anonymous translator whose work was discovered by Bernard Weinberg, 'Une traduction française du "Sublime" de Longin vers 1645', *Modern Philology*, 59 (1961–62), 159–201 (see Introduction, n. 9), and expanded upon in Emma Gilby, ed., *De la sublimité du discours: traduction inédite du XVIIe siècle* (Paris: Éditions Comp'Act, forthcoming 2006). John Logan is the only critic I have found to make even a very brief mention of Weinberg's article ('Longinus and the Sublime', in *The Cambridge History of Literary Criticism*, III: *The Renaissance*, ed. by G. Norton (Cambridge: Cambridge University Press, 1999), pp. 529–39 (p. 538)). The lack of attention is due in part, no doubt, to the fact that the journal *Modern Philology* was not, in the 1960s, the best medium for getting Weinberg's message across to the French audience to whom it would have been of particular interest (and for whom, being written in French, it was presumably intended).

3. Jules Brody, *Boileau and Longinus* (Geneva: Droz, 1958), pp. 94–95 (the passage from Boileau is on pp. 348–49).

4. 'Platonisme et classicisme', in *French Classicism: A Critical Miscellany*, ed. by Jules Brody (Englewood Cliffs, NJ: Prentice-Hall, 1966), pp. 186–207 (p. 206). Brody follows the 'revisionist' stance towards French classicism expounded in E. B. O. Borgerhoff's seminal *The Freedom of French Classicism* (Princeton: Princeton University Press, 1950). See also Brody's 'What *Was* French Classicism?', in *Rethinking Classicism: Overviews*, ed. by David Lee Rubin (= *Continuum*, 1 (1989)), pp. 51–77. Brody writes here that 'the major values and tenets of French "classicism" — its preoccupation with form, universality, perfection, etc. — should be regarded as coded variants in the Platonic-Platonistic paradigm of the Good' (p. 75, n. 30).

5. Slobodan Vitanovic, 'La Place de la mythologie dans la poétique de Boileau', in *La Mythologie au XVIIe siècle: actes du XIe colloque du CMR 17* (Marseilles: CMR 17, 1982), pp. 25–31 (p. 27).

6. Nicholas Cronk, *The Classical Sublime: French Neoclassicism and the Language of Literature* (Charlottesville: Rookwood Press, 2002), pp. 42, 108.

7. See *Huetiana, ou pensées diverses de M. Huet, esveque d'Avranches*, ed. by L'Abbé d'Olivet (Paris: Jean Estienne, [1722, misprinted as 822]), pp. 80–81: 'C'est ainsi que dans ces paroles de la Genese, 1.3. *Dixitque Deus, fiat lux, & facta est lux*, Longin a cru trouver du sublime, faute de savoir que cette expression concise, qui paroît vive & forte dans la langue Grecque, dans la Latine, & dans celles qui en sont dérivées, à cause de cette répétition des mêmes termes qui semble avoir été étudiée & recherchée, est un Ebraïsme très-commun & très-simple dans les langues Orientales.' See also Huet's *Demonstratio evangelica*: 'Ce que Longin rapporte ici de Moïse, comme une expression Sublime et figurée, me semble très simple. Il est vrai que Moïse rapporte une chose qui est grande, mais il l'exprime d'une façon qui ne l'est nullement' (cited in Boileau, *Œuvres complètes*, p. 1072).

8. In 1701, Boileau makes an equally safe addition to his Preface: 'J'ai rapporté ces paroles de la Genese, comme l'expression la plus propre à mettre ma pensée en jour, et je m'en suis servi

d'autant plus volontiers que cette expression est citée avec éloge par Longin même, qui au milieu des tenebres du Paganisme, n'a pas laissé de reconnoître le divin qu'il y avait dans ces paroles de l'Ecriture' (p. 338).

9. Brody, *Boileau and Longinus*, p. 55. Socrates describes the soul as possessing an element of the 'divine, immortal, intelligible, uniform, indissoluble, and ever self-consistent and invariable' in *Phaedo*, 80b, trans. by Hugh Tredennick, in Plato, *The Collected Dialogues*.

10. Antoine Adam notes the historical facts about the *Dissertation sur Joconde*, which arose out of a literary 'pari' between Boileau and a chevalier de Saint-Gilles regarding the relative merits of La Fontaine's and Bouillon's translations of Ariosto's *Joconde*; that 'Brienne, un secrétaire de cabinet nommé M. de Langlade, Pierre Cyrano de Bergerac formaient le jury, Molière avait été désigné pour rapporteur', and that the event was reported in the 'Journal des Savants' in 1665. The *Dissertation* was first published in 1668 in a Dutch edition of La Fontaine, though 'ce fut en 1702 que dans une conversation avec Brossette il [Boileau] revendiqua la Dissertation'. *Histoire de la littérature française au dix-septième siècle*, 5 vols (Paris: Domat, 1948–56), III (1952), 84. René Bray, in 1931, compared the piece to Boileau's translation of the *Traité*, drawing attention to the similarity in certain turns of phrase. 'La Dissertation sur Joconde est-elle de Boileau?', *RHLF*, 38 (1931), 497–517.

11. For a full-length study of the term 'je ne sais quoi' in early modern literature, see Richard Scholar, *The Je-Ne-Sais-Quoi in Early Modern Europe: Encounters with a Certain Something* (Oxford: Oxford University Press, 2005). Cronk, in *The Classical Sublime*, brings up the 'je ne sais quoi' in order to state that for Boileau, this term was less powerful and coherent than the 'sublime'. This is because the appropriation of the 'je ne sais quoi' as a literary critical term had already been effected by Bouhours, who had used it 'as an attempt to produce a more reader-oriented theory of poetic discourse that can account for the idea of full expressivity' (p. 63). The power Boileau attributes to the term 'sublime', on the other hand, stems from the inconsistency with which it was used prior to Boileau's publication of his translation of Longinus. These very inconsistencies mean, for Cronk, that Boileau is subsequently able to define the term at will: 'Since "le sublime" was not an established critical term [...] [it] allowed him more easily to underscore the affective aspects of language and to suggest that the language of strong emotional appeal might as effectively be achieved by simple means as by elaborate rhetoric' (p. 96).

12. Brody, *Boileau and Longinus*, p. 142.

13. Louis Marin speaks of 'une altération, une défaillance de l'identité du sujet, une désappropriation du sujet à soi-même (qu'il s'agisse du ravissement, du transport, de l'enlèvement, ou de la stupéfaction, de l'étonnement, de la sidération)'. 'Le Sublime dans les années 1670: un "je ne sais quoi"?', *Papers on French Seventeenth-Century Literature*, 25 (1986), 185–201 (p. 188).

14. Louis Marin, 'On the Sublime, Infinity, Je Ne Sais Quoi', in *A New History of French Literature*, ed. by Denis Hollier (Cambridge, MA: Harvard University Press, 1989), pp. 340–45 (p. 341) (Marin's italics).

15. See *Boileau and Longinus*, p. 95, and my discussion at the beginning of this chapter.

16. Marc Fumaroli, *Héros et orateurs: rhétorique et dramaturgie cornéliennes* (Geneva: Droz, 1990), p. 346.

17. See Marin, 'On the Sublime, Infinity, Je Ne Sais Quoi', p. 341.

18. *Traité du sublime*, p. 335.

19. *Dyonisii Longini Liber de grandi sive sublimi genere orationis, latine redditus, et ad oram notationibus aliquot illustratus a Gab. De Petra* (Geneva: J. Tournai, 1612), p. 55. Petra has realized that the gap in Longinus's text refers to an anecdote to be found in Plutarch, *Life of Alexander*, 29. As noted in my Introduction, Petra's translation was reproduced in subsequent editions of Longinus brought out by Langbaine (1636), Manolesius (1644) and Le Fèvre (1663).

20. All folio references are marked in Gilby, ed., *Pseudo-Longin, De la sublimité du discours*; see the critical introduction to this volume for further discussion of this text and the examples cited in what follows.

21. 'He fell on the host as a wave of the sea on a hurrying vessel, | Rising up under the clouds, a boisterous son of the storm-wind. | The good ship is lost in the shroud of the foam, and the breath of the tempest | Terribly roars in the sails; and in their hearts tremble the sailors, | By the breadth of a hand swept out from under the jaws of destruction.' Longinus, *On the Sublime*, 10.5.

22. See the Greek text of the passage from Homer cited above (n. 21; the prepositions in question are translated as 'from under').

23. Boileau, by contrast, has 'les Orateurs' ('voyons, pour l'amour de vous, si nous n'avons point fait sur cette matiere quelque observation raisonnable, et dont les Orateurs puissent tirer quelque sorte d'utilité' (p. 341)); the Loeb edition has 'let us then see whether my observations have any value for public speakers' (1.1). The terms 'emploi' and 'maniement' are interesting given that, at a point at which Montaigne's *Essais* resonate with the treatise on the sublime — with Longinus's praise for those poets who can, as we saw above, force 'into an abnormal union prepositions not normally compounded' (10.6) — Montaigne also couples these two nouns: 'Le maniement et emploite des beaux espris donne pris à la langue, non pas l'innovant tant comme la remplissant de plus vigoreux et divers services, l'estirant et ployant. Ils n'y aportent point de mots, mais ils enrichissent les leurs, appesantissent et enfoncent leur signification et leur usage, luy aprenent des mouvements inaccoustumés, mais prudemment et ingenieusement.' *Essais*, ed. by P. Villey, 2nd edn (Paris: Presses universitaires de France, 1965), III. 5, p. 873.

24. 'Tout ce qu'il dit est simple et naturel,' writes Boileau of La Fontaine in the *Dissertation sur Joconde*, 'et ce que j'estime surtout en lui, c'est une certaine Naïveté de Langage, que peu de gens connoissent, et qui fait pourtant tout l'agrément du discours' (p. 315).

25. 'Poetic needs', writes Aristotle in *Poetics*, 61b11–12, 'make something plausible [pithanon] though impossible preferable to what is possible but implausible [apithanon]'; this is in spite of the fact that 'it is probable [eikos] that improbable [para to eikos] things occur' (61b14–15). On the other hand, 'if then a thing is incredible and not probable [mē eikos], it will be true; for it is not because it is probable and credible [eikos kai pithanon] that we think it true' (*Rhetoric*, 1400a8). What Aristotle seems to be saying here (see note d in the edition cited) is that if a statement is made which is incredible and improbable, we grant it an irrationally high truth value on the grounds that it is so extraordinary that it would not have been made unless it were true.

26. René Rapin, *Réflexions sur la poétique de ce temps, et sur les ouvrages des poetes anciens et modernes*, 2nd edn, rev. and enlarged (Paris: François Muguet, 1675), p. 36.

CHAPTER 9

❖

The *Querelle des Anciens et des Modernes* and the Sublime

Another of the concrete additions made to the text of *Peri hypsous* by the 1612 editor Gabriele de Petra is Homer's description of the goddess of discord, which follows on directly from Alexander's response to Parmenio, discussed above, and has a similar exemplary status, as we see in Boileau's translation:

> Et c'est en cette partie qu'a principalement excellé Homere, dont les pensées sont toutes sublimes: comme on le peut voir dans la description de la Déesse Discorde, qui a dit il:
>
> > La teste dans les Cieux, et les piés sur la Terre.
>
> Car on peut dire que cette grandeur qu'il luy donne est moins la mesure de la Discorde, que de la capacité et de l'élévation de l'esprit d'Homere.[1] (pp. 351–52)

This passage carries, as we shall now see, a particular burden of polemic. This becomes evident in the *Réflexions critiques*, where Boileau goes to work with unrestrained energy upon one particular author who has failed to understand.

Perrault's Reasoning

Charles Perrault, in his *Parallèle des anciens et des modernes*, makes emphatic objections concerning the excessive unreality of Homer's depiction of discord. In making discord a giantess, Homer 'la met au rang des contes de peau d'asne' (p. 509). Boileau's retort is revealing. Homer's point, he states, is that 'la Discorde regne par tout sur la terre, et mesme dans le Ciel entre les Dieux; c'est-à-dire, entre les Dieux d'Homere' (p. 509). Homer's point, then, is the unpredictability and the discordance of existence. We are not to engage with his depiction in terms of its verticality (in envisaging a mythical being who might stretch from the earth to the heavens) but rather in terms of its different, parallel, strata (the stratum that is the earth and the stratum that is the heavens), which mirror each other in their discordant messiness. The capacity to get this across, then, is Homer's sublime 'capacité' and 'élévation' (p. 351 — although in saying of Homer that his 'pensées sont toutes sublimes' Boileau contradicts Longinus's point about the *Odyssey* lacking the sublimity of the *Iliad* later in Chapter 9: 'Henceforth we see the ebbing tide of Homer's greatness, as he wanders in the realm of the fabulous and the incredible', 9.13).

Perrault, though, is missing the point completely when he writes: 'C'est que, tant qu'on poura voir la teste de la Renommée sa teste ne sera point dans le Ciel; et que si sa teste est dans le Ciel, on ne sçait pas trop bien ce que l'on voit' (p. 510).[2] 'O l'admirable raisonnement!', exclaims Boileau (p. 510). If Perrault's 'raisonnement' were flexible enough, he would see that the disorder of the Gods allegorizes the chaos on earth: 'Ce n'est point la description d'un Géant, comme le prétend nostre Censeur, que fait icy Homere; c'est une allegorie tres-juste: et bien qu'il fasse de la Discorde un personnage, c'est un personnage allegorique qui ne choque point, de quelque taille qu'il le fasse' (p. 509). Homer is conveying his concern with the unpredictability of existence. It is in this connection that, for Longinus as for Boileau, his thoughts can be qualified as 'sublime', his 'esprit' as 'élevé'. Homer makes space for heterogeneity in a way that Perrault cannot: thus his discourse is sublime. And we might say that any allegory (knowledge through the rethinking of similitude and difference) is beyond an author who thinks only in 'parallèles'.

These comments open up, as I shall go on to argue, a new way of understanding the sublime in relation to the debate generally known as the *Querelle des Anciens et des Modernes*. First, though, it is worth considering briefly the terms of this *Querelle*, which pits 'Ancients' such as Boileau or Anne Dacier against 'Moderns' such as Desmarets de Saint-Sorlin, Perrault, and Pradon. The 'Ancients' are seen by the 'Moderns' as demanding a return to the classics, and as tracing out a trajectory, in their reading and thinking, which is more or less cyclical: a continuous movement from the present to the past and back again. Such a movement is opposed to the 'Modern' model of a progressively linear development culminating in the seventeenth century of 'Louis le Grand'.

Desmarets has been held up by critics as the first 'Modern', preceding other contributors to the debate by a number of years with vehement tracts such as *La Comparaison de la langue et de la poésie française avec la grecque et la latine, et des poètes grecs, latins, et français* (1670) and *La Defense du poëme héroïque* (1674). Indeed Joan DeJean comments, in terms almost as polemical as those of her subject, that 'it is hard to imagine why [these works ...] did not set the Ancients off'.[3] Desmarets handed over the baton to Perrault in 1675 in his testamentary *La Défense de la poësie, et de la langue françoise, adressée à Monsieur Perrault*:

> Vien deffendre, Perrault, la France qui t'appelle,
> Vien combattre avec moy cette troupe rebelle,
> Ce ramas d'ennemis, qui foibles & mutins
> Preferent à nos chants les ouvrages Latins.[4]

Desmarets cannot countenance the relevance of 'les ouvrages Latins' for a modern, self-enclosed and self-sustaining world:

> Nous qui d'inventions ayant nos sources pleines,
> Dêdaignons de puiser aux antiques fontaines.
> Nous parlons un langage & plus noble & plus beau
> Que le triste Latin qu'on tire du tombeau. (p. 23)

And with Desmarets, other Moderns attribute to their Ancient counterparts a confidence in a redundant standard of knowledge and beauty, which they counter with Cartesian rationalism: in Fontenelle's words, 'c'est lui [Descartes], à ce qu'il me semble, qui a amené cette nouvelle méthode de raisonner', and with it 'une précision et une justesse qui, jusqu'à présent, n'avoient été guère connues'.[5]

Fontenelle's valorization of newness, his avowal that 'sur quelque matière que ce soit, les Anciens sont assez sujets à ne pas raisonner dans la dernière perfection' (p. 420), is manifested with equal force in Perrault's *Parallèle des anciens et des modernes en ce qui regarde les arts et les sciences* (1688). The 'Modern' of Perrault's dialogues is a representative figure who, we are told, 'a pris soin de cultiver son propre fonds', who 'en tire par de fréquentes réflexions mille pensées nouvelles', and who 'juge du mérite de chaque chose en elle-même'.[6] This kind of reasoning is posited by Perrault as available to all, rather than simply to an educated elite. His concomitant equation of the study of the classics with intellectual stagnation is taken up by DeJean in her analysis of the *Querelle*: 'The Ancients went to war because [...] they feared that the literary world was changing too fast and too completely, and because they hoped that, if they could humiliate the Moderns, they could reverse the shifting tide of literary values.'[7]

In discussions of the *Querelle*, the term 'sublime' is often aligned with transcendence and seen as the polar opposite of a 'modern' regulatable reason. When Fumaroli cites Montaigne's rapture at classical authors ('leurs écrits ne me satisfont pas seulement et me remplissent; mais ils m'étonnent et transissent d'admiration') to state that 'l'apologétique du sublime par les Anciens de la fin du XVIIe siècle, un Boileau, une Anne Dacier, est déjà toute formée dans l'enivrement qui remplit Montaigne à la lecture des poètes antiques', he forges a steadfast link between the sublime, the ancient, and 'enivrement'.[8] Fumaroli's account here is very similar to the accounts of Antoine Adam — '[Boileau] n'ignorait pas que les Modernes ne voyaient dans les enthousiasmes de l'inspiration que divagations et délires'[9] — and Théodore Litman: '[Perrault] devait se heurter à un élément esthétique à la fois mystérieux et divin'.[10] And one seventeenth-century anecdote suggests that the term 'sublime' was closely associated with the *Querelle* from the inception of debate:

> Madame de Thianges a donné à M. du Maine en étrennes une chambre grande comme une table, toute dorée. Au-dessus de la porte il y a écrit *Chambre sublime*, et dedans un lit, un balustre et un grand fauteuil, dans lequel est assis M. du Maine fait en cire en petit, fort ressemblant. Auprès de lui M. de la Rochefoucauld auquel il donne des vers pour les examiner; derrière le dos du fauteuil, madame Scarron. Autour de lui M. de Marsillac et M. de Condom; à l'autre bout de l'alcove, madame de Thianges et madame de la Fayette lisant des vers ensemble. Au dehors des balustres, Despréaux, avec une fourche, empêchant sept ou huit mauvais poëtes d'approcher. Racine auprès de Despréaux et un peu plus loin la Fontaine auquel il fait signe de la main d'approcher. Toutes ces figures sont faites en cire, en petit; et chacun de ceux qu'elle représente a donné la sienne. On les appelle la *cabale sublime*.[11]

As Fumaroli puts it, 'Il ne fallait pas être grand clerc pour deviner que parmi les bannis de liasse figuraient Perrault et Quinault.'[12]

One 'Modern', Pradon, reveals 'une obsession révélatrice envers ce mot de 'sublime' accaparé par ses adversaires'.[13] And Pradon's vituperative comments in his *Préface* to *Phèdre et Hippolyte* and in his later works *Le Triomphe de Pradon sur les Satire du Sieur D★★★* (1684), *Nouvelles remarques sur tous les ouvrages du Sieur D★★★* (1685), and the 1694 *Réponse à la Satire X du Sieur D★★★*, do indeed revolve around a sublime supposed to be the province of Boileau and, by association, Racine. The *Préface* to *Phèdre et Hippolyte* reads as follows:

> En verité, n'en déplaise à ces grands Hommes, ils me permetront de leur dire en passant que leur procedé & leurs manieres sont fort éloignées de ce Sublime qu'ils tâchent d'atraper dans leurs Ouvrages: Pour moy, j'ay toûjours crû qu'on devoit avoir ce caractere dans ses mœurs, avant que de le faire paroître dans ses Ecrits, & que l'on devoit estre bien moins avide de la qualité de bon Autheur, que de celle d'honneste Homme, que l'on me verra toûjours préferer à tout le sublime de Longin.[14]

Pradon understands the sublime as the pretentiously elevated; something Boileau and Racine think they have to aim towards and 'atraper'. In his satirical *Nouvelles remarques sur tous les ouvrages du Sieur D★★★*, he maintains this definition of sublimity:

> Tâche de polir mieux & ta prose & ta rime,
> Fais qu'on ne trouve plus de bas dans ton Sublime;
> On voit que ton Esprit bronche à chaque moment,
> Et qu'il manque à son feu le froid du jugement.[15]

Boileau's work betrays the vacillation of his mind, a form of 'feu' which, like the irrational elements of ancient culture, precludes 'le froid du jugement' of Fontenelle's 'nouvelle méthode de raisonner'.[16]

Censors and Pedants

Boileau's *Réflexions critiques* are clearly set up from the start to make Longinus participate in the *Querelle*: they are subtitled *sur quelques passages du rheteur Longin, où, par occasion, on répond à quelques objections de Monsieur P★★★ contre Homère et contre Pindare*. Each *Réflexion* begins with a passage from Longinus. However, since the *Réflexions* do not deal in any way with the irrational ecstasy associated, as we see in Pradon and in modern critics such as Fumaroli, with the sublime, and since they present a very personal attack on Perrault, the role played by the Longinian sublime within them has often been puzzled over. Cronk comments that 'the title *Réflexions sur Longin* is deliberately ironic'.[17] Boileau's editor, Françoise Escal, states of the *Réflexions critiques* that 'Longin ne sert souvent que de prétexte ou de point de départ' (p. 1095). Kerslake opines that 'the first nine, published in 1694, form part of Boileau's quarrel with Perrault and have at most a tenuous connection with the sublime'.[18] Boileau's comment, at the end of the ninth reflection, that 'encore n'y en ai-je mis [des fautes que Monsieur P. a commises] qu'une tres-petite partie, et selon que les paroles de Longin m'en ont donné l'occasion' seems, for these critics, to be entirely disingenuous. The *Querelle des Anciens et des Modernes* is summarized as a battle pitting 'sublime contre style sublime, génie créateur contre travail poétique, décadence culturelle contre progrès artistique'; and the *Réflexions* do not seem to participate.[19] But there is, as I have observed throughout, more to the interactive Longinian sublime than a 'génie créateur'. And any form of thought which sees itself as self-regulating and self-sufficient is therefore shown, in the *Réflexions*, to be disastrous in this context. Boileau juxtaposes Longinus and Perrault to suggest that Perrault is incapable of sublime discourse as Longinus defines this.

Boileau's repeated characterization of Perrault as 'nostre Censeur' takes on a particular force here. The discourse of a censor is by necessity homogeneous: it brings into line, excluding all that which does not correspond to its own angle of vision and thereby obviating dialogue. Furetière's definition of the term 'censeur' brings out this monologizing effect: 'Il faut se conduire de telle sorte, que les censeurs n'y trouvent rien à redire.'[20] One of Boileau's epigrams is telling:

> D'où vient que Ciceron, Platon, Virgile, Homere,
> Et tous ces grands Auteurs que l'Univers revere
> Traduits dans vos écrits nous paroissent si sots?
> P★★★, c'est qu'en prestant à ces Esprits sublimes
> Vos façons de parler, vos bassesses, vos rimes,
> Vous les faites tous des P★★★. (p. 263)

Boileau shows that Perrault defers only to the structures of his own singular perceptions. In Boileau's personification of censorship in the *Réflexions*, its action is to 'sali[r] tout ce qu'il touche' (p. 506). Thus, 'Toute la grossiereté prétenduë du mot d'Homere appartient entierement à nostre Censeur, qui salit tout ce qu'il touche, et qui n'attaque les Auteurs anciens que sur des interpretation fausses qu'il se forge à sa fantaisie.'

Boileau makes the specific point, therefore, that his own discourse is infinitely more flexible than a censorious 'forging':

> Et je ne regle point l'estime que je fais d'eux par le temps qu'il y a que leurs Ouvrages durent: mais par le temps qu'il y a qu'on les admire. C'est de quoy il est bon d'avertir beaucoup de gens qui pouroient mal-à-propos croire ce que veut insinuer nôtre Censeur; qu'on ne louë les Anciens, que parce qu'ils sont Anciens, et qu'on ne blâme les Modernes, que parce qu'ils sont Modernes; ce qui n'est point du tout veritable, y ayant beaucoup d'Anciens qu'on n'admire point, et beaucoup de Modernes que tout le monde louë (p. 527).

There is a rejection, here as in other texts I have examined in this book, of blanket, homogenizing regulation: different instances of this rejection, taking the ancient–modern divide as their specific context, have been seen with the 'Modern' Saint-Evremond, who defines a modern 'bon goust' in part through a discriminating 'bon goust de l'antiquité', and Pascal, who states that we can only 'surpasser' the Ancients 'en les imitant'.[21] And here, Boileau establishes the elastic judgement of his own work in contrast to the generalization attributed to it by Perrault. He concomitantly reverses the poles of the debate, turns Perrault's accusation ('qu'on ne louë les Anciens, que parce qu'ils sont Anciens, et qu'on ne blâme les Modernes, que parce qu'ils sont Modernes') against him, to show Perrault as guilty of this narrowly univocal (and so anti-Longinian) discourse himself.

Perrault's *Mémoires* are particularly instructive when they reach the founding episode of the *Querelle des Anciens et des Modernes*, and the reading, at the seat of the Académie française, of a poem 'qui blâmaient les plus grands hommes de l'antiquité'.[22] Boileau, as Perrault notes, famously took umbrage: 'Depuis cette avanture, le chagrin de M. Despreaux lui fit faire plusieurs épigrammes, qui n'alloient qu'à m'offenser, mais nullement à miner mon sentiment touchant les anciens' (p. 202). But Racine, on the other hand, seems to have supposed Perrault's reading to be a mere exercise in demonstrative rhetoric. Perrault writes that 'M. Racine me fit compliment sur cet ouvrage qu'il loua beaucoup, dans la supposition que ce n'était qu'un pur jeu d'esprit qui ne contenoit pas mes véritables sentiments, & que dans la vérité je pensois tout le contraire de ce que j'avois avancé dans mon poëme' (p.202). The idea that Perrault might have been trying out, or on, a set of opinions which would provide an ironic coating for his own is distasteful to him: 'Je fus fâché qu'on ne me crût pas, ou du moins qu'on fît semblant de ne pas croire que j'eusse parlé sérieusement' (p. 202). The idea that Racine might be demonstrating his own capacity for irony — 'ou du moins qu'on fît semblant de ne pas croire' — only makes more urgent Perrault's need to refute entirely the suggestion that he might function, as a critic, in the same way: 'Je pris la résolution de dire en prose ce que j'avois dit en vers, & de le dire d'une manière à ne pas faire douter de mon vrai sentiment là-dessus. Voilà quelle a été la cause & l'origine de mes quatre tomes de Paralleles' (p. 202). Watertight partitions keep Perrault's 'vrai sentiment' away from the boggy relativism of irony.

Boileau's condemnation of Perrault as a 'censeur', in the *Réflexions*, is closely linked to the status he grants him as a 'pédant'. The appropriation and reappropriation of this term, as it is employed first by one party and then the other, offer further insights into the nature and significance of the debate about censorship and univocality. The following quotation has Boileau summing up Perrault's understanding of the term:

> Mais à propos de hauteur pédantesque, peut-estre ne sera-t-il pas mauvais d'expliquer icy ce que j'ay voulu dire par là, et ce que c'est proprement qu'un Pédant. Car il me semble que Mr P. ne conçoit pas trop bien toute l'étenduë de ce mot. En effet, si l'on en doit juger par tout ce qu'il insinuë dans ses Dialogues, un Pédant, selon luy, est un sçavant nouri dans un Collége, et rempli de Grec et de Latin, qui admire aveuglément tous les Auteurs anciens, [...] qui croirait faire une espèce d'impieté, s'il avoit trouvé quelque chose à redire dans Virgile: qui ne trouve pas simplement Terence un joli auteur, mais le comble de toute perfection; qui ne se pique point de politesse. (p. 515)

The discussion of pedantry attributed to Perrault bears comparison to Malebranche's definition of the term in *La Recherche de la vérité*: 'Les pédants sont donc vains et fiers, de grande mémoire et de peu de jugement, heureux et forts en citations, malheureux et faibles en raisons, d'une imagination vigoureuse et spacieuse, mais volage et déréglée, et qui ne peut se contenir dans quelque justesse.'[23] 'Justesse', here, is Furetière's 'précision, exactitude, régularité', the last term condensing the 'juste' into the spatially justified, the precisely aligned, the non-individuated.[24] Pedantry, on the other hand, is unregulated citation. Quotation is rejected as a mode of utterance, so Malebranche's theory seems to go, because to subordinate oneself to the thoughts of others is to devalue the reasoning self which should be conscious of the 'justesse' of its own functioning.[25] Boileau's counter-definition of pedantry is crucial: 'qu'un Pédant est presque tout le contraire de ce tableau, qu'un Pédant est un homme plein de luy-meme, qui, avec un médiocre sçavoir décide hardiment de toutes choses: qui se vante sans cesse' (p. 515). Pedantry, in the sense Boileau gives to the term, is a secularized *amour-propre*, the propensity to 'se vanter'; 'un homme plein de luy-meme' is incapable of a projection — in writing, reading, or living — towards others.

One author condemned as a 'pédant' by many of Boileau's contemporaries is Montaigne. Montaigne exemplifies the 'imagination vigoureuse et spatieuse, mais volage et déreglée' of Malebranche's definition of pedantry; as the latter notes, 'Il ne sera pas maintenant fort difficile de prouver que Montaigne était aussi pédant que plusieurs autres selon cette notion du mot de pédant.'[26] It is a critical commonplace that 'seventeenth-century reactions to Montaigne demonstrate vividly the growing intolerance of multivocal and self-consciously dialogic discourse'.[27] But Boileau, apparently, views just such a multivocal mode of writing as exemplary in its opposition to pedantry: 'Balzac & M. Despreaux', we are told, '[...] n'estoient point effrayés de la grande liberté de Montaigne.'[28] Boileau is reported to have asked: 'Qu'est-ce [...] qu'un Saint-Evremond, que les Sots osent comparer à Montaigne? Les écarts de l'un valent mieux que tout le concert et l'arrangement de l'autre' (p. lx). Boileau's appreciation of Montaigne's structure of 'écarts' reveals once again his opposition to the univocality, 'le concert et l'arrangement', of pedantic 'politesse'.[29] And because univocality is the target here, the intensely personal form of Boileau's attacks on the way Perrault conducts himself — on the self-imposing way in which Perrault reads and writes — is the relevant and indeed necessary structure of debate. Perrault is closed off to texts that can convey, sublimely, the dialogues of existence. The structures of Boileau's *Querelle* are also those of the Longinian sublime.

It makes sense, given all this, and as I mentioned in introducing this discussion of the *Querelle des Anciens et des Modernes*, that Perrault should distrust allegory; and it makes sense that this distrust should extend to more isolable cases of comparison or metaphor. As Boileau notes, Perrault's mouthpiece in his *Parallèle des anciens et des modernes*, the Abbé,

> declare en un endroit qu'il n'approuve point ces comparaisons d'Homere où le Poëte, non content de dire précisément ce qui sert à la comparaison, s'étend sur quelque circonstance historique de la chose dont il est parlé: comme lors qu'il compare la cuisse de Menelas blessé à de l'yvoire teint en pourpre par une femme de Mœonie et de Carie, etc.[30]

Homer's metaphors, like his allegories, amount (says the Abbé's admirer, the Chevalier, quoted here in Boileau's *Réflexions*) disreputably to 'visions'; they are 'peu sensées':

> *Il faut que Dieu ne fasse pas grand cas de la reputation de bel Esprit: puisqu'il permet que ces titres soient donnez preferablement au reste du genre humain à deux hommes, comme Platon et Homere, à un Philosophe qui a des visions si bizarres, et à un Poëte qui dit tant de choses si peu sensées.* (p. 538)

Homer's metaphors, in other words, are *'comparaisons à longue queuë'* (p. 519). The distance between the two points of comparison is too great to be validated by Perrault. Perrault polices the terrain of metaphor, constructing formal guidelines for tropes of comparison. The authority to which we ought to turn, he says, is common opinion as to what is acceptable. The only possible words of support for Homer are put into the mouth of the Abbé's adversary, the President: 'Comme dans les ceremonies on trouveroit à redire aux queuës des Princesses, si elles ne traînoient jusqu'à terre; de même les comparaisons dans le Poëme Epique seroient blâmables, si elles n'avoient des queuës fort traînantes' (p. 520).

Boileau finds the highest comic potential in the way that the Abbé then adjusts this analogy by extending it, 'avoüant [...] qu'à la verité on peut donner de longues queuës aux comparaisons, mais soûtenant qu'il faut, ainsi qu'aux robbes des Princesses, que ces queuës soient de même étoffe que la robbe. Ce qui manque, dit-il, aux comparaisons d'Homere, où les queuës sont de deux étoffes differentes' (p. 520). For Boileau, what Perrault illustrates with this whole episode is merely the way that, in language, anything can be compared to anything else: '*Quel rapport*', Boileau asks disparagingly, 'ont les comparaisons à des Princesses?' (p. 520, my emphases). It is not just the matter of the comparison which Boileau finds extravagant — the comparison of comparisons to dresses — but also the fact that these characters find themselves capable of making arguments, and extended value judgements, on the basis of the vagaries of fashion design: 'De sorte que s'il arrivoit qu'en France, comme cela peut fort bien arriver, la mode vînt de coudre des queuës de differente etoffe aux robbes des Princesses, voilà le President qui auroit entierement cause gagnée sur les comparaisons' (pp. 520–21).

Boileau's 'quel rapport?', then, rather like his condemnation of Perrault as a 'pédant', takes the terms of Perrault's criticism — a lack of rapport in Homer's metaphors — and turns his own accusations against him. Thinking he is deferring to the rules and regulations of rhetoric, Perrault gets it extravagantly wrong. Moreover, in criticizing a lack of precision in Homer, Perrault cannot see that he is aiming to circumscribe a domain which is defined only by inexactitude. 'C'est une verité universellement reconnuë', says Boileau, 'qu'il n'est point necessaire, en matiere de Poësie, que les points de la comparaison se répondent si juste les uns aux autres: qu'il suffit d'un rapport general, et qu'une trop grande exactitude sentiroit son Rheteur' (p. 519). The relationship between the tenor and the vehicle of a metaphor is motivated only by a 'rapport general'. The universality of this fact allows for an infinity of instantiations of it. We cannot fix 'une verité universellement reconnuë' into a single frame of reference or regulation. 'Metaphor asks us not only to balance but to value balancing.'[31] Boileau ackowledges this in a way that Perrault does not, noting of Homer that:

> Non seulement toutes les comparaisons, mais tous les discours sont pleins d'images de la nature si vrayes et si variées, qu'estant toûjours le mesme, il est neanmoins toûjours different; instruisant sans cesse le Lecteur, et lui faisant observer dans les objets mêmes, qu'il a tous les jours devant les yeux, des choses qu'il ne s'avisoit pas d'y remarquer. (p. 519)

When DeJean writes on the *Querelle*, she sees Boileau's work as standing for 'the transcendental values of a timeless "we"', to which Perrault 'opposes the right to individual choices and the infinitely varied and contemporary values of an "I" determined to maintain its critical independence'.[32] And similarly, Robert J. Nelson writes that 'for [Boileau] language was not a secondary, transparent signifier of *present* signifieds, but the primary if paradoxical site of *eternal* truths transcending language and other signifying systems'.[33] But I hope to have shown that Boileau can be understood to counter a moral myopia he sees as that of the Moderns. The consequences of a 'perte de vue', as we saw at the beginning of Chapter 8 with Boileau ('ces hommes accoûtumez aux débauches et aux excés des Poëtes modernes, et qui n'admirant que ce qu'ils n'entendent point, ne pensent pas qu'un Auteur se soit élevé, s'ils ne l'ont entierement perdu de veuë', p. 337), are fatal in the context of the Longinian sublime. Longepierre's *Discours sur les anciens* provides us with an interesting point of comparison here:

> Concluons donc en ajoutant que ne pouvoir perdre son siècle de vue est le fruit d'un amour-propre entièrement aveugle et d'un génie extrêmement borné. Un esprit vaste est de tous les temps et de tous les siècles. Il les voit tout d'une vue, et si je peux parler ainsi, *d'un seul coup d'œil*. Il entre sans peine dans leurs goûts différents.[34]

Boileau's translation of and comments on Longinus need to be identified with this assumption that it is not useful to leave unqualified any talk of the blandly transcendent, transhistorical, or transparent. The *Réflexions* are important from the start in Boileau's analysis of knowledge gained through populated texts and our proliferating responses to them.

The *Réflexions critiques* and their refutation of Perrault's work, then, are of the highest relevance to our examination of Longinus and of sublimity. Boileau grants the *Querelle* a particular moral force through his interrogation of the sublime. His criticism of Perrault is not just that the latter fails at classical scholarship, but that his censorious, pedantic discourse makes him incapable of understanding the sublime. Boileau, in his reception of the Longinian sublime, puts forward a view of sublimity that consists not in seizing, holding, trapping, or controlling, but in encountering, in engaging with, in the words of another translator, 'l'emploi et le maniement des affaires du monde' (see Chapter 8). A cognitive interest in human 'affaires' can, both as a way of writing and a way of reading, encourage the sublime experience with which Longinus is concerned. Texts that figure encounters, and readers who seek them out, can come together in a moment of sublime experience. With their belief in a linear, constantly improving, and univocal reason, the 'Moderns' cannot countenance the unpredictability of knowledge gained through encounter, nor that this unpredictability might both pleasurably and troublingly define the course of our existence as human beings.

Every element in Longinus's treatise serves to activate part of Boileau's own body of work. We have seen that, in the sublime, absorption (a commingling of oneself as reader with the thought of an author) is modified by self-examination. Just as important as this for Boileau, though, is the way that the Longinian sublime consists of an interplay of hermeneutic standpoints. Boileau himself follows Longinus in this, and does so as a means of modelling ethical thought. His expansion of Longinus's examples and his reflections on the sublime acknowledge the vulnerability of the unitary, the centred, or the grounded and make a case for the importance of discourse about human relations.

Notes to Chapter 9

1. The reference is to the *Iliad*, Book IV, verse 443. All that can be read in Longinus at this point, where the suspension points signal six missing pages, is 'Alexander's answer to Parmenio when he said "For my part I had been content" [...] the distance between earth and heaven. One might say too that this measured the stature not of Strife so much as of Homer' (9.4).

2. Virgil imitates Homer's turn of phrase in writing about 'la Renommée' rather than discord; Perrault, while criticizing Homer, is confusing Homer and Virgil.

3. Joan DeJean, *Ancients against Moderns: Culture Wars and the Making of a Fin de Siècle* (Chicago: University of Chicago Press, 1997), p. 46.

4. Geneva: Slatkine reprints, 1972 (Paris: Nicolas le Gras, 1675), p. 20.

5. M. de Fontenelle, 'Digression sur les Anciens et les Modernes', in *Œuvres complètes*, ed. by Alain Niderst, 7 vols (Paris: Fayard, 1989–96), II (1991), 413–31 (p. 420).

6. Charles Perrault, *Parallèle des anciens et des modernes en ce qui regarde les arts et les sciences*, 4 vols (Paris: Jean-Baptiste Coignard, 1692–97), I, 3–4.

7. *Ancients against Moderns*, p. 42.

8. Marc Fumaroli, 'Les Abeilles et les araignées', in *La Querelle des Anciens et des Modernes*, ed. by Anne-Marie Lecoq (Paris: Gallimard, 2001), pp. 7–218 (pp. 9–10). The citation of Montaigne is taken from 'De la présomption'.

9. Antoine Adam, *Histoire de la littérature française au dix-septième siècle*, 5 vols (Paris: Domat, 1948–56), V, 76.

10. Théodore Litman, *Le Sublime en France, 1660–1714* (Paris: Nizet, 1971), p. 162.

11. 'Lettre à Bussy', 12 January 1675, attributed to Mlle Dupré, in *Correspondance de Roger de Rabutin, Comte de Bussy, avec sa famille et ses amis*, ed. by Ludovic Lalanne, 6 vols (Paris: Charpentier, 1858–59), II (1858), 415–16. M. du Maine, then five years old, was the eldest illegitimate son of Mme de Montespan and Louis XIV, and the nephew of Mme de Thianges. Mme Scarron, the governess of M. du Maine, was to become Mme de Maintenon, and M. de Marsillac was the son of La Rochefoucauld.

12. 'Les Abeilles et les araignées', pp. 175–76.

13. Jacques Pradon, *Phèdre et Hippolyte*, ed. by O. Classe (Exeter: Exeter University Press, 1987), p. xiv.

14. Ibid., p. 4.

15. Jacques Pradon, *Nouvelles remarques sur tous les ouvrages du Sieur D**** (The Hague: Strik, 1685), p. 20.

16. Fontenelle, 'Digression', p. 420.

17. Nicholas Cronk, *The Classical Sublime: French Neoclassicism and the Language of Literature* (Charlottesville: Rookwood Press, 2002), p. 151.

18. Lawrence Kerslake, *Essays on the Sublime: Analyses of French Writings on the Sublime from Boileau to La Harpe* (Berne: Peter Lang, 2000), p. 50, n. 16.

19. Philip Lewis, 'L'Anti-sublime, ou la rhétorique du progrès', in *Rhétoriques fin de siècle*, ed. by Mary Shaw and François Cornilliat (Paris: Christian Bourgeois, 1992), pp. 117–45 (p. 135).

20. *Dictionnaire universel d'Antoine Furetière* (The Hague: Arnout & Reinier Leers, 1690).

21. Saint-Evremond, 'Dissertation sur le grand Alexandre', in *Œuvres en prose*, ed. by René Ternois, 4 vols (Paris: Didier, 1962–69), II (1965), pp. 84–102 (p. 90). Pascal, 'Préface sur le traité du vide': 'Partageons avec plus de justice notre crédulité et notre défiance, et bornons ce respect que nous avons pour les anciens. [...] Comme ils ne se sont servis de celles [les connaissances] qui leur avaient été laissées que comme de moyens pour en avoir de nouvelles, et que cette heureuse hardiesse leur avait ouvert le chemin aux grandes choses, nous devons prendre celles qu'ils nous ont acquises de la même sorte, et à leur exemple en faire les moyens et non pas la fin de notre étude, et ainsi tâcher de les surpasser en les imitant'. *Œuvres complètes*, ed. by Jean Mesnard, 7 vols (Paris: Desclée de Brouwer, 1964–), II (1970), 777–82 (p. 780).

22. *Mémoires de Charles Perrault, contenant beaucoup de particularites et d'ánecdotes interessantes du ministére de M. Colbert* (Avignon: [n. pub.], 1759), p. 201.

23. Nicolas Malebranche, *La Recherche de la vérité*, ed. by Geneviève Rodis-Lewis, 3 vols (Paris: Vrin, 1962), I, 359.

24. *Dictionnaire universel.*
25. See Nicholas Cronk on the way that 'the Cartesian theory of mind and the emergence of the ideas of the individual conscious subject are clearly crucial for the way in which monologism develops in the seventeenth century'. 'The Singular Voice: Monologism and French Classical Discourse', in *Rethinking Classicism: Overviews*, ed. by David Lee Rubin (= *Continuum*, 1 (1989)), pp. 175–202 (p. 196). Cronk cites Bakhtin, whose work on the philosophy of language opposes 'individualistic subjectivism' to 'a stable, immutable system [...] which the individual consciousness finds ready-made', and traces the latter back to seventeenth-century rationalism: 'There can be no doubt that the second trend has profound interconnections with Cartesian thought and with the overall world view of neoclassicism and its cult of autonomous, rational, fixed form.' M. M. Bakhtin, *Marxism and the Philosophy of Language*, trans. by L. Matejka and I. R. Titunik (Cambridge, MA: Harvard University Press, 1973), pp. 48, 57, cited in Cronk, p. 176.
26. *La Recherche de la vérité*, p. 362.
27. Cronk, 'The Singular Voice', p. 182. Antoine Compagnon supposes that, for the seventeenth century, 'ce n'est pas la démarche introspective de Montaigne qui est en elle-même reprouvée, mais qu'elle soit rendue publique, qu'elle soit détachée du rituel de l'aveu et de la pénitence'. *La Seconde Main*, p. 312.
28. *Bolaeana: les œuvres de M. Boileau Despreaux, avec des éclaircissements historiques*, ed. by M. de Monchesnay (Paris: Veuve Alix, 1740), p. lx.
29. The opposition to 'concert' and 'arrangement' that I have noted here finds acute expression, of course, both in Boileau's *Satires* and in his frequently satirical correspondence with Racine. For a discussion of the latter body of work, in which Boileau and Racine put forward a mobile kind of ethical modelling whereby they judge themselves judging others, see my article 'Being Discrete: The Singularity of Judgement in the Correspondence of Racine and Boileau' in the proceedings of a 2001 conference on 'Discontinuities', *Seventeenth-Century French Studies*, 24 (2002), 209–15.
30. *Œuvres complètes*, pp. 518–19.
31. Christopher Ricks, *Allusion to the Poets* (Oxford: Oxford University Press, 2002), p. 246.
32. DeJean, *Ancients against Moderns*, p. 49.
33. Robert J. Nelson, 'The Quarrel of the Ancients and the Moderns', in *A New History of French Literature*, ed. by Denis Hollier (Cambridge, MA: Harvard University Press), pp. 364–69 (p. 367) (Nelson's italics).
34. H.-B. de Requeleyne, baron de Longepierre, *Discours sur les anciens* (Paris: P. Ambouin, 1687), p. 100.

CONCLUSION

❖

We saw in Longinus that 'hypsos' equates to something other than a 'movement upwards' or an 'improvement' in any straightforwardly linear sense: it equates to an engagement with an author or speaker via a text. Because this is the case, the sublime is tied to the endlessly variable rather than to the intrinsic or absolute, and Longinus supplies the sublime with categories which ineffable experience might be thought to subsume. With his recognition of the force of affectivity comes his interest in the human interaction whose extinction this force could be held to imply. And making sublime experience inseparable from communication, from encounters with words, Longinus is also interested in discourse which itself frequently dramatizes encounter, dealing in temporality, locality, the fragmented background of lived experience, 'images drawn from real life' (9.13). 'The sublime is a documentary technique.'[1]

Recognizing that Longinus was, from the mid-sixteenth century, important in the world of the *Respublica litteraria* to which 'les écrivains en langue française, médiateurs entre deux degrés de culture, avaient naturellement accès',[2] we also need to recognize that 'les écrivains en langue française' would have been able to find more in the treatise (would have had to, given its contradictory emphases) than notions of 'grandeur' or powerfully simple language. Thus I have sought to add my commentary here to the statements, for instance, that '[Pascal] ne cesse de répondre à la question que pose le traité [du sublime], et qui était ouverte obstinément depuis le XVIe siècle: qu'est-ce que la grandeur ?', or that 'la poétique de Corneille est une poétique de la grandeur, c'est-à-dire du sublime'.[3] My approach throughout has been a reading of early modern textual structures which form 'un ensemble de perturbations textuelles',[4] spin out from the term 'sublime', and function to delineate, tentatively, interrogations about knowledge and experience.

Corneille, I have shown, touches on the textures of our own lived experience in a sophisticated and tangential referentiality that is played out through his creative, possessive use of the term 'sublime'. Immanent greatness or goodness, here as in *Peri hypsous* itself, offers no sublime cognitive satisfaction. The most successful tragedies, says Corneille, are 'le plus sublime et le plus touchant', and this sublimity, and an associated 'extraordinaire', define themselves by their enquiry into the unpredictability of existence. Those sublimely tragic heroes who 'connaissent, entreprennent et n'achèvent pas' embody, on stage, this unpredictability. Their experiences and encounters, vulnerable to 'changements de fortune', to the 'pouvoir' of others, force a Cornelian 'commisération'. And in important seventeenth-century texts which associate Corneille and Longinus, it is less the concept of the 'grande ame' that is of interest than the fact that Corneille is seen, as we found in Saint-

Evremond, to 'entrer dans l'interieur, et tirer du fond de ces grandes ames [...] leurs plus secrets mouvements', thereby facilitating the evocation of a responsive echo in the reader or spectator.[5]

Pascal's writing, too, charts Longinian *tropismes* of reason and meaning and the question of how knowledge can be secured within, and not just beyond, the world of ordinary lived experience. The *Pensées* look, via passages which casually furnish themselves with the term 'sublime', at moments of human 'connaissance' and ask, or demand that the reader asks, at what point these integrate to become knowledge of the divine. If the answer to this question comes only at the moment when God's grace is granted, Pascal remains no less alert to the transformative potential of text which is packed with 'les entretiens ordinaires de la vie' (S618/L745). His own readerly relationships to Descartes, to Montaigne, and to Augustine, his interlocutory relationships to the Jansenists of Port-Royal, connect palpably with his epistemological enquiry.

For Pascal, mankind unites, in a generalized truth, unavoidably paradoxical characteristics: 'la nature nous rendant toujours malheureux en tous états' (S529/L639); 'le bonheur n'est ni hors ni dans nous; il est en Dieu et hors et dans nous' (S26/L407); 'le bien universel est en nous, est nous-même et n'est pas nous' (S471/L564). Pascal's achievement is to 'particulariser', to 'particulariser cette proposition générale' (S529/L639), to make the sheer banality and predictability of the generalized clash with the pain, and the pleasure, of individual engagement with this. The *Pensées* demand, on close reading, a redistribution of the privilege so often accorded by critics to fragment S494/L597 and its 'moi haïssable', and also to Arnauld and Nicole's renowned anecdote: 'Feu M. Pascal, qui savait autant de véritable rhétorique, que personne en ait jamais su, portait cette règle jusques à prétendre, qu'un honnête homme doit éviter de se nommer, et même de se servir des mots *je*, et de *moi*.'[6] First-person pronouns are too easy a target, as Proust shows mordantly when his character Brichot is criticized for overusing them:

> A partir de ce moment Brichot remplaça *je* par *on*, mais *on* n'empêchait pas le lecteur de voir que l'auteur parlait de lui et permit à l'auteur de ne plus cesser de parler de lui, de commenter la moindre de ses phrases, de faire un article sur une seule négation, toujours à l'abri de *on*.[7]

A vital spectacle within Pascal's discursive procedures is the rethinking of divisions between the particular and the general, as experience in the world becomes a reviewing of the terms of knowledge and of self-perception.

Longinus's seventeenth-century translators, famous and anonymous, are fully preoccupied with the way that he dramatizes the complex relationships between subject and object positions. They exploit certain of Longinus's examples by giving these notable space in their versions of the treatise. Boileau's *Réflexions critiques* are also a good phenomenological study of the complexity and the necessity of taking account of otherness. They move in the domain of the Longinian suggestion that excellence or virtue should not be thought through as being something (merely) of a person's own, but should rather be seen to find both origins and completion in an openness to encounter — to encounters with texts and to encounters depicted within them. The references to Longinus in the *Réflexions critiques* show us that the structures of the Longinian sublime define Boileau's contribution to the *Querelle des Anciens et des Modernes*. The self-sufficient reason characterized by Fontenelle as a 'nouvelle méthode de raisonner' is shown to have disastrous consequences for the sublime.[8]

Longinus's discourse, with the examples he gives, and the rigour and exhibitionism which these examples straddle, makes for live dilemmas. Like the work of Corneille, Pascal, and Boileau, the Longinian sublime brings into play, in its invitations and challenges to readers, a dimension of ethical responsiveness not amenable to the rigid morality of certain critics. Seventeenth-century examples have been given throughout this book: D'Aubignac, for instance, or Pascal's Jesuits, or Boileau's 'Modernes'. The ensuing clashes need to be read on the level of the tiniest textual detail. They have often been collapsed by critics under the weight of subsequent developments: under later conceptions of the sublime, or under the weight that modern criticism has attributed to the Cartesian rejection of the 'livre du monde' as epistemic shift. The authors I have considered deal in an intricate economy of forceful knowledge, tentative understanding, and different hermeneutic standpoints. They track readers who spread themselves wide, writers who write vividly about the seen and the heard. They are interested in the multiplicity and the aberrations of the everyday. Boileau's interest comes with his translating and reflecting upon Longinus; Pascal's comes with his modulations of divine veracity and human 'volupté'; Corneille's is channelled through his professional fascination with the transporting force of the theatrical. The reader of all partakes, if close attention is paid to the terms of debate, in a seventeenth-century self-interrogation, where footings for the passing of judgement and the gaining of experience are found with the sublime mediation of other people.

Notes to Conclusion

1. Anne Carson, '(Essay with Rhapsody): On the Sublime in Longinus and Antonioni', in *Decreation: Poetry, Essays, Opera* (New York: Knopf, 2005), pp. 43–51 (p. 45).
2. Marc Fumaroli, 'Rhétorique d'école et rhétorique adulte: remarques sur la réception européenne du traité "Du Sublime" au XVIe et au XVIIe siècle', *RHLF*, 86 (1986), 33–51 (p. 36).
3. Ibid., p. 50; Georges Forestier, *Essai de génétique théâtrale: Corneille à l'œuvre*, 2nd edn (Geneva: Droz, 2004), p. 277.
4. The phrase is Terence Cave's, in *Pré-histoires: textes troublés au seuil de la modernité* (Geneva: Droz, 1999), p. 15.
5. 'Dissertation sur le grand Alexandre', in *Œuvres en prose*, ed. by René Ternois, 4 vols (Paris: Didier, 1962–69), II (1965), 84–102 (p. 92).
6. Antoine Arnauld and Pierre Nicole, *La Logique ou l'art de penser*, ed. by Charles Jourdain (Paris: Gallimard, 1992), p. 250.
7. Marcel Proust, *A la recherche du temps perdu*, ed. by J.-Y. Tadié, 4 vols (Paris: Gallimard, 1987–89), IV, 371.
8. M. de Fontenelle, 'Digression sur les Anciens et les Modernes', ed. by Alain Niderst, 7 vols (Paris: Fayard, 1989–96), II (1991), 420.

BIBLIOGRAPHY

❖

Primary Sources

ANONYMOUS, 'Recueil d'Extraits en diverses langues', Paris, Bibliothèque nationale de France, fonds italien, 2028

ARISTOTLE, *The 'Art' of Rhetoric*, trans. by J. H. Freese, Loeb Classical Library, 193 (Cambridge, MA: Harvard University Press, 1994)

—— *The Metaphysics*, trans. by Hugh Tredennick, Loeb Classical Library, 287 (Cambridge, MA: Harvard University Press, 1933)

——*Nicomachean Ethics*, trans. by H. Rackham, Loeb Classical Library, 73 (Cambridge, MA: Harvard University Press, 1990)

——*Poetics*, trans. by Stephen Halliwell, in *Aristotle, 'Poetics', Longinus, 'On the Sublime', Demetrius, 'On Style'*, Loeb Classical Library, 199 (Cambridge, MA: Harvard University Press, 1995)

——*La Poétique d'Aristote*, trans. and ed. by André Dacier (Paris: Barbin, 1692)

——*Politics*, trans. by H. Rackham, Loeb Classical Library, 264 (Cambridge, MA: Harvard University Press, 1932)

ARNAULD, ANTOINE, *Réflexions sur l'Eloquence des Predicateurs* (Paris: Florentin and Pierre Delaune, 1695)

——and PIERRE NICOLE, *La Logique ou l'art de penser*, ed. by Charles Jourdain (Paris: Gallimard, 1992)

AUBIGNAC, FRANÇOIS HÉDELIN, ABBÉ D', *Dissertations contre Corneille*, ed. by N. Hammond and M. Hawcroft (Exeter: University of Exeter Press, 1995)

——*La Pratique du théâtre*, ed. by P. Martino (Geneva: Slatkine Reprints, 1996; orig. publ. Paris: Antoine de Sommaville, 1657)

AUGUSTINE, *Concerning the City of God against the Pagans*, trans. by Henry Bettenson (Harmondsworth: Penguin, 1972)

—— *Confessions*, trans. by Henry Chadwick (Oxford: Oxford University Press, 1998)

—— *Confessions*, trans. by Arnauld d'Andilly, ed. by Philippe Sellier (Paris: Gallimard, 1993)

——*De Trinitate*, trans. by Paul Agaësse, in *Œuvres de saint Augustin*, XV–XVI (Paris: Études augustiniennes, 1991)

BALZAC, GUEZ DE, *Socrate chrestien par le Sr de Balzac; & autres oeuvres du mesme autheur* (Paris: Augustin Courbé, 1652)

BOILEAU-DESPRÉAUX, NICOLAS, *Dissertation sur la Joconde, Arrest Burlesque, Traité du sublime*, ed. by Charles-H. Boudhors (Paris: Les Belles Lettres, 1966)

——*Œuvres complètes*, ed. by Antoine Adam and Françoise Escal (Paris: Gallimard, 1966)

BOSSUET, JACQUES-BÉNIGNE, *Discours sur l'histoire universelle* (Paris: Garnier-Flammarion, 1966)

——'Dissertio de Psalmis', in *Liber Psalmorum* (Lyons: Anisson, Posuel, and Rigaud, 1691)

——*Œuvres choisies*, ed. by Jean Calvet (Paris: Hatier, 1928)

BOUHOURS, DOMINIQUE, *La Manière de bien penser dans les ouvrages d'esprit* (Brighton: Sussex Reprints, 1917; orig. publ. Paris: Michel Brunet, 1715)

BRÉBEUF, GEORGES DE, *La Pharsale de Lucain* (Paris: A. de Sommaville, 1665)

BURKE, EDMUND, *A Philosophical Enquiry into the Origin of our Idea of the Sublime and the Beautiful* (Oxford: Oxford University Press, 1990)

BUSSY, ROGER DE RABUTIN, COMTE DE, *Correspondance*, ed. by Ludovic Lalanne (Paris: Charpentier, 1858)

CHAPELAIN, JEAN, *Opuscules critiques*, ed. by Alfred C. Hunter (Paris: Droz, 1936)

CHARRON, PIERRE, *De la sagesse*, ed. by Barbara de Negroni (Paris: Fayard, 1986)

CORNEILLE, PIERRE, *Œuvres complètes*, ed. by André Stegmann (Paris: Éditions du Seuil, 1963)

——*Trois discours sur le poème dramatique*, ed. by Bénédicte Louvat and Marc Escola (Paris: Garnier-Flammarion, 1999)

——*Writings on the Theatre*, ed. by H. T. Barnwell (Oxford: Blackwell, 1965)

COSTAR, PIERRE, *Defense des ouvrages de Monsieur de Voiture, à Monsieur de Balzac* (Paris: Courbé, 1653)

——*Suite de la Defense* (Paris: Courbé, 1655)

DESCARTES, RENÉ, *Discours de la méthode*, ed. by Geneviève Rodis-Lewis (Paris: Garnier-Flammarion, 1966)

——*Œuvres philosophiques*, ed. by F. Alquié, 3 vols (Paris: Garnier, 1988–89)

Dictionnaire de l'Académie française (Paris: Jean-Baptiste Coignard, 1694)

DIONYSIUS, PSEUDO-, *The Complete Works*, trans. by Colm Luibheid (New York: Paulist Press, 1987)

ESTIENNE, HENRI, *Anacreontis et aliorum lyricorum aliquot pöetarum odæ. In easdem Henr. Stephani Observationes Eædem Latinæ* (Paris: G. Morel & R. Estienne, 1556)

FÉNELON, FRANÇOIS DE SALIGNAC DE LA MOTHE-, *Œuvres*, ed. by J. Le Brun, 2 vols (Paris: Gallimard, 1983–97)

FONTAINE, NICOLAS, *Mémoires ou histoire des solitaires de Port-Royal*, ed. by Pascale Thouvenin (Paris: Champion, 2001)

FONTENELLE, M. DE, 'Digression sur les Anciens et les Modernes', in *Œuvres complètes*, ed. by Alain Niderst, 7 vols (Paris: Fayard, 1989–96)

FURETIÈRE, ANTOINE, *Le Dictionnaire universel d'Antoine Furetière* (The Hague: Arnout & Reinier Leers, 1690)

GARASSE, FRANÇOIS, *Somme théologique des véritez capitales de la religion chrestienne* (Paris: S. Chappelet, 1625)

HUET, PIERRE-DANIEL, *Mémoires (1718)*, trans. by Charles Nisard, ed. by Philippe-Joseph Salazar (Toulouse: Klincksieck, 1993)

JAUCOURT, LOUIS DE, 'Sublime', in *Encyclopédie ou Dictionnaire raisonné des sciences, des arts ou des métiers*, ed. by Denis Diderot and Jean le Rond d'Alembert (Neufchastel: Samuel Faulche, 1765), pp. 566–70

KANT, IMMANUEL, *Critique of Judgement*, trans. by James Creed Meredith (Oxford: Oxford University Press, 1991)

——*Observations on the Feeling of the Beautiful and the Sublime*, trans. by John T. Goldthwait (Berkeley: University of California Press, 1991)

LA BRUYÈRE, JEAN DE, *Les Caractères ou les mœurs de ce siècle*, ed. by Robert Pignarre (Paris: Garnier-Flammarion, 1965)

LE MAISTRE DE SACY, LOUIS-ISAAC, *La Genese traduite en François, avec l'explication du sens litteral & du sens spirituel* (Paris: Lambert Roulland, 1682)

——*La Genèse traduite en françois, avec l'explication du sens litteral & du sens spirituel, tirée des saint Peres et des Auteurs ecclesiastiques*, new edn (Paris: Guillaume Desprez and Jean Desessatz, 1725)

——*Lettres chrestiennes et spirituelles de Messire Isaac Louis Le Maistre de Sacy*, 2 vols (Paris: Elie Josset, 1690)

——(trans.), *La Sainte Bible*, ed. by l'Abbé Jacquet (Paris: Garnier, [n.d.])

LONGEPIERRE, H.-B. DE REQUELEYNE, BARON DE, *Discours sur les anciens* (Paris: P. Ambouin, 1687)

LONGINUS, PSEUDO-, *De la sublimité du discours: traduction inédite du XVIIe siècle*, ed. by Emma Gilby (Paris: Éditions Comp'Act, forthcoming 2006)

——*Dionysii Longini de Sublimi dicendi genere liber a Petro Pagano latinitate donatus* (Venice: Vincentius Valgrisius, 1572)

——*Dionysii Longini rhetoris praestantissimi Liber de grandi orationis genere, Dominico Pizimentio Vibonensis interprete)* (Naples: Scotus, 1566)

——*[Dionysiou Longinou rhetoros Peri hypsous biblion]* = *Dionysii Longini rhetoris praestantissimi liber, De grandi, sive sublimi orationis genere. Nunc primum a Francisco Robortello vtinensi in luce[m] editus, eiusdemq[ue] annotationibus latinis in margine appositis, quae instar commentariorum sunt, illustratus* (Basle: Jean Oporin, 1554)

——*Dionysius Longinus of the Height of Eloquence*, trans. by John Hall (Oxford: Roger Daniel for Francis Eaglefield, 1652)

——*Dyonisii Longini Liber de grandi sive sublimi genere orationis, latine redditus, et ad oram notationibus aliquot illustratus a Gab. de Petra* (Geneva: J. Tournai, 1612)

——*On Great Writing (On the Sublime)*, trans. by G. M. A. Grube (Indianapolis: Hackett, 1991)

——*On the Sublime*, ed. by D. A. Russell (Oxford: Clarendon Press, 1964)

——*On the Sublime*, trans. by W. Hamilton Fyfe and rev. by Donald Russell, *Aristotle, 'Poetics', Longinus, 'On the Sublime', Demetrius, 'On Style'*, Loeb Classical Library, 199 (Cambridge, MA: Harvard University Press, 1995)

——*Peri hypsous libellus, cum notis emendationibus, et præfatione Tanaquilli Fabri* (Saumur: J. Lenerius, 1663)

MALEBRANCHE, NICOLAS, *La Recherche de la vérité*, ed. by Geneviève Rodis-Lewis, 3 vols (Paris: Vrin, 1962)

MONCHESNAY, M. DE, ed., *Bolaeana. Les œuvres de M. Boileau Despreaux, avec des éclaircissements historiques* (Paris: Veuve Alix, 1740)

MONTAIGNE, MICHEL DE, *Essais*, ed. by P. Villey, 2nd edn (Paris: Presses universitaires de France, 1965)

——*Journal de voyage en Italie*, ed. by M. Rat (Paris: Garnier, 1955)

MURET, MARC-ANTOINE, ed., *Catullus et in eum commentarius M. Antonii Mureti* (Venice: Paulus Manutius, 1554)

NICOLE, PIERRE, *Essais de morale*, ed. by Laurent Thirouin (Paris: Presses universitaires de France, 1999)

OGIER, FRANÇOIS, *Apologie pour Monsieur de Balzac*, ed. by Jean Jehasse (Saint-Étienne: Publications de l'Université de Saint-Étienne, 1977)

OLIVET, L'ABBÉ D', ed., *Huetiana, ou pensées diverses de M. Huet, esveque d'Avranches* (Paris: Jean Estienne, [1722, misprinted as 822])

PASCAL, BLAISE, *Entretien avec M. de Sacy (original inédit)*, ed. by Pascale Mengotti-Thouvenin and Jean Mesnard (Paris: Desclée de Brouwer, 1994)

——*Œuvres complètes*, ed. by Louis Lafuma (Paris: Éditions du Seuil, 1963)

——*Œuvres complètes*, ed. by Jean Mesnard, 7 vols (Paris: Desclée de Brouwer, 1964–)

——*Pensées*, ed. by Gérard Ferreyrolles (Paris: Livre de Poche, 2000)

——*Les Provinciales*, ed. by Louis Cognet (Paris: Garnier, 1965)

PERRAULT, CHARLES, *Mémoires de Charles Perrault, contenant beaucoup de particularites et d'ánecdotes interessantes du ministère de M. Colbert* (Avignon: [n. pub.], 1759)

——*Parallèle des anciens et des modernes en ce qui regarde les arts et les sciences*, 4 vols (Paris: Jean-Baptiste Coignard, 1692–97)

PLATO, *The Collected Dialogues Including the Letters*, trans. by various, ed. by Edith Hamilton and Huntingdon Cairns (Princeton: Princeton University Press, 1961)

——*Republic*, trans. by Robin Waterfield (Oxford: Oxford University Press, 1993)

PRADON, JACQUES, *Nouvelles remarques sur tous les ouvrages du Sieur D**** (The Hague: Strik, 1685)

——*Phèdre et Hippolyte*, ed. by O. Classe (Exeter: Exeter University Press, 1987)

RABUTIN, ROGER DE, COMTE DE BUSSY, *Correspondance*, ed. by Ludovic Lalanne, 6 vols (Paris: Charpentier, 1858–59)

RACINE, JEAN, *Œuvres complètes*, ed. by Luc Estaing (Paris: Éditions du Seuil, 1962)

RAPIN, RENÉ, *Réflexions sur la poétique de ce temps, et sur les ouvrages des poetes anciens et modernes*, 2nd edn, rev. and enlarged (Paris: François Muguet, 1675)

ROBORTELLO, FRANCESCO, *In librum Aristotelis De arte poetica explicationes* (Florence: L. Torrentinus, 1548)

RICHELET, PIERRE, *Le Nouveau Dictionnaire françois de Pierre Richelet* (Lyons: Jean-Baptiste Girin, 1719)

SAINT-CYRAN, JEAN DUVERGIER DE HAURANNE, ABBÉ DE, *Somme des fautes et faussetez capitales contenues en la Somme Theologique du Pere François Garasse de la compagnie de Jesus, qui contient un nombre innombrable de fautes et de faussetez qu'il a commises alleguant les saincts Peres & autre autheurs seculiers* (Paris: Joseph Bouïllerot, 1626)

SAINT-EVREMOND, CHARLES DE MARGUETEL DE SAINT-DENIS, SIEUR DE, *Lettres*, ed. by René Ternois, 2 vols (Paris: Didier, 1967–68)

——*Œuvres en prose*, ed. by René Ternois, 4 vols (Paris: Didier, 1962–69)

SAINT-SORLIN, JEAN DESMARETS DE, *La Défense de la poësie, et de la langue françoise, adressée à Monsieur Perrault* (Geneva: Slatkine, 1972; orig. publ. Paris: Nicolas le Gras, 1675)

SCUDÉRY, GEORGES DE, *L'Apologie du théâtre* (Paris: Augustin Courbé, 1639)

SÉVIGNÉ, MARIE DE RABUTIN-CHANTAL, MARQUISE DE, *Correspondance*, ed. by R. Duchêne (Paris: Gallimard, 1972–78)

SEXTUS EMPIRICUS, *Outlines of Pyrrhonism*, trans. by R. G. Bury, Loeb Classical Library, 273 (Cambridge, MA: Harvard University Press, 1990)

SILVAIN, FRANÇOIS, *Traité du sublime, à M. Despreaux* (Geneva: Slatkine, 1971; orig. publ. Paris: Pierre Prault, 1732)

SOPHOCLES, *The Theban Plays*, trans. by E. F. Watling (London: Penguin, 1968)

TALLEMANT DES RÉAUX, GÉDÉON *Historiettes*, ed. by Antoine Adam (Paris: Gallimard, 1961)

VOITURE, VINCENT DE, *Lettres et autres œuvres* (Brussels: Lambert, 1687)

Secondary Sources

ADAM, ANTOINE, *Histoire de la littérature française au dix-septième siècle*, 5 vols (Paris: Domat, 1948–56)

ANNAS, JULIA, *An Introduction to Plato's Republic* (Oxford: Oxford University Press, 1981)

BARNWELL, H. T., 'Saint-Evremond et la tragédie classique', *XVIIe siècle*, no. 57 (January–March 1962), 24–42

——*The Tragic Drama of Corneille and Racine: An Old Parallel Revisited* (Oxford: Oxford University Press, 1982)

BARTHES, ROLAND, *Le Plaisir du texte* (Paris: Éditions du Seuil, 1973)

BAYLEY, PETER, 'Les Sermons de Jean-Pierre Camus et l'esthétique borroméenne', in *Critique et création littéraires en France au XVIIe siècle* (Paris: CNRS, 1977), pp. 93–101

BÉNICHOU, PAUL, *Morales du grand siècle* (Paris: Gallimard, 1948)

BEN MESSAOUD, SAMY, 'Lettre de Boileau à Antoine Arnauld: étude critique d'une copie inédite', *XVIIe siècle*, no. 201 (October–December 1998), 709–14

BERSANI, LEO, *The Culture of Redemption* (Cambridge, MA: Harvard University Press, 1990)

BOASE, ALAN, *The Fortunes of Montaigne: A History of the Essays in France* (London: Methuen, 1935)

BOLD, STEPHEN C., *Pascal Geometer: Discovery and Invention in Seventeenth-Century France* (Geneva: Droz, 1996)

BORGERHOFF, E. B. O., *The Freedom of French Classicism* (Princeton: Princeton University Press, 1950)

BOWIE, MALCOLM, *Freud, Proust and Lacan: Theory as Fiction* (Cambridge: Cambridge University Press, 1987)

——*Lacan* (London: Fontana, 1991)

BRAHAMI, FRÉDÉRIC, 'L'Articulation du scepticisme religieux et du scepticisme profane dans l'*Histoire du scepticisme d'Erasme à Spinoza*, de Richard H. Popkin', in *Histoire du scepticisme de Sextus Empiricus à Richard H. Popkin*, ed. by Pierre-François Moreau and Eric Brian (= *Revue de synthèse*, 42.2–3 (April–September 1998)), pp. 293–305

BRAY, RENÉ, 'La Dissertation sur Joconde est-elle de Boileau?', *RHLF*, 38 (1931), 497–517

——*La Formation de la doctrine classique* (Paris: Hachette, 1927)

BRODY, JULES, *Boileau and Longinus* (Geneva: Droz, 1958)

——'Platonisme et classicisme', in *French Classicism: A Critical Miscellany*, ed. by Jules Brody (Englewood Cliffs, NJ: Prentice-Hall, 1966), pp. 186–207

——'What *Was* French Classicism?', in *Rethinking Classicism: Overviews*, ed. by David Lee Rubin (= *Continuum*, 1 (1989)), pp. 51–77

CAMPOS LEYZA, ÉTIENNE DE, *Analyse étymologique des racines de la langue grecque* (Bordeaux: Émile Crugy, 1874)

CARR, THOMAS M., *Descartes and the Resilience of Rhetoric* (Carbondale: Southern Illinois University Press, 1990)

CARRAUD, VINCENT, *Pascal et la philosophie* (Paris: Presses universitaires de France, 1992)

CARSON, ANNE, '(Essay with Rhapsody): On the Sublime in Longinus and Antonioni', in *Decreation: Poetry, Essays, Opera* (New York: Knopf, 2005), pp. 43–51

——*If Not, Winter: Fragments of Sappho* (London: Virago, 2002)

——'"Just for the Thrill": Sycophantizing Aristotle's *Poetics*', *Arion*, 1.1 (1990), 142–54

CAVE, TERENCE, *Pré-histoires: textes troublés au seuil de la modernité* (Geneva: Droz, 1999)

——*Pré-histoires*, II: *Langues étrangères et troubles économiques au XVIᵉ siècle* (Geneva: Droz, 2001)

——*Recognitions* (Oxford: Oxford University Press, 1988)

CHADWICK, HENRY, *Augustine* (Oxford: Oxford University Press, 1986)

CLARKE, DESMOND M., 'Pascal's Philosophy of Science', in *The Cambridge Companion to Pascal*, ed. by Nicholas Hammond (Cambridge: Cambridge University Press, 2003), pp. 102–21

COLEMAN, DOROTHY GABE, 'Montaigne and Longinus', *Bibliothèque d'humanisme et de renaissance*, 47 (1985), 405–13

COMPAGNON, ANTOINE, *La Seconde main, ou le travail de la citation* (Paris: Éditions du Seuil, 1979)

COURCELLE, PIERRE, *L'Entretien de Pascal et Sacy: ses sources et ses énigmes* (Paris: Vrin, 1960)

CRONK, NICHOLAS, *The Classical Sublime: French Neoclassicism and the Language of Literature* (Charlottesville: Rookwood Press, 2002)

——'The Singular Voice: Monologism and French Classical Discourse', in *Rethinking Classicism: Overviews*, ed. by David Lee Rubin (= *Continuum*, 1 (1989)), pp. 175–202

CROQUETTE, BERNARD, *Pascal et Montaigne: étude des réminiscences des Essais dans l'œuvre de Pascal* (Geneva: Droz, 1974)

CROSSETT, JOHN M., and JAMES A. ARIETI, *The Dating of Longinus* (University Park: Department of Classics at Pennsylvania State University, 1975)

CULLER, JONATHAN, *The Pursuit of Signs: Semiotics, Literature, Deconstruction* (London: Routledge, 1981)

DEAR, PETER, *Discipline and Experience: The Mathematical Way in the Scientific Revolution* (Chicago: University of Chicago Press, 1995)

DECLERCQ, GILLES, 'Topique de l'ineffable dans l'esthétique classique (rhétorique et sublime)', *XVII* *siècle*, no. 207 (April–June 2000), 199–220

DEJEAN, JOAN, *Ancients against Moderns: Culture Wars and the Making of a Fin de Siècle* (Chicago: University of Chicago Press, 1997)

DELEUZE, GILLES, and FÉLIX GUATTARI, *Capitalisme et schizophrénie*, I: *L'Anti-Œdipe* (Paris: Éditions de Minuit, 1972)

DEPRUN, J., 'La Parabole de la seconde *Provinciale*', in *Méthodes chez Pascal: actes du colloque tenu à Clermont-Ferrand, 10–13 juin 1976* (Paris: Presses universitaires de France, 1979), pp. 241–52

DESCOTES, DOMINIQUE, *L'Argumentation chez Pascal* (Paris: Presses universitaires de France, 1993)

DOUBROVSKY, SERGE, *Corneille et la dialectique du héros* (Paris: Gallimard, 1963)

DUMONT, JEAN-PAUL, *Le Scepticisme et le phénomène* (Paris: Vrin, 1972)

EAGLETON, TERRY, *Sweet Violence: The Idea of the Tragic* (Oxford: Blackwell, 2003)

ERNST, POL, *Les 'Pensées' de Pascal: géologie et stratigraphie* (Paris and Oxford: Voltaire Foundation, 1996)

FONTAINE, JACQUES, 'Genres et styles dans les *Confessions* de saint Augustin', *L'Information littéraire*, 42.1 (1990), 13–20

FORCE, PIERRE, 'Géométrie, finesse et premiers principes de Pascal', *Romance Quarterly*, 50.2 (2003), 121–30

——*Le Problème herméneutique chez Pascal* (Paris: Vrin, 1989)

FORESTIER, GEORGES, *Essai de génétique théâtrale: Corneille à l'œuvre*, 2nd edn (Geneva: Droz, 2004)

——'Passions purgées ou passions épurées? Le problème de la *catharsis*', in *Passions tragiques et règles classiques* (Paris: Presses universitaires de France, 2003), pp. 141–54

FOSTER, DENNIS A., *Confession and Complicity in Narrative* (Cambridge: Cambridge University Press, 1987)

FOUCAULT, MICHEL, *Histoire de la sexualité*, I: *La Volonté de savoir* (Paris: Gallimard, 1976)

FREUD, SIGMUND, *The Interpretation of Dreams* (New York: Avon, 1965)

——*The Standard Edition of the Complete Psychological Works of Sigmund Freud*, trans. and ed. by James Strachey, 24 vols (London: Hogarth Press, 1953–74)

FUMAROLI, MARC, 'Les Abeilles et les araignées', in *La Querelle des Anciens et des Modernes*, ed. by Anne-Marie Lecoq (Paris: Gallimard, 2001), pp. 7–218

——*L'Âge de l'éloquence: rhétorique et 'res literaria' de la Renaissance au seuil de l'époque classique* (Paris: Albin Michel, 1994; orig. publ. Paris: Droz, 1980)

——'Apprends ma confidente, apprends à me connaître: les *Mémoires* de Retz et le traité *Du Sublime*', *Versants*, no. 1 (1981), 27–56

——*Héros et orateurs: rhétorique et dramaturgie cornéliennes* (Geneva: Droz, 1990)

——'Pascal et la tradition rhétorique gallicane', in *Méthodes chez Pascal: actes du colloque tenu à Clermont-Ferrand, 10–13 juin 1976* (Paris: Presses universitaires de France, 1979), pp. 359–72

——'Rhétorique d'école et rhétorique adulte: remarques sur la réception européenne du traité "Du Sublime" au XVIe et au XVIIe siècle', *RHLF*, 86 (1986), 33–51

GAGNEBET, M. R., 'La Théologie augustinienne type de théologie affective', *Revue Thomiste*, 44.1 (1938), 3–39

GENETTE, GÉRARD, *Figures II* (Paris: Éditions du Seuil, 1969)

GILBY, EMMA, 'Being Discrete: The Singularity of Judgement in the Correspondence of Racine and Boileau', *Seventeenth-Century French Studies*, 24 (2002), 209–15

——'Émotions' and the Ethics of Response in Seventeenth-Century French Dramatic Theory', *Modern Philology* (forthcoming 2007)

——'Models of Imagination in the *Pensées*: Re-reading Pascal and Montaigne', *Seventeenth-Century French Studies*, 25 (2003), 65–73

——'*Œdipe*, *L'Anti-Œdipe* et la logique des multiplicités', *Dialogue avec la critique dix-septiémiste américaine* (Paris: Presses de la Sorbonne Nouvelle, forthcoming 2006)

——'Reflexivity in the *Pensées*: Pascal's Discourse on Discourse', *French Studies*, 55 (2001), 315–26

——'Sous le signe du sublime: la rencontre de Boileau et Longin', *Papers on French Seventeenth-Century Literature*, 31 (2004), 416–26

GIOCANTI, SYLVIA, 'Histoire du fidéisme, histoire du scepticisme', in *Histoire du scepticisme de Sextus Empiricus à Richard H. Popkin*, ed. by Pierre-François Moreau and Eric Brian (= *Revue de synthèse*, 42.2–3 (April–September 1998)), pp. 193–210

GOUHIER, HENRI, *Blaise Pascal: conversion et apologétique* (Paris: Vrin, 1986)

GRUBE, G. M. A., 'Notes on the ΠΕΡΙ ΥΨΟΥΣ', *American Journal of Philology*, 78 (1957), 355–74

GUERLAC, SUZANNE, *The Impersonal Sublime: Hugo, Baudelaire, Lautréamont* (Stanford, CA: Stanford University Press, 1990)

——'Longinus and the Subject of the Sublime', *New Literary History*, 16 (1985), 275–90

HACHE, SOPHIE, *La Langue du ciel: le sublime en France au XVIIe siècle* (Paris: Champion, 2000)

HALLIWELL, STEPHEN, *The 'Poetics' of Aristotle: Translation and Commentary* (London: Duckworth, 1987)

HAMMOND, NICHOLAS, 'Pascal and "Descartes inutile et incertain"', *Seventeenth-Century French Studies*, 16 (1994), 59–63

——*Playing with Truth: Language and the Human Condition in Pascal's 'Pensées'* (Oxford: Oxford University Press, 1994)

HARRINGTON, THOMAS M., 'Le Pari de Pascal', *Romanische Forschungen*, 109.2 (1997), 221–51

HERTZ, NEIL, 'A Reading of Longinus', *Critical Inquiry*, 9 (1983), 579–96

HINDS, STEPHEN, *Allusion and Intertext* (Cambridge: Cambridge University Press, 1998)

JONES, J., *On Aristotle and Greek Tragedy* (London: Chatto & Windus, 1962)

KAHN, CHARLES H., *Plato and the Socratic Dialogue: The Philosophical Use of a Literary Form* (Cambridge: Cambridge University Press, 1996)

KENNY, NEIL, *Curiosity in Early Modern Europe: Word Histories* (Wiesbaden: Harrassowitz, 1998)

——*The Uses of Curiosity in Early Modern France and Europe* (Oxford: Oxford University Press, 2004)

KERSLAKE, LAWRENCE, *Essays on the Sublime: Analyses of French Writings on the Sublime from Boileau to La Harpe* (Berne: Peter Lang, 2000)

KRAILSHEIMER, ALBAN J., *Studies in Self-Interest: From Descartes to La Bruyère* (Oxford: Oxford University Press, 1962)

LACAN, JACQUES, *Écrits* (Paris: Éditions du Seuil, 1966)

LAMB, JONATHAN, 'Longinus, the Dialectic, and the Practice of Mastery', *ELH*, 60 (1993), 545–67

LAPLANCHE, JEAN, and J.-B. PONTALIS, *Vocabulaire de la psychanalyse* (Paris: Presses universitaires de France, 1967)

LE GUERN, MICHEL, *Pascal et Descartes* (Paris: Nizet, 1971)

LEWIS, PHILIP, 'L'Anti-sublime, ou la rhétorique du progrès', in *Rhétoriques fin de siècle*, ed. by Mary Shaw and François Cornilliat (Paris: Christian Bourgeois, 1992), pp. 117–45

LICOPPE, CHRISTIAN, *La Formation de la pratique scientifique: le discours de l'expérience en France et en Angleterre (1630–1820)* (Paris: Éditions de la découverte, 1996)

LIDDELL, H. G., and ROBERT SCOTT, *Greek–English Lexicon*, rev. by Henry Stuart Jones and Roderick McKenzie (Oxford: Oxford University Press, 1968)

LIMBRICK, ELAINE, 'Le Pyrrhonisme est le vrai', in *Mélanges sur la littérature de la Renaissance, à la mémoire de V.-L. Saulnier* (Geneva: Droz, 1984), pp. 439–55

LITMAN, THÉODORE, *Le Sublime en France, 1660–1714* (Paris: Nizet, 1971)

LOCKWOOD, RICHARD, *The Reader's Figure: Epideictic Rhetoric in Plato, Aristotle, Bossuet, Racine and Pascal* (Geneva: Droz, 1996)

LOGAN, JOHN, 'Longinus and the Sublime', in *The Cambridge History of Literary Criticism*, III: *The Renaissance*, ed. by G. Norton (Cambridge: Cambridge University Press, 1999), pp. 529–39

—— 'Montaigne et Longin: une nouvelle hypothèse', *RHLF*, 83 (1983), 354–70

LYONS, JOHN D., *Before Imagination: Embodied Thought from Montaigne to Rousseau* (Stanford, CA: Stanford University Press, 2005)

—— *The Tragedy of Origins: Pierre Corneille and Historical Perspective* (Stanford, CA: Stanford University Press, 1996)

—— *Kingdom of Disorder: The Theory of Tragedy in Classical France* (West Lafayette, IN: Purdue University Press, 1999)

LYOTARD, JEAN-FRANÇOIS, 'L'Instant, Newman', in *L'Inhumain: causeries sur le temps* (Paris: Galilée, 1988), pp. 89–99

MCKENNA, ANTONY, *Entre Descartes et Gassendi: la première édition des 'Pensées' de Pascal* (Oxford: Voltaire Foundation, 1993)

MACKSEY, RICHARD, 'Longinus Reconsidered', *MLN*, 108 (1993), 913–34

MACLEAN, IAN, *Interpretation and Meaning in the Renaissance: The Case of Law* (Cambridge: Cambridge University Press, 1992)

—— *Montaigne philosophe* (Paris: Presses universitaires de France, 1996)

MAGNIONT, GILLES, *Traces de la voix pascalienne: examen des marques de l'énonciation dans les 'Pensées'* (Lyons: Presses universitaires de Lyon, 2003)

MAN, PAUL DE, 'Pascal's Allegory of Persuasion', in *Allegory and Representation*, ed. by Stephen Greenblatt (Baltimore: Johns Hopkins University Press, 1981), pp. 1–25

—— 'Phenomenality and Materiality in Kant', in *The Textual Sublime and its Differences*, ed. by H. J. Silverman and G. E. Aylesworth (Albany, NY: SUNY Press, 1990), pp. 87–108

—— 'The Rhetoric of Temporality', in *Blindness and Insight: Essays in the Rhetoric of Contemporary Criticism*, 2nd edn (Minneapolis: University of Minnesota Press, 1985), pp. 187–228

MARIN, LOUIS, 'On the Sublime, Infinity, Je Ne Sais Quoi', in *A New History of French Literature*, ed. by Denis Hollier (Cambridge, MA: Harvard University Press, 1989), pp. 340–45

—— 'Le Sublime dans les années 1670: un "je ne sais quoi"?', *Papers on French Seventeenth-Century Literature*, 25 (1986), 185–201

—— *Sublime Poussin* (Paris: Éditions du Seuil, 1995)

MELZER, SARA E., *Discourses of the Fall: A Study of Pascal's 'Pensées'* (Berkeley: University of California Press, 1986)

MERLIN-KAJMAN, HÉLÈNE, *L'Excentricité académique* (Paris: Les Belles Lettres, 2001)

—— *Public et littérature en France au XVIIe siècle* (Paris: Les Belles Lettres, 1994)

MESNARD, JEAN, 'Pascal et la vérité', *Chroniques de Port-Royal*, 17–18 (1962), 21–40

—— *Les 'Pensées' de Pascal* (Paris: SEDES, 1993)

MICHEL, ALAIN, 'Rhétorique et poétique: la théorie du sublime de Platon aux modernes', *Revue des Études Latines*, 54 (1976), 278–307

MONK, SAMUEL H., *The Sublime: A Study of Critical Theories in XVIII-Century England* (Ann Arbor: University of Michigan Press, 1960)

MORIARTY, MICHAEL, *Early Modern French Thought: The Age of Suspicion* (Oxford: Oxford University Press, 2003)

NANCY, JEAN-LUC, 'Le Sublime offrande', in *Du Sublime*, ed. by Jean-François Courtine (Paris: Belin, 1988), pp. 37–75

NAU, CLÉLIA, *Le Temps du sublime: Longin et le paysage poussinien* (Rennes: Presses universitaires de Rennes, 2005)

NELSON, ROBERT J., 'The Quarrel of the Ancients and the Moderns', in *A New History of French Literature*, ed. by Denis Hollier (Cambridge, MA: Harvard University Press, 1989), pp. 364–69

NORMAN, BUFORD, *Portraits of Thought, Knowledge, Methods and Styles in Pascal* (Columbus: Ohio State University Press, 1988)

NUSSBAUM, MARTHA, *The Fragility of Goodness: Luck and Ethics in Greek Tragedy and Philosophy*, 2nd edn (Cambridge: Cambridge University Press, 2001)

—— 'Tragedy and Self-Sufficiency: Plato and Aristotle on Fear and Pity', *Oxford Studies in Ancient Philosophy*, 10 (1992), 107–60

OLSON, ELDER, 'The Argument of Longinus' *On the Sublime*', in *Critics and Criticism Ancient and Modern*, ed. by R. S. Crane (Chicago: University of Chicago Press, 1952), pp. 232–59

ORCIBAL, JEAN, ed., *Les Origines du jansénisme*, I: *Correspondance de Jansénius* (Paris: Vrin, 1947)

PARISH, RICHARD, '"Mais qui parle?" Voice and Persona in the *Pensées*', *Seventeenth-Century French Studies*, 8 (1986), 23–40

—— *Pascal's 'Lettres Provinciales': A Study in Polemic* (Oxford: Oxford University Press, 1989)

PHILLIPS, HENRY, *Church and Culture in Seventeenth-Century France* (Cambridge: Cambridge University Press, 1997)

—— *The Theatre and its Critics in Seventeenth-Century France* (Oxford: Oxford University Press, 1980)

POPKIN, RICHARD H., *The History of Scepticism from Erasmus to Spinoza* (Berkeley: University of California Press, 1979)

POTTS, D. C., '"Une carrière épineuse": Neoplatonism and the Poet's Vocation in Boileau's *Art poétique*', *French Studies*, 47.1 (1993), 20–32

PRINS, YOPIE, 'Sappho's Afterlife in Translation', in *Re-reading Sappho: Reception and Transmission*, ed. by Ellen Green (Berkeley: University of California Press, 1996), pp. 36–67

PROUST, MARCEL, *A la recherche du temps perdu*, ed. by J.-Y. Tadié, 4 vols (Paris: Gallimard, 1987–89)

REY, ALAIN, ed., *Dictionnaire historique de la langue française* (Paris: Le Robert, 1993)

RICKS, CHRISTOPHER, *Allusion to the Poets* (Oxford: Oxford University Press, 2002)

RUSSELL, D. A., 'Longinus Revisited', *Mnemosyne*, 34 (1981), 72–86

RUSSIER, JEANNE, *La Foi selon Pascal, 2: Tradition et originalité dans la théorie pascalienne de la foi* (Paris: Presses universitaires de France, 1949)

SAINT GIRONS, BALDINE, 'Avant-propos', in Edmund Burke, *Recherche philosophique sur l'origine de nos idées du sublime et du beau* (Paris: Vrin, 1973)

—— *Fiat lux: une philosophie du sublime* (Paris: Quai Voltaire, 1993)

SCHMITT, CHARLES, 'The Rediscovery of Ancient Skepticism in Modern Times', in *The Skeptical Tradition*, ed. by Myles Burnyeat (Berkeley: University of California Press, 1983), pp. 225–31

SCHOLAR, RICHARD, 'La Force de l'imagination de Montaigne: Camus, Malebranche, Pascal', *Littératures classiques*, 45 (2002), 127–38

—— *The Je-Ne-Sais-Quoi in Early Modern Europe: Encounters with a Certain Something* (Oxford: Oxford University Press, 2005)

SCREECH, MICHAEL, *Montaigne and Melancholy: The Wisdom of the Essays* (London: Duckworth, 1983)

SEDLEY, DAVID L., 'Sublimity and Skepticism in Montaigne', *PMLA*, 113 (1998), 1079–92

SEGAL, CHARLES P., '῞ΨΟΥΣ and the Problem of Cultural Decline in the *De Sublimitate*', *Harvard Studies in Classical Philology*, 64 (1959), 121–46

SELLIER, PHILIPPE, *Pascal et saint Augustin* (Paris: Albin Michel, 1995)

SHIOKAWA, TETSUYA, '*Justus ex fide vivit* et *fides ex auditu*: deux aspects de la foi dans l'apologétique pascalienne', in *Pascal: l'exercice de l'esprit*, ed. by Christian Meurillon (= *Revue des sciences humaines*, no. 244 (December 1996)), pp. 159–78

SKINNER, QUENTIN, 'Meaning and Understanding in the History of Ideas', *History and Theory*, 8 (1969), 3–53

STURROCK, JOHN, *The Language of Autobiography: Studies in the First Person Singular* (Cambridge: Cambridge University Press, 1993)

TAYLOR, CHARLES, *Sources of the Self: The Making of the Modern Identity* (Cambridge: Cambridge University Press, 1989)

TOURNIER, MICHEL, *Le Vol du vampire: notes de lecture* (Paris: Gallimard, 1983)

TOURNON, ANDRÉ, 'Images du pyrrhonisme selon quelques écrivains de la Renaissance', in *Les Humanistes et l'antiquité grecque*, ed. by Mitchiko Ishigami-Iagolnitzer (Paris: CNRS, 1991), pp. 27–37

——*Montaigne, la glose et l'essai* (Lyons: Presses universitaires de Lyon, 1983)

TRINQUET, ROGER, *La Jeunesse de Montaigne: ses origines familiales, son enfance et ses études* (Paris: Nizet, 1972)

UNDERHILL, EVELYN, *Mysticism: A Study in the Nature and Development of Man's Spiritual Consciousness*, 12th edn, rev. (London: Methuen, 1930)

VARNER GUNN, JANET, *Autobiography: Toward a Poetics of Experience* (Philadelphia: University of Pennsylvania Press, 1982)

VILLIERS, ANDRÉ, 'Illusion dramatique et dramaturgie classique', *XVIIᵉ siècle*, no. 73 (January–March 1966), 3–35

VITANOVIC, SLOBODAN, 'La Place de la mythologie dans la poétique de Boileau', in *La Mythologie au XVIIe siècle: actes du XIe colloque du CMR 17* (Marseilles: CMR 17, 1982), pp. 25–31

WALSH, GEORGE B., 'Sublime Method: Longinus on Language and Imitation', *Classical Antiquity*, 7 (1988), 252–69

WEINBERG, BERNARD, 'Translations and Commentaries of Longinus, *On the Sublime*, to 1600: A Bibliography', *Modern Philology*, 47 (1949–50), 145–51

——'Une traduction française du "Sublime" de Longin vers 1645', *Modern Philology*, 59 (1961–62), 159–201

WEISKEL, THOMAS, *The Romantic Sublime: Studies in the Structure and Psychology of Transcendence* (Baltimore: Johns Hopkins University Press, 1976)

WILLIAMS, BERNARD, *Moral Luck: Philosophical Papers, 1973–1980* (Cambridge: Cambridge University Press, 1981)

WILSON, EMMA, *Sexuality and the Reading Encounter: Identity and Desire in Proust, Duras, Tournier, and Cixous* (Oxford: Clarendon Press, 1996)

ŽIŽEK, SLAVOJ, *The Sublime Object of Ideology* (London and New York: Verso, 1989)

INDEX

❖